# BLUE SKIES & Black Olives

JOHN HUMPHRYS has reported from all over the world for the BBC and presented its frontline news programmes on both radio and television, in a broadcasting career spanning forty years. He has won a string of national awards and been described as a 'national treasure'. He owned a dairy farm for ten years and has homes in Wales, London and Greece.

CHRISTOPHER HUMPHRYS is John Humphrys' eldest son. He has lived in Greece for the past seventeen years and is a cellist with the hugely popular Camerata Orchestra based in Athens.

# BLUE SKIES & Black Olives

A survivor's tale of housebuilding and peacock chasing in Greece

JOHN HUMPHRYS
& CHRISTOPHER HUMPHRYS

HODDER

First published in Great Britain in 2009 by Hodder & Stoughton
An Hachette UK company

First published in paperback in 2010

1



A CIP catalogue record for this title is available from the British Library.

ISBN 978 0 340 97884 9

Typeset in Sabon MT by Palimpsest Book Production Limited,
Grangemouth, Stirlingshire
Printed and bound by Clays Ltd, St Ives plc

Hodder & Stoughton policy is to use papers that are natural, renewable and recyclable products and made from wood grown in sustainable forests. The logging and manufacturing processes are expected to conform to the environmental regulations of the country of origin.

Hodder & Stoughton Ltd
338 Euston Road
London NW1 3BH

www.hodder.co.uk

For Catherine

# *Acknowledgements*

I suppose Christopher and I should thank (through gritted teeth) the many and varied builders in Greece who've been driving us mad, one way or another, for the past four years. There'd have been no book without them. Christopher's in-laws have been wonderful, and his wife Peppy was an invaluable source of information. She endured his histronics and my endless demands with her customary good nature and kept us both in line. Here in Britain I'm grateful for their encouragement to Rowena Webb and the folk at Hodder – especially Helen Coyle, now tango dancing in Argentina, Anna Swan, who stepped in at the last minute and took over the editing and my agent Luigi Bonomi. This is the first time I've tried to write a book that sets out to amuse rather than provoke and I couldn't have done it without Catherine Bennett offering her merciless and invaluable observations at every stage.

# Contents

# I

*In which John makes his debut as a mime artist in a Greek café and his cellist son encourages him in a rash decision*

It was the sort of rain you expect climbing an exposed hillside in the Lake District in February or tramping around the edge of a Scottish loch: cold rain, driven hard by an easterly wind, stinging the face. It was not the sort of rain you expect in Greece. With the benefit of hindsight I should have seen it as a harbinger of worse things to come. If I had known then, as I struggled to find my rental car in the vast car park of Athens airport, what the next couple of years were going to bring I would probably have turned around and caught the next plane back to London. The fact that I didn't says more about my stubbornness than it does about my common sense.

Ahead of me, if I ever managed to find the blasted car, lay a long drive that would take me across the Corinth Canal onto the Peloponnese peninsula. The last leg of the journey involved crossing two mountains and by the time I reached them it would be dark. The mountain roads of Greece are pretty fearsome at the best of times. The double lines in the middle of the most treacherous stretches are not so much laws that must be obeyed on pain of severe penalties as helpful guidelines. They do not tell you: 'If you overtake at this point you will probably be killed and if not you will be fined heavily and disqualified for dangerous driving.' Instead they say: 'It's probably wise not to try it, but if you do overtake and get killed don't say we didn't warn you.'

But at least there is beauty in the mountains and on a summer's day the breathtaking scenery lifts the spirits. On a black night in driving rain there are no views at all and the only things to see are the little roadside shrines, candles burning inside some of them to mark the passing of the poor unfortunates who had made the same journey as I was about to make and had either ignored the road markings or were the victims of someone else who had. I once tried counting the shrines. I gave up by the time I had calculated that there were roughly two of them for every mile of road. Not the best odds, I thought.

Still, there would be some consolation at the end of the journey – assuming it did not end with a blazing wreck at the bottom of a cliff or on a hairpin bend squashed by a big Greek truck. I was driving to what would one day be my new home in the Peloponnese. There was already a home there when I bought the land – though 'home' is stretching it a bit. It was a dilapidated old cottage whose only inhabitants for the last seven years or so had been a colony of rats. But it was in a stunning location – right on the beach – and high above it, cut into the hillside, in an even more stunning position, were the foundations of what could become a glorious villa. All I had to do was get it built. That's all.

Waiting for me in the cottage would be Daniel, the builder who had become a friend. He was working on making the cottage habitable and would then start work building the new house. He was a charming and clever Englishman who had come to do some work in Greece twenty years earlier and liked it so much he stayed. He had learned to speak the fiendishly difficult language so well he was indistinguishable from the natives – which was good. As I was to learn to my great cost, he had also learned the Greek approach to life in general and building in particular, which was bad. But I did not know that on this bitter winter's night. All I knew was that he had promised he would be there when I arrived from London. He would have a fire blazing in the grate, of course, and maybe a hot meal on the cooker. He might even have uncorked a bottle of the local wine – pretty rough but very drinkable and the perfect restorative after a hellish four or five hours on the road.

I got there eventually, but he had not. No Daniel. Therefore there was no fire and no food. I also discovered, after fumbling around in the secret hiding place under an old tile, that there was no key to the cottage either. I considered my options. I could try breaking in. This would not be easy because the windows were shuttered and I had no tools and it was dark: not city dark, where your eyes grow gradually accustomed to the background light from a thousand street lamps but the kind of total blackness you get only when you are many miles from a town and there is not a sliver of moon or a single star in the sky. I could wait for Daniel but I knew there was a very good chance that, like Godot, he would never come. One of the ways he had adapted to Greek life, as I should have realised, was that 'I'll be there at seven tomorrow evening' really meant: 'I might be there at seven tomorrow. Or eight. Or the day after tomorrow. Then again, I might simply not come at all.' *Mañana* may be a Spanish word but they learned it from the Greeks.

I considered other options. I could try sleeping in the car, but it was getting very cold and I would probably be frozen solid by morning. Or I could simply walk into the water and put an end to it all. But the water in my bay is pretty shallow until you've crossed the reef and it would be very painful having to clamber over the reef in the dark to get to the deep water.

Death by a thousand coral cuts would be unpleasant: death by a thousand sea urchin spines is surely worse. And anyway there was a slightly less melodramatic option: I could get back into the car and drive to Metamorfosi, the village above my property, to seek help.

There were two obvious flaws with this plan. One was that I spoke no Greek and the other was that the locals speak no English. For all its appeal, this was not the charming little Aegean village so familiar from the cover of holiday brochures: pretty whitewashed villas with tumbling bougainvillea, pink roof tiles and blue shutters clinging to the side of the hill, the streets full of colourful tavernas whose owners make their living from British holidaymakers and realise it is just as important to speak a little English as it is to have bright pink taramasalata on the menu to satisfy British palates. Metamorfosi is not like that. It is authentically Greek.

'Authentic', I've come to recognise, is a tricky sort of notion. We all claim to want it when we're in foreign parts – but only up to a point. What we actually want is our version of it. A bit of 'authentic' food is very nice – just so long as there's no risk that it will give us the runs in the morning and there's something on the menu that the kids will eat: preferably something involving chips, beans and either sausages or fish fingers. And, of course, it's terribly annoying if the locals haven't taken the trouble to learn even a little of our language. How on earth are we meant to communicate? Authenticity is all very well, but let's not overdo it, eh?

The closest thing to a cheery taverna in Metamorfosi is a slightly forbidding café – not quite the sort of place where plates are smashed to loud bouzouki music on boozy Saturday nights. The coffee is highly authentic and quite delicious, I've no doubt, if you drink it with four or five spoons of sugar in a very small cup. If you don't take sugar it tastes like mud. Starbucks this ain't. Not that it mattered on that grim night because it appeared to be closed. In fact, when I pushed the door it opened and I found myself on the set of that strange film *An American Werewolf in London*. Or at least that's what it felt like.

I was the American and dozens of pairs of eyes swivelled towards me. What appeared to be half the population of the village was here in this room behind the little shop, warming themselves in front of a fire of olive logs. In one chair was a pile of old clothes which moved when I looked at it . . . then got up and made its way very slowly to the door. Inside it was a tiny woman – bent so far over that her face was almost level with her waist – and very, very old. The proprietor said good-night to her and nodded to me in recognition. I recognised him too. He had served cups of mud to my son Christopher and me when we had first come to Metamorfosi on one of our house-hunting trips. That had been some months earlier on a beautiful sunny day, when the idea of finding a house in Greece had seemed such a lovely idea.

Christopher (much more of him later) speaks good Greek, though not as good as Daniel. Nor has he yet, after eighteen years of living in the country, become a real native, though I fear he is learning. He had asked the proprietor about the property and the man had shaken his head very slowly from side to side. Were we really, honestly interested in buying it? Didn't we realise that the owner was asking a ludicrous amount of money for what was no more than a derelict cottage and a building site? Why, in the name of every Greek god who ever existed, would a couple of foreigners like us want to buy such a place in Metamorfosi? And if it was such a good idea to build a big villa in that particular spot why had it been abandoned for several years?

That conversation had taken place many months ago and, in spite of his warnings, I had gone ahead and bought it. Now here I was, on this bleak winter's evening, wondering why I had not heeded his advice and returned swiftly to London.

The proprietor said something to the other villagers (to his credit, there was only the merest hint of a snigger) and they looked at me half in wonder and, I suspect, half in pity. What then followed was the most bizarre game of charades I had ever played. You try it. You try acting out the pantomime that says: 'I am the foreign idiot who spent a small fortune on a derelict cottage and now cannot get into it because the key is no longer in its hiding place and the builder has not arrived and I have nowhere to sleep and will somebody PLEASE HELP ME!'

I try to picture now what I must have looked like then, standing in front of this audience and doing my best to mimic the action of a key being inserted into a lock, then vigorously shaking my head to illustrate that the door would not open because the key did not, in reality, exist and then affecting a look of despair. Actually, I think I did the despair bit rather well – not that it made any great demands on my acting skills since it was entirely genuine.

My audience sat through this bizarre pantomime entirely impassively, seemingly unmoved even when I got to the despairing scene. You'd have thought that their winter nights were frequently disturbed by strange Englishmen (it took some years to get around to my Welshness) bursting in on them and providing an impromptu floor show. When it was clear that I had finished they discussed my performance at some length. I half expected them to hold up score cards, the way they do at ice skating contests, but instead one of them uttered a name – Babageorgos – and it was clear that salvation was at hand.

I knew the name. He was the old man who had been keeping

an eye on the property for half a century or more. He, of course, would have a key. A search party was formed to find him and I tagged along. He was also very old – perhaps not as old as the bent-over lady, but certainly in his eighties if not his nineties. He had clearly been dozing in front of his fire, but he insisted on leaving his house and coming with me down to the cottage. Maybe he didn't trust me not to lose this key too, but I think he was just being friendly.

And so I spent my first night alone in Villa Artemis, a rather grand name for a decrepit cottage. Not quite alone, as it happened. My sleep was disturbed by a thriving colony of rats who clearly regarded it as their home, though they did have the good grace that night to confine themselves – albeit noisily – to the roof space above my bed rather than pay a social call on me personally. They became more sociable with the passing of time, as Christopher's Greek auntie-in-law was to discover when she slept in the same room some months later and woke to find a pair of them sitting at the end of her bed regarding her with great curiosity. The auntie-in-law did not return. But I did.

I have spent many days and nights since then in that little cottage, some more eventful than others. Here are a few of the things that have happened during the building of the new house that made me wonder occasionally whether it might not have been wiser after all to wade into the black water on that winter's night:

- a small but scary earthquake;
- the worst forest fire in the history of modern Greece;
- a drunken, incontinent, over-familiar peacock;
- an angry old man accusing me of stealing his olive trees;
- assorted contractors demanding vast amounts of money for work I never ordered including one who has not set foot on the property since I've owned it;

- assorted foremen builders who actually did carry out some work but would have been more help if they, too, had never turned up;
- the threat of invasion by people-smugglers who scared one contractor so much he lit flaming torches at night and planted them on the beach;
- Greek bureaucracy

That last entry is the one that still, after all this time, causes me to whimper pathetically. I know I will not do justice to it in the pages that follow. It deserves a book all of its own. Dealing with Greek officialdom is like trying to wade through a lake of treacle wearing a heavy overcoat and lead-lined boots with your eyes blindfolded, knowing that if you ever make it to the shore there will be another official waiting to push you back in again. And then jump on your head and hold you down. If anybody ever again complains to me about the British planning process or British plumbers or British builders in general I shall take them to Villa Artemis and feed them to the rats – having filled in the appropriate forms beforehand, obviously.

But we persevered in spite of everything and now a splendid villa sits on the hillside overlooking what may be the most beautiful bay in the world. There are, admittedly, one or two minor problems still. The water that comes from the bathroom taps has an annoying tendency to electrocute unwary guests and the swimming pool seems determined to slide down the hill into the sea – which rather defeats the point of having one, I suppose. That's because some abnormally heavy rain has undermined the terrace on which it's built. Not that the rain will matter too much in the long run if we get any more earthquakes because the whole garden will disappear – and maybe the house too.

But let's look on the bright side. The job is, more or less, complete and for that I have to thank Christopher's beautiful wife Peppy, who is a Greek lawyer capable of playing the bureaucrats at their own game, and Peppy's father Thakis. He is a civil engineer who not only makes the best *stifado* on the planet and several other classic Greek dishes besides, but is capable of putting the fear of God into incompetent officials. And then, of course, there is my first-born son, Christopher.

Christopher is an optimist. He sees every cup as half full and every opportunity – no matter how fraught with risk – as a golden one, to be seized with maximum enthusiasm and minimum caution. For Christopher, problems do not exist. The future stretches away to a golden horizon and the sun rises each morning on a world of opportunity and harmony full of joy and prosperity for all – except, possibly, in the few hours after waking with a hangover. When someone makes a promise to Christopher he believes deep in his soul that the promise will be fulfilled. It does not occur to him that the person making it may well be a gross incompetent barely capable of erecting a shelf in the kitchen, let alone a seven-bedroomed villa on a steep hill, or an unprincipled rogue and vagabond – or possibly a combination of both. Christopher believes in the milk of human kindness and that all will be well in the best of all possible worlds, no matter that every scintilla of available evidence and experience suggests exactly the opposite.

In truth, the world would probably be a better place if there were fewer crusty old cynics like me and more trusting young souls like my son. It is also true that his virtues are perfectly acceptable (if not desirable) in a musician, which is what he is. He has made his living as a cellist since he left the Royal College of Music in 1990. One of the proudest moments of my life was watching him in his first solo concert playing

Elgar's cello concerto. He was clearly transported with the beauty of the music – and so was I, the nervous father in the front row, watching him. But the qualities needed to play divine music on a cello are not exactly the same as those needed to oversee the building of a house in Greece.

It would be unfair to blame Christopher for the various crises we endured and it is certainly true that I should have exercised a little more control. Every time he phoned me in London to tell me that he had just hired the finest building contractor on the mainland of Europe, who was absolutely guaranteeing to complete the whole job on time for the price of little more than a decent bottle of wine and a cheese sandwich, I should have caught the next flight to Athens, driven at speed to his home and tied him to a chair until the scales fell from his eyes. But I never did. The truth, of course, is that I wanted to believe him. More to the point, I needed to believe him: I had no choice. Supervising a difficult building project is bad enough if you're on the spot but if you're a thousand miles away and can't speak the language, it's impossible.

So his natural enthusiasm invariably trumped my instinctive caution and it would not be until several months later, when the finest contractor in Europe had turned out to be incapable of building a doll's house from Lego bricks, that he would reluctantly agree that, yes, on balance it might not have been the wisest choice and the money thrown at him might have been better used lighting the barbecue. Not that he was unduly dismayed, because by then he would have found another contractor and this one really *was* the finest . . . you may fill in the rest of this sentence as you wish.

Nor can I blame Christopher for setting this whole thing in motion – except in the widest sense that if he had not decided to move to Athens, the idea of a home in Greece would never have entered my head. But he did and I started going there regularly and hugely enjoyed our walking holidays in the Peloponnese and I became fascinated with Greece. It was at the end of one of our walks that I made one of my more rash decisions: to buy a building site in a meltingly beautiful corner of the Peloponnese. Not that it seemed rash at the time because Christopher encouraged me to believe that building a house on a steep hill would be a walk in the park. A doddle, as he put it.

I believed him. Can you credit that? I had been a fresh-faced 22-year-old struggling to make a name for myself on a Welsh newspaper when Christopher bawled his way into the world and for forty-two years I had watched him grow into the amusing, intelligent, accomplished young man he is today. I know his strengths and I thought I knew his weaknesses. Had I given it a moment's thought I would have realised that his judgement on how long it would take to build a house and what the problems might be would prove about as useful as a mink coat in a Greek summer. But I didn't.

That was in January 2006. Within six weeks I was the owner of the building site, four acres of forested hillside, one wreck of a beach cottage, one charming lemon grove and heaven knows how many ancient olive trees. Summer came and went and so did several more summers and the building site remained just that: a building site. This book tells the story of those years and it should, in all fairness, include Christopher's version of events as well as mine – and also his own reflections on what it's like to be a foreigner living in one of the world's most fiercely patriotic and tradition-bound countries. Those of us who have been there on holiday at some time or another might think we know a bit about it. As I discovered to my cost after a few years, most of us don't.

# 2

*In which Christopher falls in love and ends up half-naked in the biggest Orthodox church in Christendom*

*Christopher writes:*

If I'm being strictly honest I suppose Dad has a point when he blames my irrational optimism for some of our problems with the housebuilding. I'd prefer to think of it as me having a sunny disposition that matches the climate of my adopted country and him being a bit of a grumpy old man, but maybe it's because I've had an easier life than him. He was born during World War Two into a poor working-class family and there was never any money to spare. Like millions of others in the years after the war my grandfather had to struggle desperately to make a living and although Dad has always said he can't remember going really hungry, there was never anything to spare. When I was little and had apparently been complaining about being made to eat my meat and two veg he gave me a sandwich made of two slices of bread with margarine and sugar. It was disgusting and I refused to eat that too. I realised afterwards that he'd done it to make a point: sugar sandwiches were what he and his siblings often got to eat when money was very short, so what the hell did I have to complain about!

And God help us if we ever wasted anything. Anything at all. For both Dad and Mum, waste was one of the Seven Deadly Sins. And that applied to wasting energy just as much as food. Having never lived in Cardiff (we left when I was a baby) I can only assume that Wales must be one of the coldest, dampest places on earth. It's the only thing that can explain Dad being so oblivious to the cold. Either that or he genuinely disliked central heating: maybe a bit of both.

My sister Catherine and I wonder to this day how we managed to survive the Arctic temperatures of the various houses in which we were brought up. Moving to South Africa was a joy because we could finally stay warm – until we realised that they have winter there as well. And no central heating – at least, not in our house. We didn't really need fridges in most of our houses: the living rooms were usually quite cold enough. I was grateful for the hot water from the tap, so I could warm my fingers for five minutes every time I went to practice my cello. He must have wondered why his gas bills were so high despite the central heating being off. Catherine and I still joke with each other about Dad's frugal ways. If we are ever cold in one another's houses we will invariably come out with his stock response: 'Put a bloody jumper on!' muttered in our time-honoured 'Grumpy Dad' voice. I don't think he ever realised quite how difficult it is to play the cello when you're wearing five jumpers and look like the Michelin Man on steroids.

Now, of course, we have the great fear of global warming and these days we are all considered to be antisocial yobs if we waste energy instead of trying to save the planet. Happily, Dad is not the sort of man to say 'I told you so' . . . well, not more than two or three times a day at most.

Even when Dad became successful at the BBC and started making a bit of money, not much changed. He and my mother reckoned it made no difference how much money you had, there was still no excuse to waste food or buy things you didn't need just for the sake of it. You might think that because he was on telly every night reading the news he'd have splashed out a bit on expensive clothes, but that wasn't how he operated. Not that it seemed to make any difference: he was voted 'Best dressed man in Britain' one year and the fanciest suit in his wardrobe had come from Marks and Spencer. Maybe that tells us something.

And yet for all his loathing of waste, Dad could be a big spender. A very big spender. He may save the pennies, but he can definitely spend the pounds. He blew a small fortune on a rundown farm in Wales when he didn't know the first thing about farming. He'd always wanted some land of his own and he thought it would be good for the family to live on a farm, so he went ahead and did it – even though everyone told him he was crazy.

As for Greece, it's true that I bear part of the blame because I was dead keen on him buying a house there – for obvious reasons – but even I was astonished at the way he went about it. When he finally saw the place he wanted he made the decision to buy it in about five seconds flat. He looked at the view, looked at me, and said: 'This is it.' And so it was. He committed himself to spending all that money – the equivalent of about fifty years' salary playing the cello for a Greek orchestra – without so much as looking inside the cottage. I don't think I've ever heard of anyone buying a house without going into it and this was, after all, the only remotely habitable building on the property. Actually, it wasn't really habitable at all but we didn't learn that until quite a bit later. So why did he do it?

The easy answer is that he saw it as a challenge. He's always looking for challenges – not that he'll admit it or even recognise the word. It annoys him intensely when idiotic business people or politicians talk about 'challenges' when what they mean is dirty great problems. Then again, almost everything about modern jargon annoys him. The fact is, he's intensely competitive – he stopped playing ping-pong and snooker with me when I started beating him – and he always wants to be doing something that makes ridiculous demands on him. Time is something else he hates wasting. We used to have wonderful holidays but I'm not sure that I can remember him ever relaxing. Once we drove clear across the United States, down to Mexico and back the long way – camping in fabulous national parks as we went. But he wasn't content just to enjoy the experience. He didn't stop writing and doing broadcasts for the BBC about things we'd seen, filing his despatches to 'From Our Own Correspondent' at every possible opportunity. In fact, during our seven weeks of 'holiday' he was on the air more often than the correspondent the BBC had sent to Washington to replace him.

Again, maybe it's because of his tough childhood: from the age of thirteen he'd be out of bed by six to deliver the morning newspapers and then rush back from school to deliver the evening ones. He even had an allotment when he was fourteen to grow the family's veg.

So, yes, he saw the Greek building project as one of his many 'challenges'. The idea of spending the money on lovely long holidays in exotic parts of the world being waited on hand and foot simply wouldn't have occurred to him – any more than it occurred to him to buy a holiday home when he was in his thirties and had saved some money, rather than a working farm in Wales.

I think it's true to say that I'm not like that. Why should I be? I had it easy: a comfortable middle-class upbringing, fully aware that we'd never have to want for anything and, unlike

Dad, I have always enjoyed the good life, which was one of the reasons why I was so keen to take a job as a cellist in a new Greek orchestra. After college I had worked in a Spanish orchestra for a year but it didn't work out so a friend of mine told me about the Greek one. Still in my early twenties, I relished the idea of sunny days on Greek islands and everything that went with that sybaritic lifestyle. And I was right – it was brilliant – for the first ten years anyway.

Just as in Britain, orchestral musicians in Greece don't earn very much – but enough for me to be able to spend a couple of months every year lounging on my idea of the perfect beach on my idea of the perfect Greek island: Naxos. Whenever we had a few days (or weeks) off, I would throw a few clothes in the top box of my scooter, jump on a ferry and get there before the sun had set. A small basic room cost me a tenner a night. A decent lunch was a fiver and I would make do in the evening with a souvlaki in town for a couple of quid. Drinking was even cheaper because after a couple of beers my friend who owned the bar would stop counting. It was blissful. Then I met Peppy.

Sadly, classical musicians are not like pop stars – chased wherever they go by pretty young women – but I like to think that our concerts attract the more up-market class of groupies. Peppy certainly came into that category – not only very pretty but very clever too. And I met her at a concert. It was a warm summer evening and I was playing at the small theatre in Epidavros, directly across the bay from what would much later become our new home. It may have been the magic of Mozart or the wild folk music of Hatzidakis at the nightclub after the concert, but either way we fell in love. And this time it was serious.

Getting married in Greece turned out to be a bit of a problem and resulted in what was easily the most embarrassing experience of my life – and it was partly Dad's fault. He had been delighted with my choice of bride. In fact, I think he fell in love with her almost as much as I had done. Peppy is beautiful, intelligent, funny and full of life. But she is also an Orthodox Christian and that was the problem.

It's not that she is deeply religious, any more than I am. But almost everyone in Greece is, on paper at least, a member of the national religion and if you haven't been baptised you can't be married in church. The constitution might rule that Greece is a secular state, but that's neither here nor there. If you are Greek, you are an Orthodox Christian – whether you believe in God or not. That is what tradition dictates and in Greece, tradition is obeyed. So Peppy had been christened and I had not. Mum and Dad had taken the view when Catherine and I were babies that no one is born believing in a particular faith and it has to be a choice for every individual. I was perfectly happy to remain a heathen and take my chances on whether I'd get to heaven – until I met Peppy. We could have had a civil union of course, but I had already decided on the church I wanted to be married in long before I even set eyes on Peppy. It was a tiny chapel overlooking my favourite beach on Naxos. Where else?

So there was nothing for it but to be christened. We lived at the time in a very posh suburb of Athens where most of the embassies had their residences. It seemed safe to assume that the priest would therefore be fairly understanding towards foreigners wanting to marry Greeks and would be helpful. Not a chance. I was told very sternly that if I wished to become Greek Orthodox as an adult I would need to attend six months of lessons. This was a slight problem as the wedding was four months off.

Peppy's father saved us. He had a chat with the local priest in his area who agreed to wave the six-month rule in return for a small contribution to the church. This was much more like it, I thought. I had visions of waltzing in to see the priest in some small rundown old church, handing over my donation and signing a bit of paper.

I began to get nervous when it appeared that several members of Peppy's family would need to be at the baptism. This puzzled me as I was thinking in terms of a five-minute transaction with a priest. But no, I needed a godfather. That's fair, I thought, maybe they need the godfather's signature on some papers. It made sense. Then I learned that Peppy's parents would be there. This was stretching it a bit but then again, if they wanted to witness this small scene as a build up to the marriage of their only daughter, I could hardly complain. Next Peppy told me that my best man should be present. Now this seemed a bit much but by now I was resigned to it all being one of those strange Greek practices and stopped worrying about it.

I wish I had done the six months of lessons. I would have done six years. On the fateful day, I arrived at the in-laws' house in a smart shirt and the money in my pocket. Most of Peppy's immediate family was there. Aunties, cousins, the lot. Plainly this was going to be a bit more of a ceremony than I thought. I wasn't unduly worried. Years of performing on stage meant that I didn't mind being the focus of attention.

We left the house as a group and walked round the corner to the church. 'You are joking, Peppy,' I said with mounting dread. I had presumed that Peppy's Dad had found a small unassuming local church. Oh no, we were heading for THE church. Not just the biggest church in the neighbourhood. Not just the biggest church in Athens. Not just the biggest church in Greece. This was actually the biggest church in the whole of the Balkans. I was beginning to understand why Peppy had been a bit vague about the details. There was no turning back now so in we strode. I had a moment of hope when the priest ushered me in to a small office. Maybe it was just going to be a formality after all, I thought. Not exactly. He was asking me if I had remembered to bring a pair of swimming trunks and a towel. Peppy sheepishly admitted that yes, we did have the items, as I looked at her in horror. 'What is going on?' I hissed at her. 'Just do what the priest says,' she hissed back.

It has been eight years now and I still cringe when I think about it. I may have skipped the lessons but we were going to do the full Orthodox christening service, down to the letter. It started quite well. I stood with my 'godfather', Peppy's brother Adonis, in front of the altar while the priest chanted and read from a book. It felt a bit like a gay wedding but it wasn't bad, and Peppy's brother is a handsome bloke. It was about to get much, much worse. The priest ushered me in to a side chamber and told me to change into the swimming trunks. I couldn't believe what I was hearing. I checked with him several times but he just told me to hurry up. As I stripped off and put them on I consoled myself with the fact that at least this part of the service appeared to be private. It was just Adonis, the priest and me. I was wrong again. The priest then told me to follow him. We were heading for the glorious central nave of the church. The biggest in the Balkans. I was standing in the middle of it in front of half of Peppy's family wearing nothing but my bathers. Some of Peppy's younger cousins were beginning to giggle. They were being half-heartedly shushed by the older ones.

I had been to many christenings in Greece and knew the next stage. I was confident at least of escaping this humility. The 'baby' is held by the priest and dipped into a bowl of water while it is anointed with olive oil. I was pretty damn sure there was no way this seventy-year-old priest was going to lift up my fourteen stones and fit me into any bowl. But then

I hadn't been to an adult christening before, had I? Standing to one side of us was a magnificent object, which I had first taken as church ornamentation. It was a giant copper urn standing a good six feet tall with ornate religious inscriptions covering its sides. The priest gestured to me. And gestured to the urn. I looked at Peppy for help but she was desperately trying to support one of her cousins who was silently giggling so badly she couldn't stand up.

There was nothing for it. All my dignity had left me a long time before so, with the feeling of a condemned man, I walked slowly to the urn and climbed in. At least the water was warm. I began to consider staying in there until everyone including the priest had given up and gone home. I could wait until it got dark and then slink off. It didn't matter if I wasn't christened. It didn't even matter if I got married or not. It wasn't like I was ever going to speak to Peppy again and I certainly wouldn't be able to look any of her bloody relatives in the eye for many years to come. In fact I almost did stay in there forever. I had forgotten the anointment with olive oil. Just as I was beginning to feel comfortable the priest tipped a gallon of the stuff on my head. As if chiding me for beginning to enjoy any part of the process. This was the cue to get out and reveal myself to the world in all my sodden, glistening glory. Except that I couldn't. Back then I was still quite fit and strong and could easily haul my body up with my arms – but you try holding on to the sides of a copper urn when everything is covered in a mixture of oil and water. I was like a spider stuck in the bath. Every time I slithered up a few inches I slipped back down again. The priest was beginning to look concerned. Eventually, with every shred of dignity washed away along with many sins, I managed to release myself and was handed a towel for my efforts. Surely, I thought, it can't get worse. I was mistaken.

I was told later that for the audience (sorry, congregation) the grand finale was the funniest bit of all. I was mercifully allowed to keep the towel but now had to hold hands with Adonis. We then started a procession. The priest led, holding his bible in front of him and chanting gravely. Next came a very serious Adonis looking splendid in his smart suit. Holding on to his hand was me, probably most resembling something that had just drowned in an olive oil vat. I was holding on to him for dear life because I was barefoot and the marble floor was slippery as hell with the oil still dripping off me. My hair was plastered to my face and I could hardly see. Our little procession had to make a very solemn circuit of the offending urn. Not just once but three times. Enough to guarantee that there wasn't a dry eye in the house. Even my lying, deceiving so-called fiancée was doubled up with laughter.

So now I was eligible to get married – assuming, of course, that I was able to resist the temptation of throwing my beloved off the top of the Acropolis by way of retaliation for my public humiliation. Yet there still remained a serious obstacle in the way of my dream wedding. Greeks do not believe in punctuality and the timing of the service was crucial. It was planned down to the last minute. Peppy and I, the radiant newlyweds, would walk from the church to the beach below just as the sun was beginning to slide towards the horizon, and I would join my string quartet in playing the sort of music that would deliver the perfect climax to the perfect day. There had to be enough light remaining so that we could read the music and our guests (having drunk large amounts of champagne) could avoid falling into the sea. I suspect that Peppy thought that because it was her special day the sun would wait for her before it set.

Even by Greek standards, Peppy and her family's time-keeping is heroically bad. Dad summed it up nicely when he said that Peppy would be late for her own funeral. He'd had first-hand experience of her special talent. I had gone to Naxos a good two weeks before the wedding in order to organise things. Peppy was to come a few days before the wedding with Dad, who spent the night at our house in Athens. They were booked on the morning ferry that left at eight and were to be driven to the port by Peppy's brother. Dad woke early as usual and was slightly puzzled that Peppy was still sleeping. He was even more surprised that when she did wake, shortly before they were due to be picked up, she hadn't packed.

Adonis was late arriving as well so that by the time they finally left the house they had virtually no chance of making the ferry. En route Peppy realised that they had forgotten the ferry tickets. That was bad but not catastrophic: she could always buy more tickets, assuming the ferry wasn't sold out. But she had also forgotten her wedding dress. It's not easy buying a new wedding dress at eight in the morning on your way to a ferry. She realised at about the same time that she had also left the front door of our house open. All things considered it would be necessary to return.

So far, none of this surprises me in the slightest. Indeed, I might have been surprised if it had been otherwise. Peppy, as I may already have mentioned, is to time-keeping what a flame-thrower is to a piece of tissue paper. No, it was Dad who surprised me. He kept his cool. When he is broadcasting to the British people he is a model of professionalism. I have never seen him betray the slightest anger or frustration on air when things go wrong or people behave stupidly in ways that might jeopardise the programme. But off air it's a slightly different matter. Then, it is wise to find a concrete barrier and tin helmet and crouch low. Earplugs are useful too. But there was none of that with Peppy, or so I was told later. He stayed calm and they all drove back to the house through the morning traffic, collected the tickets and wedding dress, locked the door and got to the ferry just in time to see the ramp being raised. I shall always be grateful to the man with the walkie-talkie on the dock and a captain with a large streak of romance in his soul. Had he done what he should have done and sailed off to Naxos without my future bride on board . . . well, I don't suppose I'd be writing this book because I'd have probably flown straight from Naxos to London, cursing everything Greek including my ex-fiancée.

The important point to make here is that all this was completely normal behaviour for Peppy. The difference between Greek time and English time (as the Greeks themselves often describe it) is simple. I need to be somewhere at five o'clock. It will take me half an hour to get there. I will leave at 4.20 to allow for traffic or unforeseen delays. Peppy will still be doing her make-up at 4.30 but will leave by 4.40, hoping to make up a bit of time on the way. Then she will get stuck in traffic and will be astonished to finally arrive twenty minutes late. This will not be her fault, you understand. She will blame the traffic. As if bad traffic is unheard of in Athens.

Dinner parties are ridiculous. One reason Greeks don't mind eating cold food is down to lateness. I have reached an understanding with Peppy over punctuality. I had to for reasons of my own sanity. If we are going to an English-speaking dinner I insist we are on time. This involves telling Peppy we have to leave forty-five minutes before we actually do and threatening to leave without her if she still manages not to be ready in time. This has happened and I have left without her more than once.

If it is a Greek dinner I relinquish all control. She decides when we leave, whether we should have thought a bit earlier about taking a gift and how we are going to find the place when we have no directions and have left the map at home. I just go with the flow. I take an almost malicious pleasure in seeing how late we can actually be. I think our record is an hour and a half but it may be two hours. None of this is her fault, of course, it is just circumstances that are to blame. But then most people seem to do the same so there is no bad feeling. Arriving an hour late is on time. Arriving on time is being English and is verging on rudeness as the hosts are probably running late themselves and won't even be dressed. Peppy's defence is that we 'English' get too stressed over the whole issue and shouldn't worry so much. She has a point but doesn't have a job where turning up late for a concert means instant dismissal. How musicians manage in London with the dire state of public transport I can't imagine.

It was inevitable that Peppy would therefore be late for the wedding. I should have seen it coming. I should also have foreseen the added complication of Peppy having three close girlfriends help her get ready. This was really disastrous. I think she changed her hair and make-up three times before everyone was satisfied. It left me and 150 guests standing outside the tiny church for a very long time. After half an hour people even stopped making jokes about whether she had changed her mind. I might have started to wonder the same if I wasn't so used to her lateness.

The problem, as I said, was the sunset. We had it all worked out. After the service we would walk down to a beautiful little bay set apart from the rest of the long beach by large, prehistoric boulders that looked like they had grown out of the sea. This was just below the church and happened to be one of my favourite spots on the whole five-kilometre-long beach. The only problem with using this bay was that it is so secluded it is very popular with naturists. I have no problem with a bit of nudity myself but I blanched a little at the thought of some of Peppy's aged aunties coming face to face (or worse) with some of the beach's regulars in their under-dressed state. Their husbands might not have objected, but I thought it might be expedient to put the word out the day before that we needed the bay to ourselves. In the end I needn't have bothered. Peppy was so late that the sun had already set by the time we got down to the bay. It was just as well that my string quartet was made up of good friends and we had been playing the same music for decades.

The serious partying started that night and lasted a week and at the end of it I realised how much my life had changed. No longer the footloose young hedonist, I was now a responsible married man with a wife who wanted to start a family as soon as possible. No more drunken weekends in Naxos. The cheap ferry journey with a scooter became a very expensive one with a car. The basic room had to be upgraded to a luxury one with a kitchen. And we ate twice as much. There was no way we could afford to spend even a month on Naxos during the summer. Staying in a small flat in Athens with young children and the temperature well over a hundred degrees in the shade wasn't much of an option either. Still, as Dad wrote earlier, I am the eternal optimist. Something would turn up.

It did.

It was Dad.

# 3

*In which we encounter Greek estate agents and Christopher begins to have misgivings*

I would like to say that the welfare of Christopher in his newly married state was uppermost in my mind when I started thinking about buying somewhere in Greece, but I'm afraid it was a bit more selfish than that. I had begun to develop, if not a permanent love affair, at least a serious infatuation with Greece and I wanted to spend more and more time there. But because I dislike hotels – I've spent too much time in them as a foreign correspondent and I associate them with work – I wanted my own place. It had to be somewhere big enough for my children and grandchildren to stay but far enough away from everywhere that I would have plenty of time by myself. I thought I knew all the potential pitfalls: I had bought a second home some thirty years earlier in a foreign land. Well, Wales actually, and yes, I'm well aware that I was born in Wales so I hardly count as a foreigner. But my place of birth was Cardiff and my second home – a working dairy farm – was in west Wales and I promise you that there is about as much similarity between Cardiffians and the good folk of Welsh-speaking Wales as there is between the flat-dwellers of Knightsbridge and the nomads of the Gobi Desert.

I remember wandering around the muddy farmyard a few days after we moved in, wondering quite what I'd let myself in for, when an old Land Rover came chugging down the farm road. The driver introduced himself.

'My name is David Jones,' he said without any of the usual preamble when two strangers meet for the first time, 'I own the farm on the other side of the road and I am living with a woman who is not my wife.'

I blinked a bit and almost said: 'So what? Half my neighbours in London are living with women who are not their wives.' But I thought it wiser just to wait for what followed.

'I tell you about this,' he said, with the grammatical precision often used by people who are speaking in a second language, 'only because there are those in this village who would prefer to have nothing to do with me. I shall quite understand if you feel the same. I was once a chapel warden but naturally I have resigned from that position.'

I assured him that it was none of my business, that it did not concern me in the slightest who he was living with except that I hoped they were happy together and I was grateful that he had gone to the trouble of coming to introduce himself. He nodded gravely and we said no more of it – not then, nor in the years that followed. Instead we shook hands, wished each other well, and he went his way.

Over the years that followed we became good neighbours. He was always among the first to help when I ran into trouble, which I frequently did. I think it's fair to say that the gods did not smile on my farming venture, but time smoothes most of memory's jagged edges and I managed to persuade myself there would be fewer problems buying a home on the Mediterranean.

C: We were sitting at his kitchen table in London when Dad first mentioned it to me. It seemed a brilliant idea – the answer to all my prayers – except that he'd been talking to his Turkish barber and the barber had told him the best place to buy was Turkey. Disaster! Yes, Turkey gets lots of sun and, yes, you can buy a glorious villa there for the price of a fish supper in Greece and, yes, it has some wonderful coastline and scenery but it's TOO FAR AWAY. Hadn't Dad heard of the sensible Greek tradition of having an *Exokiko*? The fact that Greeks have a specific word for the summer house says it all. No self-respecting Greek would dream of living in Athens without having somewhere to escape to in the heat of the summer. Why else would the holidays be so long? He'd have to be stopped!

I realised I'd need to be a bit subtle about this. I could hardly say: 'Look Dad, I know it's your money and you've worked very hard for fifty years to earn it and of course you should buy whatever you like wherever you like, but you must realise that what I and my family need is for you to buy somewhere close enough to Athens so that we can use it as our second home. We must have somewhere to go for long weekends and especially summer holidays when it's too hot to stay in Athens. It will transform our lives, solve all our problems at a stroke. Even if it costs you twice as much. Oh, and obviously it'll have to be big enough for our friends to stay as well.'

My challenge, then, was to persuade Dad that what he wanted and what I wanted were exactly the same even if he didn't know it yet, but it would have to be handled carefully because he can be incredibly impetuous, not to mention stubborn. So I'd have to move pretty quickly to make sure he was heading in the right direction. I mentioned as casually as I could that actually he'd be far better off buying somewhere in Greece and I'd have no trouble at all finding exactly the right place to suit my (whoops! . . .) *his* needs. And if we couldn't find exactly what we (he) wanted at the right price, there'd be no problem in buying a nice plot of land and building from scratch. Peppy would be able to take charge of all the legal details and her father Thakis could be our civil engineer. It'd be a piece of cake and probably save a lot of money too.

He looked a bit doubtful but he obviously hadn't thought it through in any detail. He's always coming up with ideas and getting involved in crazy schemes without giving them enough serious thought. He once bought half a cheese factory, which produced some wonderful cheese and which might have been a brilliant idea if only they'd found a customer for the cheese. It went bust pretty quickly. And, of course, he bought a dairy farm without knowing which end of the cow produced the milk. So I didn't really doubt that I could bring him around to my view.

My trump card was our first baby, Hector, who had been born a few months before the conversation in the kitchen. Dad may not look it, but when it comes to babies he is a great big softy. Especially when they happen to be his grandchildren. I knew that all I had to do was mention how wonderful it would be for him to be able to see his Greek grandchild and the battle would be half won.

'Look,' I said, 'why don't I just test the market and see what's out there and if I can't find anything suitable, well, you can always go back to your Turkish barber and . . .' But I didn't finish the sentence. I didn't really need to. I knew that I'd be able to find the ideal property – ideal, that is, for Peppy, me and the children – and with a bit of luck it might even suit Dad rather well too. So I went back to Athens and started looking.

I had never bought a house in Greece, just moved from one rented apartment to another, and it took me only a few hours to discover something very important about the market: outside Athens there isn't one. There are plenty of property sections in the newspapers and even a few magazines dedicated to property, but none of it made any sense. One villa on Poros Island would be on the market for three million euros and something similar ten minutes away would be priced at half a million. Across the water on the mainland it might cost three hundred thousand. Or five million. There was no logic to it and not even much choice. I started expanding my search further down the Peloponnese just to find suitable properties. The main reason for this crazy variation in prices came down to the agents – or, rather, the lack of agents.

In Britain we may regard estate agents as only slightly higher up the social scale than journalists or even politicians, but they do meet an important need – as you discover when they don't really exist. In Greece you simply cannot pop into an estate agent's high street office and immediately get an idea of what is available in any given area. The first problem is that there isn't even one big national agency – not even in Athens. You need to deal with irritable old men in a shabby office who do their best to be unhelpful and represent an area of about twenty blocks. When I first experienced an estate agent on the island of Poros I thought somebody was pulling my leg.

The agreement was that an agency in Athens would send someone across on the ferry to meet me on Poros and show me a property that had caught my eye. I duly waited to meet him at the quayside and stood there as the passengers left the boat. Having no idea what he might look like, I wasn't quite sure that I would recognise him, but I didn't worry about it. Estate agents all look pretty much the same, don't they? Neat suits, crisp shirts, an air of eagerness about them. They can be spotted a mile off, I thought, and I could be fairly sure that mine would be a typically sharp character, given that the property I wanted to see was on the market for a million euros. I hadn't actually told Dad that, but I reckoned I'd find the right place first and persuade him to cough up later.

Every time an earnest young man in a suit and a fake smile got off the boat I went as if to greet him, but he was always meeting someone else. Eventually the boat was empty and the port was thinning out. Where was my estate agent? The only people left on the quayside were a couple of very dodgy-looking mafia types. I know that particular Mediterranean mafia look fairly well because my wife is lucky enough to have a few of them as clients. I say lucky because they give her plenty of work, always pay on time in cash and offer to break the legs of anyone who is bothering her. I always hope that doesn't include me. The two hanging around the port, though, were very far down the mafia food chain. They almost looked scruffy despite their suits – or maybe because of them. Eventually one of them pulled a mobile out and dialled and my phone rang in reply.

They were friendly enough and we chatted happily as we drove up the hill to the property, but they did nothing to change my initial impression. Their language seemed much better suited to the streets of Athens than it did to addressing a client. Every girl in a short skirt we passed was commented on, usually accompanied by a colourful description of what they would like to do to her. I had little experience of agents at this stage and assumed that perhaps they were trying to bond with me in some kind of macho way, not the most subtle form of establishing client trust perhaps.

The property looked fine from the outside but the interior was a bad joke. My mafia friends did not have a clue. One of them started off by showing me where the doors were, perhaps fearing that I might not spot them for myself. Then they were at a loss for a while until the other one had the bright idea of showing me the windows as well. I agreed that they were very nice windows – ideal for looking out of. When I asked some simple questions about water supply, heating and the like they were completely stuck. One of them searched in vain for the boiler but gave up. I realised that they had never seen this property before and almost certainly had never sold a single property between them. I seriously doubted whether they were even estate agents. I felt so sorry for them that I reversed the roles and started showing them around.

'How about this lovely pink bathroom, eh?' They looked mildly interested.'And what about these mirrors on the ceiling!' This interested them more.'Look at the way this bar has been built into the corner of the room so that you can have cocktails in bed!' They loved it.

I could have sold the place to them in five minutes. It suited my mafia buddies down to the ground. The asking price – with the barest minimum of land – was a preposterous million euros. Some time later I looked at another property similarly priced but hugely more impressive. This one had it all: six bedrooms in the main house, staff quarters, stables, a tennis court, a huge pool and a helicopter pad. Dad decided that the upkeep of such a vast estate ruled it out.

*J*: The truth is that 'Dad ruled it out' – and, for that matter, ruled out all the other houses Christopher laid before me – because they were all ghastly for one reason or another. It took me a while to realise that this was no accident. Christopher, I came to realise, knew perfectly well I would hate them even before I'd seen them. Eventually I spotted his cunning plan. When Christopher said he'd been sent the details of a particular house but had decided it sounded so horrible that it wasn't even worth going to view, what he actually meant was that it did not meet his requirements. He allowed me to think that his only concern was finding me somewhere that would suit my tastes and give me endless pleasure. Trusting father that I was, I failed to spot that my much-loved son was pursuing a slightly different agenda from my own.

What I wanted was a charming little holiday cottage close enough to the sea to be able to swim every morning from a beach so secluded that even the crabs apologised for intruding on my privacy. Behind the cottage would be gentle hills rising to a magnificent mountain range so that I could go for a stroll before breakfast and more energetic hikes in the mountains when the spirit moved me. I think I pictured a combination of Snowdonia and the Pembrokeshire coast in my native Wales – but with sun and warm seas. The further away it was from any major centre of population, the better.

This, I learned eventually, was not what Christopher had in mind. What he wanted was a second home for him and his growing family close enough to Athens so that he could drive to it in a couple of hours for long weekends and pop back to the city occasionally during the long, hot summer months. It had to be large enough to allow him to entertain his many friends and relatives for days or weeks at a time and close enough to several decent restaurants where they could entertain him in return for his generous hospitality at 'his' house. A swimming pool was desirable if not essential – ideally designed for lots of small children to use safely. My own view of swimming pools is that no one in their right mind would even think of using one if the sea is even remotely accessible.

After several months of searching he managed to find one that sounded perfect. Or, rather, it sounded perfect over the phone. We had many long-distance conversations during this period. If I had been a little more suspicious I might have spotted what he was up to, but I wasn't. Not yet. This property, he told me breathlessly, had its own beach, tennis court and even a summer house that could be converted into a useful cottage. It was easily the best place he had seen and he just knew I would love it. I didn't.

When I saw it for myself I discovered one or two little drawbacks: the beach, for a start. It was entirely surrounded by brooding hills which meant it was in perpetual gloom. So it was ideal only for those unfortunate people who suffer from that medical condition that means they must never, ever be exposed to the sun. I think Christopher did concede that there would have been something distinctly perverse about buying a place in the sun and never actually being able to see it.

The main house, he also conceded, was a little cramped and might need some work. What that meant, I discovered, was that it had all the charm and space of one of those prefabricated bungalows swiftly thrown up in Britain after the war when the troops came home and needed somewhere to live. They were meant to be temporary accommodation on the basis that no one could possibly live in one for more than a few years without going stir-crazy, but they stayed for decades. We called them 'prefabs' and much ruder things too. In fact, this place made prefabs look pretty spacious. Plus, it was squat and ugly and the only way to improve it would have been to offer it to the Greek Air Force for target practice and start all over again.

It did, though, have one advantage. It was in the next bay along from the little island of Poros and it takes an hour to get to Poros by hydrofoil from Piraeus. Very convenient if you happen to live in Athens. As I say, I was beginning to get the picture. From now on, I would cast a slightly more sceptical eye over Christopher's recommendations before flying a thousand miles to see them for myself. The problem was that there weren't any. We had looked at all the houses on his shortlist – a grand total of three – and none of them was even remotely acceptable.

By now I was beginning to feel a bit despondent but also, in a way, slightly relieved. Did I really want to go to all the trouble and expense of buying a home in a foreign country when I had always felt vaguely scornful of British people who colonise the lovelier corners of Europe with their second homes, in the process helping to destroy the very culture that so attracted them in the first place? There is something dispiriting about a Saturday street market in the Dordogne where you are more likely to hear British than French voices inquiring about the cheese. Even worse are those lovely little Spanish villages where the people in the bar complaining about the size of their British pensions will outnumber the locals complaining about the grape harvest. And now I was planning to do it myself, to become one of those second-home owners. On the other hand, I reckoned I could just about claim the status of honorary Greek: Greek daughter-in-law; half-Greek son and, by now, a grandson who could switch from being Greek to being British as quickly as he could unwrap a bar of chocolate.

The one thing on which Christopher and I agreed – possibly for different reasons – was that we would not buy a house on a Greek island. Lord knows there are enough of them – more than six thousand – though only a couple of hundred are inhabited. The trouble with having a home on an island is that you've got to get there – no good for Christopher's weekend jaunts and no good for me either. Those with big airports were automatically ruled out because big airports mean too many tourists (yes, I know I'm a tourist too when I'm abroad) and those without can be difficult to get to. The ferries are all very well except when the wind blows too hard, which it often does. And anyway, why go to an island when you have the Peloponnese on your doorstep?

When Christopher moved to Greece in 1992 I could only just place the Peloponnese on a map: that funny little blob to the left of Athens under the belly of Greece, a bit like a misshapen cow's udder. I knew that it had played an important role in classical antiquity and was vaguely aware that it had both a spectacular coastline and the sort of mountains and gorges that made it a walker's paradise. That's why Christopher and I started going there regularly: to walk. We went mostly in late winter or early spring when the air was clear and sharp and the valleys were carpeted with spring flowers.

For Christopher there was a positive appeal too. It got him out of Athens. He lived in a poky little flat in the centre of the city and Athens is a dump. Maybe that's a bit unfair. If you think of it as a glorious museum to be visited occasionally, there is nowhere quite like it – the Acropolis in a setting sun will melt the hardest heart – but the problem is that every other Greek wants to live in the city and regards it as his inalienable right to ignore whatever planning regulations may or may not exist. So, since the 1950s, the city has spread like a fat man's bottom on a small chair: ugly neighbourhoods of concrete apartment blocks crammed together with barely a patch of green between them. In some areas there is an almost medieval squalor in the way one family's little balcony will overhang another's. Christopher was able to watch television on his – even though he didn't have a television set. He watched his neighbour's instead.

For decades the result of this over-population was some of the most congested roads in Europe and the filthiest air. They call it *nefos* and on a bad day the air would be so thick with pollution it seemed as though you could take a knife and carve it into slices. Eventually they built a metro to persuade Greeks to leave their cars at home and it worked. The air got gradually cleaner. But Athens sits in a bowl, surrounded by forested mountains which acted as the lungs of the city – until fires burned most of them down, of which, more later.

So Athens is a very good place to leave behind you and, on a good day, it takes very little time to drive to Corinth. Once you have crossed the Corinth Canal you are in the Peloponnese. Now here is a very curious thing about Greece. The country is broke. Its economic wellbeing depends to a very large extent on tourism. Without the cash foreign motorists bring, the government's accounts would not balance. Actually, even with the cash they don't, but that's the subject of a different book. Suffice to say, Greece needs tourism the way a pop star needs publicity: it could not survive without it. And here, only a couple of hours drive from the capital city, is one of the most glorious corners of Europe. So what happens when you call into a tourist office in Athens and tell them you would like to spend some time and money in the Peloponnese? They look at you as if you had tried to book a twin room with bath and colour television for a long weekend in the lost city of Atlantis. You might, if you're lucky, come away with a dog-eared little brochure that's about as useful for finding your way around as a compass at the magnetic North Pole, but that's it. You have to be very determined indeed or, like me, have a Greek-speaking son to plan it. If I tell you about our first trip it might give you some idea why I came to feel the way I do about the Peloponnese and why I ended up owning a small piece of it.

# 4

*In which John is reacquainted with an English war hero and Christopher embarks on a killing spree*

Christopher had decided that we should go to the Lousios Gorge, the most famous gorge in the Peloponnese, largely on the basis that if it inspired the glorious art of Poussin it might fill us with a different kind of inspiration. It did, but we had to get there first. We were looking for the little town of Dimitsana. When you approach it from the north, as we did, the mountains play a delightful trick on you. It is a place that conceals its beauty until the last moment. We had been driving through soft green hills with some snow-tipped peaks in the distance and climbing so gradually for so long that the only real signs of altitude were the changes in the vegetation. When we got there we had to leave the car in the village square. A thousand feet below us a green valley disappeared into the distance, here and there a tiny village clinging to its sides, apparently hewn from the rock of the cliffs.

Dimitsana was a delight: tiny square houses of soft stone squatting almost on top of each other along steep cobble paths winding to the top of the hill to another square. This is the heart of the village and the source of its history. There is a lot of history for such a small place. There was a settlement here before Christ.

In the fourteenth century the Turks invaded Greece and liked it so much they stayed until Greece won its independence in 1821. But they never quite managed to subdue the people of Dimitsana, a natural hiding place for the rebels. The locals helped by supplying them with cartridges. When they ran out of paper to make them, they tore up the precious books stored in the museum on the square. One of the village's tavernas has its dining rooms in the arched vaults of an old powder mill. Christopher and I wanted to see the monasteries where the monks fomented their revolution. A local man, Archbishop Yermenos, had played a central role in the rebellion – the first to raise a Greek flag in defiance of the Turks in 1821.

A map would have been handy, but not only did the tourist offices back in Athens have no information and no maps, neither did the locals. Maybe they were still using all their paper to make cartridges for the next Turkish invasion. More likely, they probably figure that if you're daft enough to get lost you deserve all you've got coming. We asked the two delightful young women who ran our little hotel for help. They tried to direct us with a few squiggles on the back of a menu card. Not terribly helpful but we thought: what the hell? It's only a valley. You can't get lost in a valley and if you do there's always someone to ask. Wrong on both counts.

If you are like me, you can get lost anywhere. I believe you are born with a sense of direction just as much as you are born with an ear for music. I have none – and I mean none. I have owned my small farm in Wales for nearly thirty years and I still can't figure out the quickest way to the cottage from the furthest field. This valley is rather bigger than my farm. And emptier. In three long days of walking we came across only four other groups – three couples and one family.

We walked down a sheep trail and caught tantalising glimpses of a gorge far below. It is not easy to reach, but the effort is worth it. This is how gorges should be: deep, forbidding, darkly magnificent. At its steepest its sides of white and orange cliffs fall almost sheer for a thousand feet. Long before you see it you can hear the Lousios River at the bottom, crashing against the rocks and carving its way ever deeper. According to Homer, Zeus once bathed in these very waters. You would need to be a god to survive in this torrent. Halfway down Christopher grabbed my arm.

'Look! Across the valley!'

It was an extraordinary sight. Hanging from what seemed to be a sheer cliff on the other side of the gorge was a cluster of wooden buildings – one of the many hidden monasteries. It could have been a giant swallow's nest because God knows how anything but a bird could have built in such a spot. More to the point, God knows how we were going to get there ourselves. The first thing we had to do was get down to the bottom of the gorge and the second was to get up the other side.

Both were easier than I had thought – thanks to the old shepherds' trails. I'd always wondered how the shepherds decided on the route for their paths. It seems what they did was tie a heavy load to a donkey's back, slap its backside and follow it. Every time it stopped they'd slap it again. Donkeys, being both extremely lazy and extremely sensible, will take the easiest route. The shepherds followed behind, clearing the trail as they went. The entire valley turned out to have a network of trails. The trick was finding the right one. We got it wrong more often than we got it right.

It proved impossible to get to the monastery from below so we climbed to the ridge and took another trail back down. This was Nea Filosofou – the newest of the valley's monasteries –

built in the seventeenth century. The entire structure leaned over the edge of the cliff, seeming to crane its neck to take in more of the glorious vista spread out beneath. Why is it that non-believers, even those most determined not to be awed by what they see as superstitious nonsense, always lower their voices in a church? I suspect it has less to do with God than with awe at the achievement of those who built it all those centuries ago. That even a modest monastery could be built in such an awesome location inspires wonder and demands respect from the most cynical. How did they do it? What resources of strength and determination and faith must have gone into it?

The church adjoining this monastery was not a grand one. The friezes covering walls and ceilings still hold their rich colours but the building is scarcely bigger than a cottage and indistinguishable from the outside from the buildings where the monks still live. Here we were – alone in the church and almost alone in this vast gorge – and yet we talked in whispers.

Then we saw another monastery. It is a hit-and-miss affair, looking for monasteries in this gorge, so thickly wooded that you can walk for an hour and see nothing. Then you stop for a drink from one of the springs that bubble almost everywhere, straighten your back – and there it is. This one, too, was on the other side of the gorge. You can see them only if they are facing you, not if they are on the same side. So here we go again – all the way down and all the way up again.

By now we were further along the gorge and the river, as it narrowed, became more ferocious. It forced its way through ever smaller gaps, polishing great boulders, thrusting aside anything more puny that stood in its way. The sides of the gorge were steeper, too, the cliffs vertical in places. But here, too, the donkeys had done their work.

With this monastery it was possible to approach from beneath. Possible, but hard going. I tried to explain to Christopher that a dutiful young son would offer to carry his aging father up the more difficult bits on his shoulders. He did not reply – just panted.

If the first monastery was impressive, this one defied belief. Imagine a row of sixteenth-century cottages with their seemingly fragile stone and timber walls bowed with age. Now imagine them set into an almost sheer thousand-feet cliff with no visible means of support. This was the monastery of Prodromou. Monks have been living and praying on this site in their breathtaking isolation for almost a thousand years. The early ones lived in caves and those caves are still in use.

This is a working monastery with twelve monks and a steady supply of guests who stay for a day or two at a time or sometimes longer. We entered through a door set in the rock: ten inches thick of black wood and rough metal studs, a reminder that this had once been a fortress as well as a holy site.

The tunnel we entered was so small and narrow we were forced to stoop. Off it is a series of small doors with more tunnels running into the cliff. We opened another door. A monk's bedroom. We retreated quickly. Then another. We were now approaching the heart of the monastery. We were in a rough chamber with a few crude benches and, at one end, a few steps hewn from the stone leading up to another door.

This was the chapel: small and simple. The light came from candles and the chairs were the only furniture: six of them on opposite walls, exquisitely carved, one for each monk.

In this place of silence, remote and shielded from the modern world, the monks have been using these chairs for their worship every day. The arms and seats are worn smooth and in the floor before each there are two perfect grooves where their sandals have worn away the stone.

The sun was now beginning to set over the western rim of the gorge. In theory the walk back to Dimitsana was a relatively easy one. There would be no more diversions to hidden monasteries, no more crossing and criss-crossing the gorge – just a simple climb up to the rim, find the road and we'd soon have our hands wrapped around a glass of cold beer. I should be old enough by now to know that, as Clausewitz once put it, no plan survives its first contact with the enemy. Sadly, age does not necessarily confer wisdom and Christopher's sense of direction is no better than mine.

An hour later we were standing at a crossroads: three tracks going in different directions. Of course there were no signs and of course we took the wrong one. It was an hour before we found that out. There comes a point in most walks when you realise how tired you are and seriously doubt your ability to make it back again – especially when you have no idea which route to take. This was that point.

And then an old monk appeared from the monastery far below. Shrouded in the mountain mist, his head covered in his rough hood, he silently guided us back to the monastery. There, we were fed a simple but nourishing meal, given beds for the night and sent on our way the next morning, both physically and spiritually refreshed. Actually that's not true. What really happened is that Christopher's mobile rang.

Yes, I know it is unspeakably naff to carry a mobile when the whole point of walking the hills is to get away from it all.

But you should know that Christopher was a young man very much in love and he had left his fiancée at home in Athens. What if she needed to get in touch with him? Four days is a long time when you are separated from your betrothed. Thirty years ago, I might have done the same.

Anyway, thank God he did – and thank God he had thought to leave the number of his mobile with one of the young women at our hotel. It was she on the other end of it. She was worried about us, bless her. He had told her we would be back well before dusk and when we failed to arrive she had got into her car and come looking for us. When she couldn't find us she phoned. She rescued us from our own stupidity.

So the hotel scored ten out of ten for its free rescue service. Breakfast was just as good. The oranges for the juice had been picked a few hours ago and the jams and honey were home-made. So were the *loukoumades*: small pieces of dough, smothered in wild thyme, honey and cinnamon and fried while you wait. Blissful.

We paid the bill before we left for our final day's walk – or, rather, we tried to. I had no cash and I offered a credit card. They did not do credit cards. Christopher said he would find a bank and come back with the cash but the sisters wouldn't hear of it. Didn't he live in Athens? Well, he could always post a cheque when he got home. No problem.

This had been my first visit to the Peloponnese and this, I knew, was where I wanted to find a home. And so I did. It happened at the end of one of our walking weekends – not in the mountains, this time, but on the coast.

We were high in the hills above the Aegean looking down on the islands of the Argo Saronic Gulf and below us, on a thickly-wooded hillside sloping down to a beach, there was a clearing and the foundations of a house. Further down the hill – almost on the beach at the bottom of the hill – was what looked from this distance like a small cottage. Since we had a couple of hours to kill before returning to Athens we thought we might as well make a detour and take a look at it. Christopher thought it might be one of the properties that had been mentioned by one of the estate agents he had contacted, but he hadn't bothered pursuing it or even mentioning it to me because of the estate agent's description of it. When we got there I understood why.

The cottage had obviously not been inhabited for many years and was effectively derelict. The roof seemed to be more or less intact – as far as we could see – but the shutters guarding the windows had rotted and the walls themselves seemed perilously cracked. It was impossible to see inside.

There was a lemon grove that had clearly been carefully tended over the years, but the land rising up from the cottage to the building site was a different matter altogether. At one stage it must have been a magnificent piece of woodland with a fine mixture of trees as well as the usual cypresses, eucalyptus, firs and (of course) olives but it had been totally neglected for many years and was overgrown, thick with thorns and vines. It took a long time and some badly scratched limbs to fight our way through, but when we finally got to the building site I knew immediately that this was what both Christopher and I had been looking for. I wanted to see a villa built on those foundations and I wanted it to be ours.

Perhaps if I had known then what I know now I might have had some reservations. I might have done well to heed the old warning: beware of what you wish for lest it come true. But I doubt it. And anyway Christopher assured me there would be no problems getting it built. With all his many contacts in Greece we'd probably get the whole thing knocked off within a few months for the price of a decent meal and I'd be able to invite my friends over for the summer. True, he didn't actually say which summer.

But in fairness to Christopher, it wasn't his absurdly optimistic assessment that swung it for me: it was the view. It was quite simply breathtaking. To our left were the mountains of the Peloponnese – snow-tipped in winter – folding away into each other to the horizon and, on one hilltop no more than five miles from us, the ancient theatre of Epidavros, one of the true wonders of the ancient world. To our right were more hills and the peninsula of Methana, forming a perfect bay. Ahead of us lay the islands of the Aegean Sea, stretching two hundred miles to the coast of Turkey.

No wonder scholars have puzzled for so long over Homer's description of this 'wine dark sea'. He uses it dozens of times in the *Iliad* and the *Odyssey* but there was nothing wine dark about this sea on this glorious January day, sparkling with light, touching the beaches of Turkey on its furthest shores two hundred miles away. Across two-thirds of the bay was a reef, partly visible through the water, which protected our beach from the rougher sea further out. If there was a finer stretch of water for swimming in, I thought, I had yet to see it.

One final detail was needed to complete this magical scene: the sun had to set in the right place. You might assume that because we were on the east coast of the Peloponnese this would be a bit tricky, but thanks to the convoluted geography of the region it did exactly that. If I had been the celestial lighting director planning my stage I could not have placed it more perfectly. One day, I told myself, I would sit on the balcony of the villa that was yet to be built and watch it as it slid behind the mountains, its dying rays reflected on the olive oil water of my bay.

You may have noticed the possessive articles in that last sentence. I was already thinking of it as 'my' bay and 'my' beach – and feeling guilty about it. I have always been pretty sniffy about the sort of people who can't see a piece of beautiful, unspoiled scenery without wanting to build something slap in the middle of it, destroying its beauty in the process. Is that what I wanted to do? I really don't think so. The damage had already been done because the site had been cleared and the foundations and pillars built. A lot of concrete had already been poured. If this became mine, I would be able to finish the job and then plant lots of trees and greenery so that it was no longer just a scar on the hillside. But there was that 'if' to be overcome first.

Buying property is never easy wherever you are and this, after all, was Greece. As anyone who has ever had any dealings with Greek officialdom will tell you, this is a country where the simplest bureaucratic task requires the patience of Job and a battalion of lawyers. The alternative is to approach the task with the bank balance of a ship owner and the morals of a Mafia don, in which case things can happen very quickly indeed. Not that I'm suggesting bribery or threats are the most effective ways of getting things done in this country: let's just say that deep pockets, brown envelopes and a lot of influence where it counts can come in very handy. As it happened, I needed none of them. Not at first anyway.

A scruffy piece of wood nailed to a tree on the dirt track leading down to the property from the village above confirmed that it was indeed for sale. We read the sign, noted the phone number written on it and, less than six weeks later, I was the owner of a cottage with the rather grandiose name of Villa Artemis, several acres of woodland and a building site with the finest views in Europe – or possibly the world.

Yes, I know how implausible that sounds but the fact is that the deal was done on the basis of one brief conversation with the owner, who happened to be a Welshman by the name of Julian Gibson-Watt. A telephone conversation at that: to this day I have never so much as set eyes on Mr Gibson-Watt. He told me how much he wanted for the property. In the time-honoured tradition of house purchases, I offered a bit less. He accepted. Deal done.

Even more implausible was the story that lay behind the original ownership of the property. By a bizarre series of coincidences this piece of land in a remote part of the Peloponnese a thousand miles from my native country of Wales was linked to me via an heroic officer in the British Army, whom I had interviewed in Wales after he became a leading politician, and his aristocratic wife who fell in love with the Peloponnese. Her name was Lady Gibson-Watt and she'd been christened Diana – which explained the name she gave the cottage. In Greek mythology Artemis was the goddess of the forests and hills and the hunt, who became identified with the Roman goddess Diana. But it was for another reason entirely that Lady Gibson-Watt was known throughout the local area: her ability to drink the most hardened Greek farmer under the table. Whenever we heard her referred to locally in the years to come it was simply as 'The English Lady', and her prodigious drinking bouts were spoken of with awe and respect.

Her husband, David Gibson-Watt, had also been much larger than life: an extraordinary character. His obituaries spoke of a man who was the epitome of the Tory gentleman farmer of a vanished age: educated at Eton and Cambridge, tall, charming and very brave indeed. He joined the Welsh Guards when war broke out in 1939 and four years later won the Military Cross when he led an assault in North Africa. Within a year he had won not one but two bars for it. Here's how his actions near Monte Cassino in 1943 were described:

> Jumping into his jeep and standing bolt upright, Gibson-Watt advanced on the enemy, firing his Tommy-gun as he went. The pursuit continued to Castel Gugliemo which was occupied by an enemy cover party for the demolition of a bridge over the Canale Biancho. As his jeep entered the town a white light was fired from the north of the bridge. At once Gibson-Watt sprang from the vehicle and advanced towards the bridge, emptying his Tommy-gun at the enemy-occupied houses on the far bank. The leading platoon leapt from their tanks and followed his example. Shortly afterwards the bridge was blown up and bazooka fire was directed at the tanks; but Gibson-Watt remained in the vicinity of the bridge and carried out a reconnaissance of the canal with a view to crossing it, until nightfall, when he was ordered to withdraw. In the words of the citation: 'Throughout this memorable day, Major Gibson-Watt continuously inspired and cheered all under his command, and his obliviousness to his own safety was complete.'

I came across him when I was a young reporter in South Wales covering the Aberfan disaster and he was appointed by the then prime minister, Edward Heath, to deal with its terrible aftermath. At about the same time his wife was building her cottage in the Peloponnese. Almost half a century later – less than ten years after her death – I was to become its owner and my son was about to get his first glimpse of what the inside of her cottage looked like. He was not exactly prepared for what he found.

C: As soon as the purchase had been completed I raced down to see the place. Peppy stayed in Athens with our son Hector. She said she didn't like the idea of spending the night in a derelict cottage with a baby. This turned out to be a very wise move. As Dad says, when we first saw the cottage we had managed to peer through a few cracks in the shutters on our whirlwind inspection but it was too gloomy to see the interior. Not exactly a full survey. So the first time I stepped through the front door I felt a bit like Indiana Jones in the Temple of Doom. What really hit me was the smell. When a small mouse dies behind your fridge the smell gets everywhere. The cottage was clearly a mass grave. Generations of mice had died here. Still, I thought, at least they're dead. And then I opened a cupboard and learned two things very quickly. First, that they definitely weren't all dead and second, that these weren't mice. These were rats. Very large rats. The cupboard I had so casually opened was at eye level. I was staring at mummy rat and her sweet little babies. Mummy was the size of a small cat and she just glared at me as if to say, 'What exactly do you think you are doing in my house?' She had a point.

I closed the cupboard door quickly and went and sat on the balcony. I had to consider my next move carefully. If the first cupboard I opened had a rat in it there was a good chance that all the others did too, I thought. The cottage was small but it had plenty of storage space. Obviously it wasn't enough just to identify where they all were. They had to be removed as well. And then I realised that it wouldn't be enough to merely shoo them out of the house. They would be back within hours. It looked like I had a big and bloody job on my hands. I really didn't know if I was up to it.

Then Babageorgos came to my rescue. When Dad agreed the sale with Julian Gibson-Watt he had also agreed to take on the gardener. Babageorgos had been working for the family for the best part of forty years and he was now an old man. It wouldn't be right to throw him off the land that he had tended for so many years. Thank God we didn't. Babageorgos may have been old but he was probably fitter than me. And he could definitely handle rats. I had no choice but to help him. My pride wouldn't allow me to do otherwise. The first thing we did was haul all the furniture outside. Rats found hiding in drawers were dealt with swiftly by a blow to the head. The worst part was the wood box. This was a big, deep chest where the firewood was stored. It also served as a kind of rodent high-rise apartment block. Under every layer of firewood we took out of the chest we found a family. It took the two of us an hour to systematically remove all the wood and bash everything that moved. Some of them were squealing as we rained down blows on them. It was one of the most unpleasant tasks I've ever been faced with. I justified our carnage by telling myself that I would soon be living in this place with my small baby and I didn't want to wake up in the middle of the night to find one of these buggers nibbling on my son's ear. It was fairly safe to assume that my wife Peppy wouldn't have been too delighted either. In fact, she would have swiftly become my ex-wife. Then there was the matter of Dad. Should I ring him up and congratulate him on buying a cottage with a bigger rat concentration than the sewers of downtown Delhi or should I gloss over some of the problems? In the end I reasoned that (as he himself frequently pointed out) he was A Very Busy Man and I really didn't need to trouble him with every little detail.

With the rats gone I found something else in almost all the cupboards: empty bottles. Ouzo, cognac, gin, whisky, you name it. Babageorgos silently watched me take these outside. Eventually I had to ask him.

'Did Mrs Diana like to drink?'

'Ach, what can I tell you? She was a very good woman. And very beautiful. As tall as me! But she had too much *Kefi*.'

*Kefi* is an important Greek word with no literal English translation and sums up the Greek character as perfectly as any single word can do. High spirits is about as close as I can find in English but it means much more than this. It has nothing to do with drunkenness. Peppy rarely drinks but in the right company, and if the mood takes her, she can spend the whole night dancing as if possessed. A great evening out will be explained later as a night with lots of *Kefi*.

Babageorgos's description of Diana struck me as somewhat circumspect. Here I was carting empty bottles out of the place by the crateful and all he would say was that she had a lot of *Kefi*. His defence of her was almost gallant. I wondered how much more there was to the story. Eventually he told me.

'You know, she was a lady. A real lady. Her husband was a big Lord. She was always very kind. But she could drink . . . po, po. One time I remember I came in the evening to water the garden and she said to me, "Babageorgos, come and have a drink with me." Me! I don't drink! Not even an ouzo with my fish! But this time I said I would have a small whisky. She gave me a big one and we were talking. Then she gave me another. I don't remember how many I had but when I left it was very late. I started to walk back to the village but I kept falling down. You know where the big hill is? I couldn't go up it! Me! I had to crawl on my hands and knees like a dog! I was cursing Mrs Diana and I was cursing the whisky. But when I got home, po, po! My wife was cursing me! She cursed me all night! And even in the morning when my head was hurting so much she kept on cursing me. I never drank again. But Mrs Diana was drinking like this every night!'

Babageorgos wasn't the only one with stories to tell. I soon learned the easy way to describe where I lived. Any local I met was naturally curious as to what a Greek-speaking foreigner was doing in their part of the woods. Initially I would start to explain where our bay was, how far from the village it was and what the house looked like. They usually got there before me.

'Ah! You live in the English Lady's house!'

After a while I realised that this was all I had to say. Even people from nearby villages seemed to know about the English Lady and her house. Her parties in the village were legendary. I think she acted as a catalyst for the locals. Their humdrum evenings where nothing ever happened were suddenly transformed by the arrival of this rare and exotic creature. If humans can come back to live as a different animal then I know exactly what happened to Mrs Diana. But that story will have to wait. First I had the cottage to deal with.

The vermin problem was just the start. There were a few other small niggles that needed ironing out. Like a new bathroom, a new kitchen and new floors. Oh, and a new roof.

The roof seemed like the main priority. Our initial assessment that it was in a reasonable condition turned out to be very wide of the mark. From inside, it looked as though it would collapse any second – which might, at least, deal with a few rats living in the eaves. My father-in-law, Thakis, scouted round the area and found a local roofer who would do it cheaply. We then had to find a cheap source of wood. As Thakis is from Megara, a town close to Athens, it made sense to use his contacts there. We got a good deal on the wood and duly ordered it. All we had to do now was get the wood from Megara to the cottage – usually much less than a two-hour drive. Again Thakis came to the rescue with a local contact with a truck that would transport all the wood. Things were going very smoothly. All I had to do was meet the truck driver, Costas, at the timber merchants, make sure it all got loaded and then drive down to the cottage with the truck driver to show him the way. Easy . . . or at least, it might have been had the truck not been even older than Costas, and Costas would never see sixty again.

Alarm bells should have rung when Costas told me he would rather take the old road to Corinth than the motorway. He claimed this was to avoid the tolls, which would save us a bit of money. The real reason, as I soon discovered, was that his top speed of 30mph would have been too dangerous on a motorway. So instead of taking forty-five minutes to reach Corinth it took two hours. I still wasn't too worried. From Corinth to the cottage is mostly a winding A-road through the mountains where even cars aren't doing much more than thirty in many places. How much slower can we go? I thought.

It was a scorching hot June day and I was in a twenty-year-old Micra with no air conditioning. This wasn't too much of a problem usually as I would just wind the windows down and let the breeze cool me. The problem now was that we were going so slowly there wasn't any breeze. I dreaded every hill. I was having to go up them in first gear so as not to leave Costas miles behind. After a while I went up the hills normally and then waited five minutes for him to catch me up. The tailback we were creating must have stretched all the way to Corinth. Just as well Greek drivers are patient types who don't like to drive fast or use their horns or anything. Even my favourite signs in the whole of Greece couldn't cheer me up this time. These are the ones that appear regularly all the way down to Epidavros and have been there for as long as I can remember. They very clearly warn drivers of the perils to be found in trying to approach the famous amphitheatre: 'WARNING! Continuous dangerous bents!'

After a couple of horrible hours we reached Epidavros. From here you can actually look across the sea to Methana. Twelve miles as the crow flies takes you straight to our beach. The old road from this point has to deal with two large mountains reaching three thousand feet. Luckily a new coastal road had been cut out from the base of the mountains and would take us to the house in no more than half an hour. This road was still dirt in places because it hadn't been completed. Local gossip said that the original contractor for the job fell off the mountainside and died. There was now a ten-year legal battle to see who would take over the contract. All the locals used this road. There were great big signs saying Danger! Road Closed! Strictly Prohibited! and more such dire warnings but everyone used it. Maybe because they didn't mention the Dangerous Bents. The potholes were murder and large chunks of the mountain regularly fell off onto the road below, but it was either this or the long way round to our cottage.

I had assured Costas that I always took this road and that his truck wouldn't have a problem with the unmade surface. After all, it had clearly been around since the days when Greece didn't even have any roads. So after four very hot and tedious hours I was looking forward to turning off onto this unfinished new road. It meant we were on the final stretch. I could get out of a boiling car and have a cool drink.

Then I saw the turn-off. The road was closed. Not closed

in the Greek way but really closed. There was a metal barrier across it. If there had been signs they would have read: 'Danger! Road Closed! And this time we really mean it!' Someone had clearly won the ten-year court battle and had been awarded the contract to finish the job. Although I was pleased about this I could not believe it was happening on the very day that I was trying to get to the cottage with the slowest truck in the world in tow. I considered ditching the guy. Just leaving him with directions, wishing him luck and telling him I would see him in a few days, or however bloody long it would take him to cover the last thirty miles. But I knew I couldn't. Either he or his truck would probably die before they found the place. And I wouldn't get my roof built. He was as upset as I was by the closed road. After all he had to make the whole trip back.

It took us the best part of another two hours to complete the final leg of the journey. A two-hour trip had taken six. My left arm had been hanging out the window for much of this time and I now had the worst case of taxi driver arm I had ever seen. People would be laughing at me for weeks afterwards with my left arm perfectly burnt up to the elbow.

I hadn't really thought through what would happen when we arrived. There was a ton and a half of wood on Costas's truck and it needed to be in the garden next to the cottage. I assumed I would offer him a hand unloading it, he would be grateful and maybe even knock a bit off the bill. It didn't quite work out like that. We arrived at the cottage. He got out of the truck and said something like 'You didn't tell me it would be so far, old chap,' but not exactly in such a polite way. He demanded his money, which I stupidly gave him while the wood was still on the truck. What I hadn't realised was that despite its age the truck was a tipper. Costas climbed into the cab, raised the back and a ton and a half of wood was dumped in the middle of the road. Then he drove off swearing.

I was almost too hot and tired to care. But the wood was blocking the road and Babageorgos had arrived right on time. He immediately started to pick up the heavy beams and carry them inside. I could hardly sit around and watch while a seventy-eight-year-old man moved all my wood. So I went for a swim. Or rather that is what I wanted to do. It was torture. The road where the wood had been dumped was right next to the beach and the sea was looking its best. Perfectly calm and deep blue. I had just done the hottest, sweatiest, most frustrating six-hour drive of my life. But some things are worth waiting for, I suppose, because after one more hot hour we had all the wood inside. And then I really did go for that swim.

# 5

*In which our neighbour burns his boat and we learn the secret of long life*

Sitting at home in London, I tried to feel guilty that Christopher was having to do all the hard work of making the cottage habitable while I mostly barked orders down the phone from London, but I didn't really succeed. I told myself that it was me who had to foot the bills and he who'd be actually living there most of the time and the guilty feeling would go away if I forgot about it. And anyway, instead of me working my fingers to the bone to make a home for him, I reckoned it was about time for a reversal of roles. In truth, there was a time when I would have leaped at the chance of doing a bit of renovating. As a young man – partly out of enthusiasm but mostly because money was scarce – I did pretty well everything myself. I've fixed slates on roofs, laid floors and concrete paths, built walls and cupboards and plaster-boarded ceilings, painted and decorated and hammered and drilled and it wasn't until I blew myself up that I decided to stop.

I was in my forties at the time and my day job was presenting the Nine O'Clock News. Before I went into Television Centre I decided to do a bit more work to a flat roof on an extension I had been working on at my house in London. I had hired a gas burner from the local builders' merchants to melt the bitumen – something I'd never done before – and, with typical arrogance, had not bothered to get any advice. How difficult could it be, after all? So I smashed up a few lumps of the rock-hard bitumen, put them in the hopper, turned on the gas, lit a match and poked it into the chamber. Nothing happened. So I lit another match and then another, poking my hand in further and further as each match went out and the gas (yes, I know now) was filling the chamber. Eventually, after many more matches, something did happen.

My neighbour heard the bang and took me to hospital. A few hours and much pain later, I gallantly showed up for work at Television Centre, expecting sympathy and respect for my dedication to duty. My editor glanced at my mutilated arm, bandaged up to the elbow, sighed at my stupidity in blowing myself up, and said: 'Better keep that out of sight when you're doing the news . . . might distract the punters.' Which is why eight million viewers that night might have wondered why I read the news with one arm resting on the desk, as you do, and the other hidden below the desk out of sight of the cameras. That was the end of my career as an amateur builder. From then on I left do-it-yourself to those who actually know how to do it themselves. It was more expensive but a lot safer and, though it took me a while to admit it, there were real advantages to having doors that closed and shelves roughly parallel to the floor.

As for the project in Greece, I rather enjoyed the idea of playing the role of absent owner: visiting from time to time; inspecting the work; complaining that it wasn't progressing quite as fast as I'd have liked; finding fault here and there and generally being a complete pain in the backside whenever I stayed in the cottage. What I did not do was help. I did, however, go for lots of long walks while other people were working. Walking is one of life's great joys. Because nobody makes any money out of it nobody can be bothered to interfere with it. It's true that if enough people decide to walk in the same area for long enough, that area will eventually become fashionable and therefore less attractive, but that has not happened in our part of the Peloponnese. Our bay is walking heaven: the perfect circular walk of about five miles along a path through olive groves rising steeply to a charming village called Taktikoupoly, descending to the sea, skirting two more bays along a little road lined with more olive groves and vineyards and back to Villa Artemis.

I expected to bump into plenty of locals during my walks and, even though my Greek is non-existent, imagined we might exchange cordial greetings, cheery nods and smiles, perhaps the occasional hand-shake, and even try a modest exchange – given that so many Greeks speak a little English. I was wrong. They ignored me totally. I learned much later that there is a reason for this: if you are a stranger to the area it is assumed that you will make the first approach and if you do not you might as well be invisible. Patrick Leigh Fermor experienced it during his journey through the Mani – one of the three fingers of land that make up the Peloponnese. Our house is on the thumb. Anyway no one took the slightest bit of interest in me, even though they must surely have been just a little curious about this skinny, grey-haired foreigner striding or jogging around the place before the sun had properly risen. At the very least, it must have struck them as an odd thing to be doing. Why on earth would I spend hours, working up a sweat to get from one village to another when I could perfectly well have driven?

It's not that they themselves never go for walks, but if they do there seems to be a very good reason for it. Many Greeks – young and old, city and country dweller – are happy to spend hours roaming the hills digging out weeds to take home and eat. The weeds – similar to dandelions – are known as *Horta*, which appears at certain times of the year on the menus of all good tavernas and in all decent Greek kitchens. There are more than thirty varieties but the best can be pretty rare and you may have to walk miles before you have gathered enough to make a decent dish but, as Christopher writes later, it's worth it. Properly cooked, it's superb.

Some of those I meet on my own walks are villagers taking their animals out for a meal. I regularly encounter one very old man with his one donkey and one goat – an ancient billy goat, bigger than the donkey and only slightly shorter than the man. Neither is ever on a lead, but the old man ambles along and they amble with him. When they stop to nibble at a piece of green in the hedge that takes their fancy, he stops too. When they have finished nibbling they all move on.

My usual route takes me to the far side of the bay where there is a charming Greek Orthodox church built on the rocks that jut out into the water – whitewashed and tiny and silent except once a year when a queue forms outside because there are so many of them and there is no room for more than a handful to stand inside. The worshippers range from the very young to the very old and what unites them is that they all come from the village that shares the name of the church. In Greece 'name days' apply not only to people with the same name as a particular saint, but also churches, villages and even neighbourhoods of a big city like Athens.

On Sundays and Saints' Days the accompaniment to my morning constitutional is the chanting of an Orthodox priest being relayed from the bigger church on the hill overlooking Taktikoupoly. On mornings when a light breeze is blowing towards us across the sea the chanting from more churches on the other side of the bay reaches me too, the water reflects the rays of the rising sun, the peaks of the mountains shimmer on the horizon with haloes of crimson light and the deep shadows on the eastern slopes gradually vanish as the sun climbs higher and I think if this isn't exactly Paradise it's pretty damn close. In August, which is usually the hottest month, I stop for refreshment – a handful of purple grapes plucked from a vine growing wild at the side of the road – and reflect on the sense of timelessness about this place. Then, rounding the last bend on the coast road, my building site comes into view halfway up the hillside and reality intrudes.

We are not exactly surrounded by neighbours. The cottage is the only house on the beach road for a mile or two in both directions. The village is on the upper road, with a long and bumpy dirt track leading down to the building site – more potholes than track. I suppose you could call it one of the luckier villages in Greece because, unlike so many, it has survived.

After the Second World War half the population of Greece decided to move to Athens, and mostly they came from the villages. A half-deserted mountain village – home to maybe just one or two ancient couples who refused to move – is a sad sight: old stone houses left to crumble; only the odd stray dog padding its way across the one busy village square; the many shepherd's paths radiating out from the village overgrown from disuse. When the village was live, the paths were its arteries. They were used to take goats to graze, to find the best wild greens for supper and, crucially, to gather firewood. When wild fires came, as they inevitably did, the area around a village would be clear of dry kindling and fallen branches so the flames might not reach into the village and, if they did, people could get out quickly. Now the road is the only way out – which helps explain why so many died in the last great outbreak of forest fires.

* * *

The beating heart of a village is its children. Metamorfosi may not be the prettiest village in Greece, but the sound of children playing there is far more important than whitewashed walls and blue shutters. A big, new school has been built a few miles away that takes children from all over the region and the old schoolhouse – the biggest building by far – is put to good use. It acts as town hall and community centre and when Metamorfosi celebrates its Saint's Day the trestle tables are put out and the entire village sits down to eat a huge meal together under the shade of a lovely old oak that grows in the courtyard. Outside the school is the village spring. People are perfectly happy to use their tap water for washing and bathing, but for drinking water, this is where they come – and so do we. It may or may not be better than the water that comes from the tap, but there's something a bit special about waiting to fill your bottles with a very old lady who would have been doing this since long before plumbing came to her village.

As for the livestock, there is one donkey, a few goats, many chickens, the usual cats and dogs and, occasionally, a flock of sheep. Their shepherd cuts a bizarre figure, wandering with his flock within a ten-mile radius of the village, depending on where the best grazing is. He's not particularly old but years of sun have darkened the part of his face that is not covered by an enormous beard and on his head he wears a large red plastic bucket. He tends not to talk to people very much and there is some dispute in the village as to whether the bucket is worn because he needs one anyway to feed or water his sheep and this is a convenient way of carrying it, or whether it's actually very sensible head gear because it protects against both sun and rain. My own theory is that it's both.

Metamorfosi, as I mentioned earlier, is not exactly pulsating with nightlife. There is a small café and a shop that sells the basics, but the best place to go for the gossip and the social scene is Tassos's shop about a mile away. Tassos is the local Mister Big in every sense: a big man with a big personality and big ambitions for the area. His mother opened the shop after the war and still serves there, but Tassos runs it – and a great deal else besides. It's more than a shop. It's a café, bar, restaurant and take-away, community centre, post office, job centre, bus station for Athens, off-license, tobacconist, estate agents and the place where you must go if you want to know what's happening. The shop sells everything needed to sustain life: fresh fruit and veg that's been grown locally, a deli counter for local cheese and yoghurt, everything you could possibly need for cooking or cleaning or getting drunk and treating your hangover. A large supermarket is said to have about 30,000 items on its shelves. Tassos looks as though he has about thirty, but his shop is a bit like a Tardis and the deeper you enter the bigger it seems to get. There might not be a choice of fifty different breakfast cereals but it's very hard to ask for something he doesn't stock. And unlike your typical supermarket he produces the two most important things himself: oil and wine.

In a shed in his yard stand vast barrels of the finest olive oil money can buy. It is not served in sweet little bottles with pictures of olive trees and gnarled old farmers on the labels: it is ladled out from the barrels by Tassos himself using an old saucepan into whatever container you choose. It costs half what you'd pay in the city and is twice as good. The wine is, if possible, even better. My favourite is a light red, almost a rosé. I've no idea what the alcoholic content is, but it's possible to drink half a bottle and wake up the next morning feeling fine – and you need to bear in mind that he sells it in bottles of one-and-a-half litres. It costs marginally less than bottled water.

Tassos offers other services too. When Christopher pulled a muscle in his back so badly that he couldn't stand, let alone walk, he phoned Tassos. An hour later one of his shop assistants, Pavlos, arrived at the cottage. After his first treatment with hot mustard oil and a vigorous massage Christopher could stand and after the second he was walking again. Try asking for that at your local supermarket.

But the most important thing about the shop is that everyone goes there – and that is because everyone goes there. You cannot keep track of what is going on or what people think about things unless you do. It is busy from early in the morning, serving breakfast, until late at night, serving supper that is actually indistinguishable from the breakfast and it is open every day. The only time we have ever seen it shut was when Tassos's first-born was baptised.

There was a brief period when Christopher was tempted to stay away. One of our less trustworthy foremen had cleared off without paying some of the workers what they were owed and it was inevitable that he would meet them at Tassos's. They were unfailingly polite – full of smiles and kind words about Peppy and the children – before wondering when they were going to get paid the money still owed to them. My only embarrassment was when the old men who sit outside under the shade nursing a glass of wine and smoking – always smoking – discovered that I had become a father in my fifties. It didn't matter that we could not communicate in words: the face-splitting grins and vigorous hand gestures made it perfectly clear that they approved.

There is a clear pecking order among the customers. The indigenous Greeks own the nearby land and the local businesses. The immigrant Albanians are the builders and general odd-job men. The Punjabis do the most basic labouring, such as working on the flower farms or, if they are successful and have stayed long enough to get official papers, they open shops catering to other Punjabis and to us. Christopher taught me years ago to appreciate good curry and it is they who provide the spices in Greece. The range is far greater than it is in Athens and it comes with lots of good advice. I once challenged Gordon Ramsay on one of his television shows to cook a better curry than me. Christopher emailed me the recipe and it was, though I say it myself, magnificent. But Ramsay's team sabotaged me. The chillies they supplied were not the sort I'd asked for and turned out to be too hot for the lily-livered judges, so I lost by one vote. As Tassos might say: Pah!

He has interests apart from the shop, including some splendid holiday apartments and another café on the beach in the next bay along from ours. I'm not quite sure how he managed it, but he got the European Union to stump up for a sizeable chunk of the development. Occasionally I point out to Tassos that since it was my taxes that helped pay for them I should be entitled to a stake in the business. Generous though he is, he does not agree. His great campaign as I write is to fight a plan under which hundreds of fish farms would be concentrated along our stretch of the Peloponnesian coast. The development, if it's allowed, would destroy one of the loveliest and most unspoiled coastlines in Europe. But there is a lot of money at stake and Tassos is ranged against not only big business interests but the Greek government in Athens and local government officials too. My money is on Tassos.

He's a hard man to pin down for lunch or dinner – he is always working – but it's worth the effort. He especially enjoys telling stories of his grandfather who was over a hundred when he died, though no one seems quite sure how much over a hundred. Inevitably he was asked time and again for the secret of his long life. Tassos loves delivering his answer after a few glasses of wine:

'Number one,' says the old man, 'wake up before the sun does. Number two, eat a good lunch but only have meat two or three times a week. Number three, have a long siesta. And most important is number four. Make sure you have fiki-fiki at least four times a week. My Grandfather did this until he was a very old man. Even after his wife died.'

At this he lets out a great roar of laughter and repeats the hand gesture that accompanies the 'fiki-fiki' so that even an English-speaker is left in no doubt as to its meaning.

'Four times a week! And he was an old man! That is the biggest secret to long life!'

I always want to ask Tassos if he follows his grandfather's recipe, but I lack the courage.

Our nearest neighbour is Nikos, an old sailor who had spent his life at sea. He was an officer in the merchant navy and his home was in the port city of Piraeus, but he always came back to this part of the Peloponnese where he was born. He loves the sea – which is why he built his house on the edge of the bay so that when he stands on his balcony he can imagine himself as a young man on the prow of one of his ships. The first thing he did when he retired was move here permanently and buy a fishing boat, which he kept at anchor in the bay.

Nikos had a good life, or so it seemed. Before dawn every morning, weather permitting, he would set off on his boat on a fishing trip and return a few hours later with enough fish to keep him, his friends and us, his only neighbours, happy. Lunch with Nikos was always the same. When you arrived, the oil would be bubbling in the pan and the fish would be cleaned and ready. There would almost always be octopus, some sea bream and often something rather more exotic. Monkfish was my favourite. But it would always be cooked in exactly the same way.

'Fish MUST be fried,' Nikos always told us. 'If it is fresh, frying in very hot oil is the only way to preserve the flavour. If it is not fresh you should not be eating it.'

So that was lunch. And with the fresh fried fish we had fresh green salad, grown in his brother's garden, freshly baked bread, freshly pressed olive oil with freshly picked lemons and local wine, which was also pretty fresh but none the worse for it. It never varied and it was always superb.

Apart from fishing and cooking, Nikos spent his time tending his olive trees, messing about on his few acres of land, occasionally looking out across the bay with the ancient telescope he had liberated from one of the first ships on which he sailed, playing with his grandchildren and generally being a good neighbour. He had a decent pension and a few little flats in Piraeus which he rented out to supplement his income, so money seemed not to be a problem. He also had a partner and that, it was to emerge, would turn out to be the problem.

If Nikos occasionally seemed a little melancholy when he gazed out across the bay, there was a good reason for it. His wife had died in these waters. She enjoyed swimming and was good at it and then one day, as she was swimming strongly across the bay, she had a stroke and drowned. She was in her fifties, in the prime of her life, with two teenage boys. Nikos, of course, was devastated. The family rallied round and he went back to sea, eventually learning to live with his grief. Then he met Marina. She was fifteen years younger than him, a striking woman and, he told us later, he was immediately smitten. After a brief courtship she moved in with him and for a while she made him very happy. So happy that he lowered his guard.

We heard Marina before we met her. So, I imagine, did the rest of Metamorfosi. It was my first summer at Villa Artemis and the little cottage was so crowded with Christopher's family and mine that we tended to spend most of our time on the balcony, often looking up at the building site and wondering when we might be able to move into rather more comfortable quarters. Not that it was unpleasant, sipping a class of something cool under the grape vine that shaded the balcony. The shriek, when it came, sounded as though a large animal – possibly a wild boar – had been trapped in one of those gruesome snares that poachers use. For a ghastly moment we imagined the poor creature, its leg crushed and bleeding in the trap's cruel jaws. But there were no boars on our land and certainly no traps. The shriek came again. It seemed to be coming from Nikos's land. From his house. From his balcony. From Marina, who was on the balcony and who was very, very angry about something. Christopher could not make out precisely what she was angry about – except that it had to do with Nikos. He, poor man, was hiding inside the house.

That was the first time we heard her but sadly it was not the last. Sometimes the shriek would pierce the air at midday, sometimes late evening. Even though we now knew who and what it was, it was still a little unnerving. Heaven knows what it must have been like to be in the same house or, God forbid, in the same room as her. The only time we could guarantee a shriek-free period was when Nikos was out on his boat – which might explain why his fishing trips seemed to take longer as time went by. Clearly things were not going well between Nikos and Marina. It was the following summer before we realised just how bad they were.

Nikos arrived on our balcony looking very unhappy. Normally a pretty garrulous man, he exchanged no more than the briefest pleasantries and asked to see Peppy. It was clear that he wanted to talk to her in private, so we all made ourselves scarce and left them to it. After a respectable interval, we went back into the cottage to find Nikos in a dreadful state. It is not unusual for Greek men to show extremes of emotion, even to shed the occasional tear in public. Peppy's father, for one, will get misty eyed at the slightest provocation: his grandson's first words; memories from childhood or even (and maybe especially) Olympiakos beating Panathinaikos at football. But here was Nikos sobbing uncontrollably, the tears streaming down his face, gasping for breath. Surely there had not been another tragedy in the family? Not quite. It was Marina. She had left him.

My first reaction was to think: lucky Nikos. That was followed, a split second later, by: lucky us. No more shrieking! Surely Nikos must be mightily relieved to be rid of her. Seemingly not. We left Peppy and Nikos to it again and it was another hour before he emerged, still sobbing but rather more in control of himself. We offered our sympathy, but what Nikos really needed even more than that was a lawyer: hence the urgent need to see Peppy. Marina, it turned out, not only had the ability to terrify half the population of the eastern Peloponnese when she was at full volume, she had another talent too. Marina was very good at offering comfort to vulnerable men and the relationships appeared to end in tears – with Marina, after a suitable interval, ending up a little wealthier than she had been at the start of the relationship.

The strategy she adopted with Nikos was simple – or so he told Peppy. Incidentally, I am not breaking any lawyer/client confidentiality here: Nikos was only too keen to tell anyone who would listen what had happened to him, often at great length and invariably with many tears. What we learned was the reason for the shrieking. It turns out that what Marina wanted was for him to put his properties in Piraeus in her name. Love her though he might once have done, he had some misgivings about this. It was when he expressed them that the shrieking began. And continued until he gave in. And then, when the deed was done, she left him. Nikos was upset not only because he was a much poorer man than he had been and was now, once again, faced with having to live alone, but there was also the question of pride. He had fallen into what seemed to have been a very obvious trap and thus had been made to look a fool.

'Everyone in the village is laughing at me,' he told us and then, raising his hands high above his head, he went on: 'I have horns like this!'

It seems that when the Greeks tell a man he has horns, it means he has been a fool in matters of the heart. The horns are thought to be deer antlers and the expression comes from the fact that your antlers (or foolishness) can be seen by everyone but yourself. You are branded for ever as a cuckold.

'They are saying in the village that next season instead of hunting deer they will be hunting me, my horns are so big.'

Over the next week Nikos came to visit almost every day and the tears flowed every time. It was all desperately sad. Nikos may or may not have been a fool in matters of the heart, but he was a decent man. Gradually he managed to come to terms with his loss and we enjoyed rather more peaceful evenings, but on my next visit to Greece I discovered something else had changed.

The first thing I do when I arrive at the cottage is to go out onto the balcony and drink in the view. It never, ever fails to lift my spirits. That first sight of the bay surrounded by mountains and the sun setting over the sea is easily the best cure I know for the soul-sapping disease that afflicts people who must live in a big city like London and, in my case, deal with politicians on a daily basis. But it was clear that something was missing – something that had been there when we first saw this bay and was as much a part of the view as the beach and the reef. It was the boat – the fishing boat that belonged to Nikos. She was called 'Meraki Mou' which roughly translates as 'My Joyful Hobby'. We were all very fond of her with her jaunty blue-and-white paint job and the sense that similar boats had been used to catch fish in these waters for generations, if not centuries. The children would spend hours climbing up the side, hauling themselves onto the deck and then hurling themselves off again. Mostly Nikos didn't mind. We adults had our own reasons for being pretty keen on her too: if Nikos had a good morning's fishing we might very well be the beneficiaries. Mostly, though, it was her presence in the bay that mattered to us. Quite simply, she looked the part and every picture I have ever taken of the bay has her sitting proudly on the water, her shape reflected in its calm surface. I knew how fond Nikos was of her too – both fond and proud. But she had gone and I couldn't think why.

For a moment I imagined the worst. Perhaps Nikos, in the depths of his despair, had climbed on board his beloved boat one night with only his sad memories and a bottle of something strong, sailed out of the bay and into the dark waters of the Aegean and simply kept going until his fuel tank ran dry. Then, with the palest of moons glinting on the black water, he had slipped over the side, to be reunited finally with his dead wife.

When I went down to the beach, I discovered something else that struck me as strange: a large patch of shingle near the shoreline where something very big had been burned to a cinder. It was not until Christopher arrived and told me all about it that I made the connection. It was less melodramatic and certainly less romantic than my fevered imaginings had conjured up – but altogether more typical of the way Greeks like Nikos deal with crises.

C: Like Dad, I had grown attached to the old boat. I was spending a lot of time at the bay by this stage, trying to make the cottage liveable and get work started on the building site, and it was always a pleasure to see her riding at anchor. So I, too, had been shocked to discover she was missing. I went straight down to the beach and was greatly relieved to find Nikos and the boat both sitting behind the rocks that had obscured my view. He'd had her hauled out of the water. Thank God for that. My relief was short-lived.

'Good morning Nikos, fixing the old girl up are you? Giving her a new coat of paint maybe?' I asked him.

'Ach, I wish I was,' he replied. 'No, she has to be got rid of. It's the fault of that bitch I was stupid enough to get involved with, the one who made such a fool of me.'

'But why do you have to get rid of the boat?'

'Because I need the money. She didn't just take my properties, she left me with debts too. How am I supposed to repay them? I have my pension and I have my olive trees but I'm not the rich man she thought I was, the cow.'

I was curious as to why he needed to drag the boat out of the water if he planned to sell her. She wasn't exactly the size of an ocean-going liner, but she was a solid old boat and it would not have been easy. But I had things to do and Nikos was getting teary again, so I made an excuse to leave him and promised to see him later. I had been in the house for about an hour when I smelled burning. Then I saw the smoke. There was an awful lot of it and it appeared to be coming from the beach. There had been nobody on the beach earlier apart from Nikos – not even campers cooking their fish over a wood fire, as they often did. I ran out to see what was going on.

The scene was like something out of an old-fashioned horror movie. Nikos's beautiful old boat was burning. There were bright orange flames shooting up and thick black smoke. Nikos himself was running around the blaze like a man demented, sloshing water on it from a big can. Blackened by the dense smoke and cursing under his breath, he looked like a deranged goblin. Obviously there had been an accident. Maybe he'd been using a blowtorch to clean off some old paint to smarten the boat up before selling her and things had gone wrong. I looked around for another container so that I could get some water from the sea and try to help Nikos extinguish the flames. And then I realised it wasn't water he was splashing on the flames. It was petrol. He's gone mad, I thought, it must have been the loneliness.

But once again I was wrong. He wasn't quite as mad as he appeared – exactly the opposite in fact. When he had said he needed to get rid of the boat he had meant just that. He could have tried selling her, but that would have taken time and effort and she probably wouldn't have fetched much money: fishermen are pretty canny when it comes to buying old boats. He had a much more lucrative plan in mind and the partner in his enterprise was rich beyond the dreams of even the richest Greek shipping magnate. It was the source of the massive sums that had been spent (and often squandered) in an effort to turn Greece into the modern, prosperous country she threatened to become before the arrival of the great credit crunch. It was the European Union.

The bureaucrats of Brussels had come up with a scheme that might not mend Nikos's broken heart, but would certainly fill a gap in his bank balance. And all he had to do to benefit from it was destroy his old fishing boat. Then the bureaucrats could put another little tick in another little box on another little form and pretend that another contribution had been made to the great scandal of over-fishing that they themselves had helped create.

The next day, with the smoke still rising from that once charming old boat, a JCB was despatched to our beach to finish off the job of wrecking her and an official was on hand with his notebook to record that the deed had been done. Score one for Brussels; one for Nikos (at least he got his cheque); nil for the European taxpayer (Dad) and nil for the cause of preserving the fish stocks of our European waters. Because the next day, of course, Nikos was out fishing again. Not for a moment had he intended to stop. He was as likely to give up fishing as a bureaucrat is likely to stop filling in forms: it would have been utterly alien to his nature.

He had a friend in the village who kept his own fishing boat in our bay so they decided to share it. They went halves on fuel, maintenance and whatever they managed to catch. Which meant – from our selfish viewpoints – that we would not, after all, have to do without our wonderful fried fish lunches. Not that Nikos would have stopped fishing even if he had not had a friend: he'd have just used his old red bath tub. It isn't really a bath tub but it looks like one and it's no bigger.

He had always kept it on the beach as a way of getting out to his fishing boat without having to swim. Nikos was nearing seventy and had a limp from an old injury to his leg. On land he was rather ungainly but as soon as he stepped into this tiny red tub he became as graceful as a tightrope walker. I once tried standing up in the bath tub and promptly fell overboard, almost capsizing it in the process. The only way to manoeuvre it was to stand up and use a long oar, much like a gondolier in Venice. Except that gondoliers didn't use bathtubs.

A few weeks after the ceremonial burning, Nikos invited himself over for lunch and said he would bring the fish. He was late – even allowing for Greek time. I looked out from the balcony and saw a red blob on the sea with Nikos standing up in it holding what looked like a very long stick. Half an hour later he was at our door with a lovely big octopus. He apologised for being late but said he'd wanted the octopus to be really fresh. It was. I asked him how he'd been so sure he would catch one, given that we'd been trying to do the same for about fifteen years in various places and had never had a nibble. It turns out you have to be pretty smart.

'The octopus is very clever,' he said. 'They aren't stupid like the fish. You must understand how they work. First you have to find their house. Every octopus has its own little cave. That is why I was over the rocks. It's not easy to find the cave. They don't like to come out unless they can see some food. The way to tell if an octopus is hiding is to look at the seabed outside the cave. If you see some small fish bones, maybe some shells, then you know this is where the octopus has been eating.'

Nikos made this sound easy and obvious. I thought it would probably take me ten years just to be able to tell the difference between an octopus's last meal and the rest of the seabed but I just nodded wisely.

'Then comes the difficult bit. You have to persuade the octopus to come out. They are very cautious. The only way is to show them something very tasty like prawns. They love prawns. But you must make the prawn swim naturally. You can't just drop a line down with a prawn on it, they will know. And you have to make sure the octopus gets far enough out of its cave. If it only comes out a little way you have no chance.'

All this sounded like it would need another ten years' experience. Nikos was basically telling me you had to think like an octopus. I could just about stretch to thinking like my cat but only because I've been living with him for ten years and can predict his every move. I wasn't sure how you could live with an octopus.

'If you get the octopus far enough away from the cave then

you can use the spear, but you have to go for the head. If you only hit a leg it will be no good.'

So Nikos is standing up in a bathtub bobbing on the surface of the sea and spearing an octopus fifteen feet below him. And aiming for its head. It all sounded so easy. I did at least manage to cut it up and cook it under Nikos's instruction. This bit really was easy – though not necessarily something for the squeamish. When you are dealing with a slippery creature with eight legs it's hard to know where to start carving. Nikos showed me how to cut down between each leg in turn and remove the mouth, the only bit that can't be eaten. Then it just got thrown in a pot with a little water and lots of oil. After it had boiled for twenty minutes a little vinegar was added and most of the water boiled off. That was it. Easy. And very, very tasty.

# 6

*In which the rats tame Oscar the wild cat and John is told he'll have to knock down the cottage*

It was now several months since I had first set eyes on Villa Artemis. My suspicions that Christopher had been just a shade optimistic when he'd told me how easy it would be to build the villa were beginning to harden. We still didn't even have the official permission we needed to start work. But at least we had the cottage to live in and the rest of the property was looking spectacular – thanks to nature rather than any of our efforts. On that first visit it had been the middle of winter and the grounds were badly neglected, in spite of old Babageorgos's best efforts, and looking pretty sad. When I went back in the spring they had been transformed. The lemon grove and hillside was a mass of wild flowers: iris, lily, twenty different orchids, poppies, primrose, buttercup, figwort, violets, crocus, cyclamen and much, much more that I had no hope of identifying.

The children's favourite looked fairly innocuous but was clearly a plant with a serious attitude problem. It stands about half a metre high and is a straggly green affair with little bulbous pods hanging down. When I first saw one of them and bent down to touch a pod I had a nasty shock. It shot off the stem, whacked me in the face and squirted me full in the eyes. I had had my first encounter with a squirting cucumber. The children were delighted and I felt rather foolish, but what a clever thing for a plant to do. The seeds are contained in the pods and the squirting spreads them far and wide – apart from deterring any hungry grazer.

Botanists say there are no fewer than six thousand species of aromatic plants and wild flowers in Greece. That's more than anywhere in Europe. Tiny, piercing blue delphiniums. Deep yellow calendulas. Tall blue-purple chicory. Multicoloured anemones. Even the cottage was beginning to look enticing now that there was less danger of the roof falling in. The vine that shaded the balcony from the increasingly fierce sun was holding out the promise of a decent grape harvest and the bougainvillea provided a riotous splash of colour. I was puzzled by the clumps of geraniums planted everywhere around the cottage. They were very pretty but why so many? It turned out that mosquitoes don't like them – or so the locals believe – and they stay away and find someone else to bite. I wish the same could have been said of the rats.

Christopher had been pretty confident that he and Babageorgos had dealt with all of them in that first savage assault, but it turned out he was wrong. They had relatives. Clearly not close relatives – or at least, not close enough to share the cottage with them – but once the first lot had been dealt with and the cottage had been cleared, the relatives decided that they would move in. The first night I slept there and heard a scrabbling noise above me I thought there was a wild animal on the roof – probably, I was told by a local, a pine marten. How delightful, I thought, being so close to nature. The following evening I saw the 'pine martens' scurrying across the vines above our heads as we sipped a glass of Tassos's wine on the balcony. They looked remarkably like rats – unsurprising, really, because that is what they were. So much for being close to nature.

To be fair, they were actually rather sweet rats as rats go. These were not the scary-looking beasts that skulk in Victorian sewers in London spreading fear and loathing and probably a spot of plague in their spare time. They had fluffy white coats and looked rather appealing. Except for the tails. It's the tails that do it every time, isn't it? If squirrels had tails like rats we'd shoot the lot of them on sight, I dare say.

As it happens, I gave quite a lot of thought to shooting them. I pictured myself sitting on the balcony with a loaded shotgun across my knee, letting loose every time a rat went for a late evening stroll with a few of its friends a couple of feet above my head. There were some obvious drawbacks. One was that the only time I have ever used a shotgun was on a clay pigeon range in Scotland and, in spite of all the pellets I blasted at them, the clays survived. Maybe these were specially designed clays with their own inbuilt avoidance systems – like the chaff helicopters throw out in war zones if a missile is detected – or maybe I'm a lousy shot. The other drawback was that even if I managed by some fluke to hit one or two rats I would destroy the delightful pergola and grape vine on which they were dancing in the process and probably take out a couple of grandchildren at the same time. So I turned to a far more effective killing machine: Oscar.

Oscar is Christopher's cat. He loves Christopher with every hair of his very hairy body because Christopher saved him from the streets of Athens when he was a kitten. The Athenian authorities have a zero tolerance approach to stray cats. They catch them and kill them and if they can't catch them they lay poison for them. Not nice. But Christopher saved Oscar from that terrible fate and Oscar has shown his gratitude ever since. If cats can love humans, Oscar's relationship with Christopher puts Antony and Cleopatra or Napoleon and Josephine in the shade. The problem is that Christopher is the *only* human he loves. There are one or two others – his children, for instance – whom he tolerates, but the rest of the human race are the enemy. He hates us all.

The children's babysitter, Judith, once phoned Christopher as he was about to go on stage for a concert in Athens. The conversation went something like this:

'Chris, you must come home now! Immediately!'

'For God's sake why?'

'Because I am in the bathroom and I cannot get out and the children are by themselves in the kitchen.'

'What! You've managed to lock yourself in?'

'No, Oscar is in the hallway and he won't let me pass.'

It wasn't the first time poor Judith had suffered at the claws of Oscar. Christopher rang me one afternoon to complain that his afternoon siesta had been disrupted by him. He was woken up by a scream from Judith, who was meant to be looking after the children. He raced into the kitchen to find her perched on the counter – with Oscar perched a few feet away looking rather pleased with himself. Apparently she had been trapped on the balcony by him and, when she thought his attention was diverted, dashed back into the kitchen. But she wasn't quick enough to slam the door behind her and had to leap onto the counter to escape.

You may think that makes Judith a bit of a wimp, but that is because you have never been attacked by Oscar. I have been, and I live to tell the tale only because I was wearing heavy boots at the time and thick trousers. That is the sort of cat Oscar is – vicious and unpredictable with a taste for living flesh – which made him the obvious alternative to the shotgun. We would put Oscar in the attic and let him finish the rats off. I was almost beginning to feel sorry for them. It wasn't easy getting Oscar up there but we managed it in the end – or, rather, Christopher did. I am as likely to try to pick Oscar up and stuff him into an attic as I am to stuff a stoat down my trousers. He slammed the trap door into place and we waited for the pathetic squealing of terrified rodents and the carnage that would surely follow. And we waited. The squealing, when it came, sounded remarkably like mewing. It was the sound of a terrified cat. Oscar had met his match and the rats survived. Maybe they ganged up on him or maybe, at heart, Oscar was just a coward – perfectly happy to terrorise human weaklings but pathetic in the presence of his natural prey.

So, since violence was clearly not the answer, we tried for some sort of compromise. We decided that we could live with the rats on the pergola and possibly even in the attic – just so long as they left the kitchen and living area to us and the children. I understand now why the term 'ratting on a deal' has entered our vocabulary. It turns out that it is not possible to negotiate a compromise with rats. In fairness to them, they did confine themselves to their own quarters for a few months but then – perhaps because they got bored – they decided to extend their territory. That's when we turned to poison.

It worked very well in the sense that it killed them, but a combination of dead rats and hot weather is not conducive to a pleasant environment. On the plus side, the smell reduced the number of unwelcome visitors hoping to cadge a bed for the night. On the minus side, the sight of a large rat's tail poking out of the housing at the back of the cooker as you prepare the evening meal has limited appeal. There are, I promise you, more pleasant ways of spending a summer's evening than dismantling a cooker, carting it out of the kitchen into the garden and removing from it a rats' nest which includes the corpses of one very large Mummy rat and several babies.

So the poison turned out to be a mistake. It would also have been wiser, with the benefit of hindsight, not to turn to the internet for helpful hints. I really did not want to know that although rats live for only about eighteen months in the wild, one colony of them can produce 2,000 babies a year. Nor did it cheer me up to learn that a single rat produces 25,000 droppings every year. Multiply those two figures and you come up with something roughly equal to the size of a bank boss's bonus at the height of the so-called boom years. Not that I'm equating the two species. Rats, after all, have a certain integrity and some people even like keeping them as pets.

Christopher and I realised that if we were not to be buried alive under a mountain of rat droppings or eaten in our beds by 2,000 starving baby rats we had to come up with yet another strategy fairly swiftly. It came to us more or less straight from the American military manual as practised in Vietnam: the way to defeat an unseen enemy is to destroy its habitat so that it has nowhere to hide. In Vietnam the Americans had the most sophisticated killing machine in the history of modern warfare: half a million military personnel armed with everything from attack helicopters to napalm and Agent Orange. I had Christopher, armed with a rusty old saw and a pair of loppers, which he used to hack down the vines and branches overhanging the cottage. It was clear what the rats were doing: leaping from the trees onto our roof and then finding little holes to get through into the attic. The trees had to go and the holes had to be filled. So that's what Christopher did and it seemed to do the trick. Within a few weeks, the attic was silent and the only smells in the cottage were those you would expect from small children.

Not that we were complacent: those rats had had decades of comfortable living and it seemed unlikely that they would reconcile themselves to being evicted. They would almost certainly be back. We pictured them eyeing the cottage from their nests somewhere out there beyond the lemon grove and

The Lousios Gorge where John and Christopher first discovered the glory of the Peloponnese.

The cottage balcony shaded with a grape vine. The rats loved it!

Nikos's boat riding in the bay, with the house just visible on the hill behind.

Poppies on the beach in the spring.

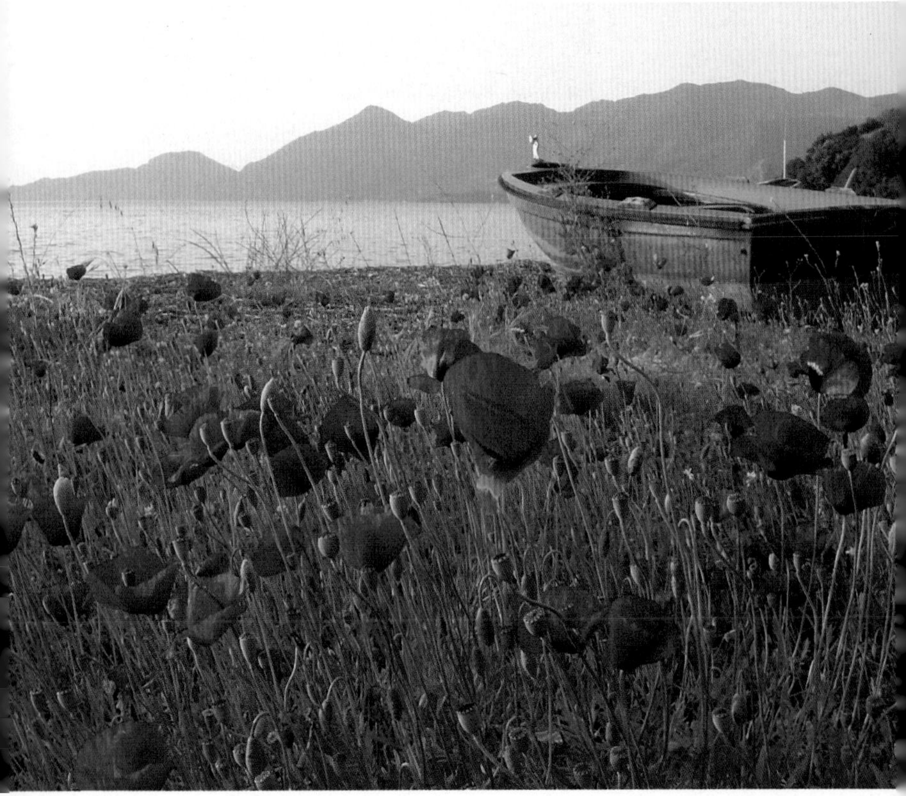

Oscar stalking Henry on their first encounter . . . and totally failing to intimidate him!

Oscar's given up trying to scare Henry and now wants to be friends . . . Henry is still unimpressed.

Dimitris on the hunt for Henry and failing to get even close to him.

The top storey gets under way.

The view from the living room before the windows were installed.

Making real progress on the house at last, but still an awful lot to do.

Peppy and Hector enjoy the sunset from the beach.

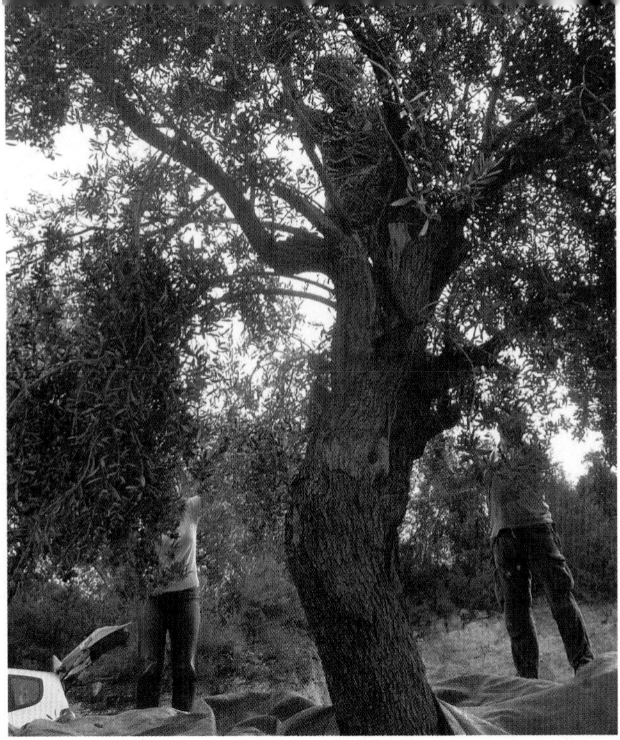

We start to harvest
our olives.

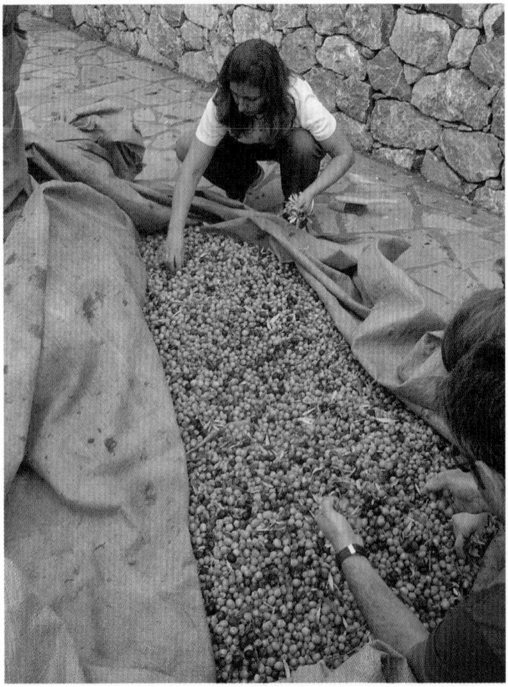

Peppy and Christopher
inspect the haul.

The magnificent ancient theatre of Epidavros.

Peppy competes with nature by stringing dragonfly fairy lights in the lemon grove.

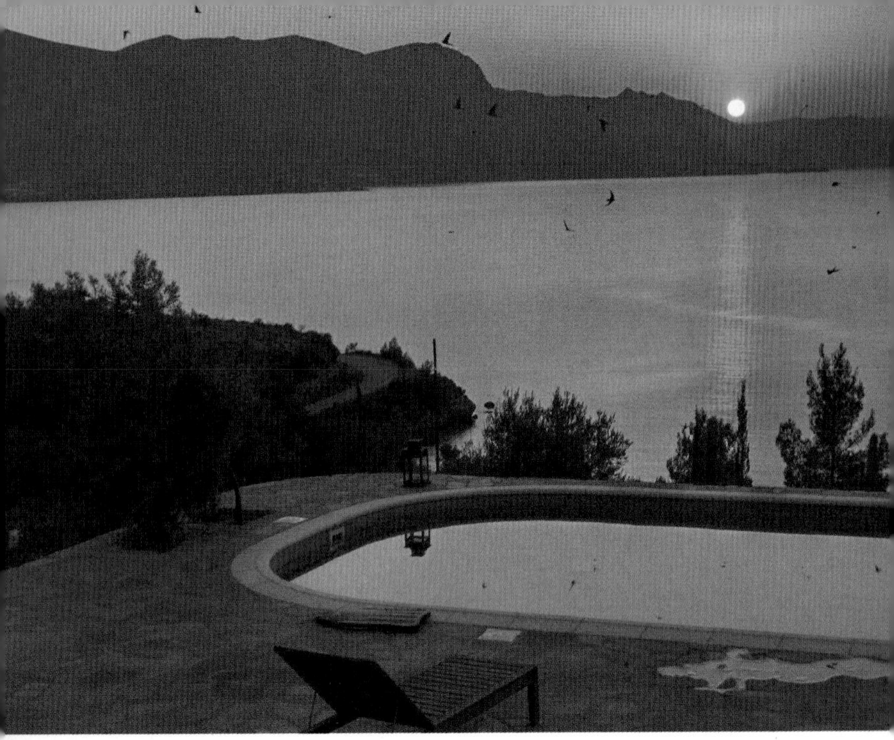

House martins hunting at sunset over the pool.

Crumbs, is it really finished! John and Christopher pose for the camera.

planning their next assault. It turns out that actually we *were* being complacent. Having employed Vietnam War tactics reasonably successfully, we should at that stage have learned lessons from an earlier conflict. In 1942, so historians would have us believe, Singapore fell to the Japanese army because the big guns defending it were pointing in the wrong direction. The Japanese were expected to attack by sea but instead they came by land from Malaya. It turned out that Christopher and I were doing something similar. All the time we were engaged in combat with the rats, another threat was building from a different source altogether: the bureaucrats in the planning office.

The population of Greece is about ten million. Most of the middle class in the cities is made up of lawyers. Outside the cities there are farmers. But everywhere there are bureaucrats. They work in the different public services, for central government and local authorities, for any one of a thousand different departments dealing with everything from applications for car licences to providing the stamp books necessary for those all-important stamps. Not in case you need to post a lot of letters, but as a way of showing that you have paid your national health insurance. Who needs computers when everyone can collect stamps?

Obviously, every country has its army of bureaucrats, but Greece is in a league of its own. That may be because working for the public sector is just about the only way to guarantee a secure income and a pension or it may be because the only way to defend yourself against the bureaucrats is to become one. I would estimate that roughly seven million of the ten million Greeks are bureaucrats. The entire public sector is one massive job creation scheme – creating jobs for more bureaucrats – and most of them are dedicated either to stopping people doing things or making it so difficult that still more bureaucrats will be needed to deal with the problems.

I came to think of it in terms of a novel by Charles Dickens. In *Little Dorrit* Dickens created a government department that existed to deal with people applying for permits to register their inventions or set up a business. They would be given a form and sent away to fill it in. Then, when they took it back for approval, it would be filed away or, more accurately, stay buried under all the other forms – a great, teetering mountain of them – and forgotten about. That was what the department existed to do and it did it so efficiently that no applications were ever dealt with. I suspect every bureaucrat in Greece is given a copy of *Little Dorrit* on their first day in the job and told to go away and learn from it.

I knew something of this before buying the property but, in my naivety, I assumed we would need to have very little contact – if any – with the bureaucrats. After all, the house we were planning to build already had planning permission; the foundations had already been built and even the pillars that would support the floors and roof were in place, sunk deep into the hillside in case of earthquakes. So it was really just a matter of informing the local planning office that we were resuming work. Or so I assumed.

It turned out that our building permission had run out because work had stopped on the site so long ago that we would have to renew it. No problem, said my ever optimistic son, it's just the standard procedure. But of course there was a problem – not with the house, but with the cottage. I learned about it in one of those telephone conversations with Christopher that I had come to dread. They invariably followed the same pattern. First he would tell me how well things were going and how wise I had been to buy the property because our area was becoming the most sought-after in the whole of

Greece and virtually the entire population of Athens was desperate to buy a house in the area, which meant we would be able to name our price if we ever decided to sell. And then, just as we were about to say goodbye and hang up, he would say: 'Umm . . . there is one thing you should know about . . . could be a bit tricky.'

That, I came to realise, could mean anything, but it was always something bad.

C: I suppose Dad has a point. The thing is, I knew he'd invested an awful lot of money and energy into the property and it's just possible that I had rather glossed over some of the problems that might arise. And obviously, since he was usually a thousand miles away and always very busy and had so many other things to think about I tended to try to shield him from the worst of it. Or at least, that's how I saw it. Anyway what this conversation consisted of was me having to give Dad a bit of bad news about the cottage . . . possibly disastrous news. Here is roughly how it went:

'It looks like the cottage might be a bit illegal,' I told him.

'Why?'

'Because it's built too near to the sea.'

'But it's ALWAYS been near the sea. Practically on the bloody beach. That's why I bought it. That's its appeal.'

'Well yes, but there are rules about how near the sea you're allowed to build and . . .'

'. . . but it wasn't me that built it, was it? It was somebody else. I was in short trousers at the time. I just bought it. So it was hardly my fault was it?'

'True, but it's still illegal.'

'Since when?'

'Since the rules were changed a few years ago.'

There was a pause . . . quite a long pause. And Dad's voice became softer – always a worrying sign.

'You're not telling me I might have to knock it down, are you?'

I contemplated hanging up and pretending we'd been cut off, but I knew there was no escape.

'Well . . . technically . . . I suppose I am.'

Another pause. This time his voice rose a bit and he switched to sarcastic mode, the approach he uses when a politician caught with his hand in the till tries to daim that actually he was acting within the rules when he'd made his nanny pregnant and then claimed expenses for her to have an abortion.

'Technically, eh? Well, what a relief that is! I never liked the bloody place anyway. I mean, that's the real reason I bought it. I wanted to knock it down all along. Who could possibly want a delightfully charming old cottage on the beach with a lovely veranda where you can sit and watch the sun set over a glorious bay. I mean obviously I hated it from the start and that's why I've spent a fortune putting a new roof on it and waging war on a colony of rats and generally making it a fit place to live in. Obviously I did all that JUST SO THAT I CAN BLOODY WELL KNOCK IT DOWN!'

I had to hold the phone away from my ear for that last bit. I tried a defence – feeble but worth a try.

'Well, I did tell you it was technically illegal.'

'True, but you also said it wouldn't be a problem.'

'Well,' I said, 'it shouldn't be really.'

'Well is it or isn't it?'

'Umm . . . I'm not sure really. What we'll have to do is make an application to the planning office.'

'You mean an application to get exemption from a demolition order?'

I took a very deep breath.

'Err . . . not exactly . . . an application FOR a demolition order. We're going to have to ask for permission to knock it down.'

The rest of the conversation is best not repeated. Let me just say that Dad was a little cross and a little puzzled . . . which was understandable. Once he had calmed down somewhat and once I'd had a very long talk with Peppy about the planning laws, I managed to convince him (more or less) that we didn't really have much option but to apply to knock it down. Simultaneously I tried to explain that we would probably never have to do it. The act of applying for the permit and renewing it every year might very well satisfy the authorities.

Let's start with the facts. The cottage is illegal. It is too near the sea. Nobody in Greece can build within thirty metres of the sea. Absolutely nobody. As it is illegal it obviously hasn't been connected to the power grid or to the water system. In order to get electricity you must supply the electricity company with a copy of the final planning approval for your completed house. If the property is illegal there is no planning approval and therefore no electricity. Except that the house has had electricity and water for forty years. So maybe it is legal after all and the answer to Dad's question is no. Or is it?

Well again . . . yes and no. Trying to explain the Byzantine workings of Greek bureaucracy to Dad makes me feel like one of the hapless politicians he is interviewing when you know, they know and he knows that they have an insupportable position. It is horrible and probably doomed to failure. Let me try to explain the so-called system and why our encounters with the bureaucrats were almost bound to end in tears.

When Greece finally won independence in 1832 the Ottomans began to depart, leaving behind them an awful lot of land which they had seized for their own purposes over the 400 years of their occupation. The new Greek state did the decent thing and divided this land up among the Greek people. By 1870 most Greek peasants found themselves the owners of about twenty acres. Not bad going when you consider how many olive trees can fit onto a plot that size. Many Greek families have deeds from the time naming their great, great grandfathers as being the owners of the land – not that the deeds contained precise boundary details. Instead of specific co-ordinates on the equivalent of an ordinance survey map, they might tell you that your property ran from the village road to the large rock on the corner or (even less helpfully) was bordered by a row of eucalyptus trees on one side and cypresses on the other. Not terribly helpful given that trees have a habit of dying or being chopped down. Anyway, the various members of Peppy's extended family had plots of land all over the place and one of them was handed down to us. Very nice too, you might think. And so it seemed. The people were happy that the Turks had left and they had unexpectedly become landowners. One snag was that, apart from no detailed maps, there wasn't even an official land register in the fledgling state of 'modern' Greece. I suppose nobody thought it mattered very much because in those days people stayed pretty much where they were. Everyone in the village knew who owned what.

It wasn't until 1923 that town planning was introduced, at about the time Greeks started moving to Athens from Asia Minor or Smyrna following the disastrous war against the Turks that lasted from 1919 to 1922 and the reprisals that followed it. Overnight the population of Athens nearly doubled to more than 700,000. In total more than a million Greeks settled here. There was another big influx after the Second World War when Greeks started to move to the capital from the islands and the countryside in search of what they thought would be a better life. Many of them had suffered horribly during the war – particularly those who lived in the mountains and continued the resistance. If the Germans didn't get them, starvation often did. And then, as if they hadn't suffered enough, the Greeks began fighting each other. The civil war was followed by the military dictatorship, which lasted until 1974.

So the birth of the new Greek nation could hardly be said to have been smooth and modern planning laws on a regional and national level did not really come into effect until the Greek Constitution of 1975. You might have thought that thirty years was enough time for Greece to have had sorted out a proper land registry. Not quite. Greece still doesn't have a comprehensive land registry. It also manages to be the only country in Europe apart from Albania that doesn't even have a registry for its forests.

The European Union gave Greece a lot of money to help it finish the land registry and after patiently waiting the agreed amount of time, asked for it back when the land registry still hadn't been finished. By which time the money had, of course, conveniently disappeared. Not that Greece is corrupt or anything. But just to give a small example of how things work here, take the example of a certain government minister. He was 'discovered' to be living in a six-thousand square feet villa built on the side of a mountain next to Athens. On forestry land. Completely illegally. The place had a staff of twenty, all illegal immigrants with no papers. He got off with a fine. The fact is, nobody seems to care very much. When I get indignant with my friends and point out that in Britain cabinet ministers have to resign because they've charged the taxpayer eighty pence for a bath plug, they simply shrug their shoulders and mutter '*Ellada*', which means 'Greece' and which says it all. It's not only politicians of course. Athens is surrounded by thousands of illegal houses. They are all connected to the national grid. The police drop by once a month for a *fakilaki*, a little envelope, and everyone is happy. I remember a seasoned old ex-pat explaining the system to me years ago. He was telling me how tricky it was. In Nigeria, he said, things had been simple. You just bribed everybody. Everything had a set price. In Greece things are more tricky. In some situations a bribe is acceptable but in others it could land you in jail. Knowing the difference is the key.

Dad may have been exaggerating the number of lawyers in Athens but not by as much as you would think. There are at least fifteen thousand of them. And many of them, including my wife, spend a lot of time trying to unravel who owns what. Family members suing each other over a few acres is common practice, but in our case we had to take the state to court. Or rather the air force. An airfield was built after the war that just happened to include an acre of the family land. The problem was that, with no land registry, it took fifteen years to prove that it was their land. They won eventually but it was just as well that they have a lawyer in the family, otherwise the legal fees would have wiped out the compensation. Which pretty much describes a lot of families' thinking. To survive in Greece you need your children to become a doctor, a lawyer and ideally someone in the civil service, or at least with plenty of contacts.

Getting the permission to continue building involved everything I've described above. Thakis spent weeks going from one planning office to another, we used every family contact we could think of and even the odd *fakilaki*. Eventually everyone was happy so we were allowed to proceed. In the end it's a question of perception. The British attitude just doesn't work here. There is no right and wrong way of doing something.

There is just *akri*, or leverage. This is where Greece resembles the East far more than the West. I first came across it when I was flying back to London and realised at the airport that I didn't have my passport. There was no time to go back home so I grabbed an old photocopy of the last page and hoped for the best.

'Passport!' demanded one of the two police officers at the immigration desk.

I told them I didn't have one. They looked at each other.

'What have you been doing in Greece?'

I explained about my job at the concert hall and the mood changed instantly.

'Ah, very nice. And do you know Dalarus?'

Dalarus is maybe the biggest star of Greek folk music and I told them that we did, indeed, have a concert coming up with him.

'Do you think you could get a few tickets for us then?'

I promised them that I could and gave them my mobile number. We agreed that when I got back from Britain they would ring me. We chatted a bit more, with me agreeing that Dalarus was the best musician in the world, and then they let me through. Immigration at London were horrified, of course, and couldn't understand how I had been allowed to leave without a valid passport. It simply wasn't in the rules. It wouldn't do.

I didn't even try to explain that it was down to Dalarus that I had been allowed to leave. And in a way it wasn't. I never got the call asking for the tickets. They probably had no intention of calling me. The point was that their honour had been satisfied enough to grant me a favour.

# 7

*In which John goes to war with one engineer and valiantly keeps his temper with another*

So here I was, with my first Greek summer beginning to turn to autumn, reflecting on what I had done six long months ago. I had paid far too much money for a building site and a derelict cottage and another big chunk of money to make the cottage habitable. I was now having to apply for permission to demolish it. I tried to cheer myself up by thinking of the house we would soon be building. Nobody could make me knock that down, could they? Not even the most vindictive bureaucrat. I had the planning permission and the foundations had been built and I even had my own civil engineer – Peppy's father, Thakis – to oversee the rest of the project. So nothing could go wrong . . . could it? Well actually it could and 'it' went by the name of Douskos.

Greek law requires that every sizeable building project must have a civil engineer in charge and Douskos was the engineer who had overseen the work when the property was owned by Lady Gibson-Watt. He wanted to hold onto the contract and did not want competition from Athens in the shape of Thakis on his home turf. I did not want anything to do with Douskos, who had given me an estimate for renovating the cottage which was a little on the steep side – or, to put it another way, the sum he quoted would have been enough to rebuild Carthage after the Romans destroyed it in 146 BC. Historians tell us that the Carthaginians had defended their magnificent city so fiercely during the siege that the women cut off their long hair to be twisted into bowstrings. I had visions of cutting off another part of the Douskos anatomy when I saw his estimate. Clearly he regarded me as a foreign mug with more money than sense who would, in the end, have to concede that I needed him and his connections in the area if the villa were ever to be built. I told Christopher to sack him. Christopher told me he was refusing to be sacked. We had another one of our long distance conversations.

'I don't see the problem,' I said. 'He's never done any work for us, so we just hand the job over to Thakis and that's that.'

'Not possible,' said Christopher. 'Douskos has to agree to go and the regulations say we can't make him. And anyway he says we have to pay him 5,000 euros for the work he's done already.'

'What! But he's already been paid for that by Gibson-Watt! You don't buy a house from someone and then pay the builder who did some work on it years before you'd even set eyes on the bloody place!'

'Not in Britain you don't, but this is Greece, remember, and the rules are different here.'

As if I could forget. The fact is, Douskos had us over a barrel and it seemed that the law was on his side. We could either give him the contract for the new house, which would cost so much I'd probably have to sell all my children and grandchildren to white slavers, or pay him to do work he'd already done and for which he'd already been paid. It would have been sensible to grit my teeth and pay him off. After all, I wouldn't just be fighting Douskos: he had the local planning office on his side. A compromise was obviously the wisest course. So I gave Christopher a message – preferably to be delivered verbatim:

'My father says you are a greedy *!$@*! and he will not give you a cent, let alone 5,000 euros, and if you ever come within a mile of this place he will personally scoop you up in a JCB and bury you in the foundations. Alive.'

Christopher said it would be difficult because there is no word in Greek for *!$@*!, which I must say, given the frequent need for it, I find surprising. But the rest of the message was duly delivered. Douskos was not even mildly perturbed. He assured us that he would continue to be our civil engineer whether we wanted him or not. He was – not unlike the Pope – unsackable. His name was on the building permit and would stay there unless he agreed to remove it and he would not. So things were looking grim. And then, for once, the gods smiled on us.

The permit, Peppy discovered, had to be renewed every four years and the present one had only a few months to run. So we sat it out, waited until the permit expired and submitted an application for a new permit with the name of Thakis in the box where Douskos should have been. It should have taken a matter of days. It actually took three weeks of meetings (Greek bureaucrats never turn down the chance of a good meeting) at various planning offices in Poros, Piraeus and Athens. One minor problem was that crucial files relating to our case had mysteriously vanished from the offices in Poros, which happened to be the island on which Douskos ran his business. But the combination of father and daughter – Thakis and Peppy – proved formidable and the permit arrived. Our celebrations – as we were to learn much later – were a little premature. The ghost of Douskos would haunt us to the very end. But we could at least get on with the building. Now all we needed was someone who could actually manage it, who could be on site and make sure that the walls were built and we had a roof over our heads.

This was not something Thakis could do on a day-to-day basis because he had a wife and family in Athens. We had to have a foreman, a site manager who would be there every day, making sure that everyone did what they were supposed to be doing and, ideally, with some building skills of his own. It should have been simple. The accepted way of going about these things was that you simply handed everything over to a local building contractor and let him get on with it. The problem with that was not only the cost – even allowing for the premium charged for being a naive foreigner – but also the fact that no contractor would give you a completion date with a penalty clause. In fact, they laughed at the idea. This was a typical conversation:

'How long will it take?'

'One year. Or thereabouts.'

'Depending on what?'

At this point the contractor says nothing but shrugs – a simple gesture that tells you all you need to know.

'You mean you can't give me a completion date?'

'Of course not. Maybe we have a problem with sub-contractors. Or the plumber . . . maybe one day he don't show up . . . or two days. Who knows? Maybe some piece of equipment breaks down. Maybe the weather gets so hot we cannot work. Who knows?'

'But surely it's your job to see that those problems are dealt with. You're the contractor after all. Isn't that what you're being paid to do?'

Another shrug, which I interpreted as meaning roughly: how stupid do you think I am? What if someone comes along and gives me another job? You really think I'm going to turn him down because I'm working for you? Still, I persisted . . .

'If I give you the contract I'd expect there to be a penalty clause so if it's not finished on time you'd have to pay up.'

This time there was no need even for a shrug. Just a look of utter incomprehension. And, of course, he had a very good point. If he was not prepared to give me even a vague indication as to when he might finish the job how could there possibly be a penalty clause? It was what I think philosophers call a category error – or, if you prefer, just plain stupidity on my part. So if I wanted the house to be built while I was still capable of getting to the bedrooms without the help of a stairlift, it was clear that we would have to handle it ourselves. We would have to find a site manager. As it happened, the site manager found us – or, more specifically, found Christopher. His name was Daniel, the man I introduced you to in Chapter One.

The first time they met, Christopher was having a fish supper at the local taverna in Methana with a group of friends. He got chatting to someone at the bar whom he assumed was a local. He didn't look exactly like a local. He was dark-skinned and dark-haired, but he was also about a foot taller than the average Greek male. But he asked the usual questions. Where are you staying? Have you come from Athens? What do you do there?

Greeks, as Christopher points out, have no fear of seeming nosy. There is none of the reserve you might find further north in Europe – especially when it comes to personal matters. Once they have established where you work and what you do, the next question may very well be about how much you earn and if it's your house you're talking about, they will want to know how much it cost. I have yet to be asked how often I make love to my partner, but no doubt it's only a matter of time. Christopher pricked up his ears when Daniel mentioned that he owned an old MG sports car. They're not exactly common in Athens, let alone out in the countryside or in a little place like Methana. When he started enthusing about other old British sports cars it finally dawned on Christopher.

'Where are you from?' he asked him.

'England,' he said.

'So why are we talking in Greek?'

That was the start of what turned out to be a long relationship between the three of us. In some ways it was rewarding and even entertaining, but mostly it was deeply frustrating. At first Christopher could scarcely believe his luck. Not only had he bumped into a local who turned out to be English but he was a builder as well. It couldn't have been better and when he told Daniel about our building project he swore that he was just the man. Sure enough, he arrived at the cottage the next morning to have a look. This, remember, was in the early days before the small matter of demolishing the cottage had been raised. We still had to get it properly habitable so that we had somewhere decent to live to use as a base before tackling the big house. We already had a new bathroom and a new roof by now but there were still a lot of things to do. We needed a new kitchen, new ceilings and some fairly crucial propping up of walls that looked as though they might fall over. Daniel assured Christopher he could do all those things and pretty much everything else. The first I knew about him was in one of Christopher's phone calls to my home in London.

'Fantastic news! I've found the perfect builder! He's English and he's brilliant and he can do absolutely everything we need! And he's a really good bloke too!'

I know there are lots of exclamation marks there, but I promise you they are justified and, in spite of my natural scepticism in the face of my son's enthusiasm, I have to say that I was impressed. Daniel did sound just the right man –

even allowing for the fact that, like most other Greek builders, he was not exactly overburdened with modesty. By his own estimation, he was probably the finest roof-builder in southern Europe. Naturally, we made a few enquiries about him in the local area. Yes, they said, we know Daniel. And is he a good builder? Oh yes, they said, he's done some very good roofs . . . very good . . . And then they would trail off and look a little evasive. After a pause they would ask: 'And what is it exactly that you are hiring him to do?'

'Oh . . . the lot. Everything. We're thinking of putting him in charge of the whole project.'

'Hmm . . .'

'Is there a problem with that?' we would ask, a little anxiously.

'Hmm . . . he builds very good roofs.'

And that was as far as we ever got. I know, I know, we should have been a little more persistent and paid a bit more attention to the way their eyes didn't quite meet ours at that point but we badly needed a good, reliable builder and Daniel was, as everyone said, a good builder. Reliability was the problem . . . not to mention one or two other character traits. But I think at this point I'd better hand over to Christopher.

C: If it's true that I am not the best judge of builders it may be because of my day job. When you play in a small chamber orchestra you are totally exposed. Your colleagues hear every note you play, even if the audience doesn't, and spot every mistake. Try telling them you are the greatest living cellist and you will be lucky not to have a violin rammed down your throat. You can't even pretend you are better than your colleague. Everybody knows exactly how good everyone is. If a fellow cellist is better than you, well you just have to live with it. Or do a lot more practice. Most jobs, including being a builder, aren't like that: you are not being judged on a daily, let alone an hourly, basis. It's relatively easy to cover up mistakes – at least for a while. So my bullshit-detecting radar is not as finely tuned as it should be – unlike Dad who has to use his all the time in his job. He's spent his life developing it. When it comes to being able to make unverifiable claims and getting away with it, politicians are the polar opposite of musicians.

Having said all this, even Dad was caught out by Daniel – at least at first. It helped enormously that he was English so Dad could talk to him directly rather than having to use me as an interpreter. I say English, but I'm not sure how English you can be when you have spent twenty years living in Methana married to a local as Daniel had done. I see it in myself and I know Dad does too. I am clearly not the same as I was when I came to Athens. But Athens is different from Methana. In Athens half of my friends are Brits or at least English speaking. We take the kids to bonfire night, see Shakespeare plays in English and generally live a reasonably cosmopolitan existence. Daniel has spent all his time living in Methana, which may be beautiful but is hardly cosmopolitan.

It has the feel of a Victorian seaside resort without the fairground combined with a Georgian spa town; failed millionaires' yachting playground and the oldest population outside Miami Beach in Florida – all set in the magnificent Aegean. If it sounds unlikely, that's because it is. To add to its charms there are more active volcanoes on Methana than in the rest of the Peloponnese put together. Short of one of them coming to life and destroying the entire peninsula (as one of them did a couple of thousand years ago) the most exciting sight on Methana is the old men playing backgammon under umbrellas on the seafront.

It is not exactly the sort of place you would expect an energetic young Englishman to settle. But that's what Daniel did and when I met him, as I say, it seemed a marriage made in heaven. It's not that I was totally inexperienced as far as Greek builders were concerned. I had only just finished renovating my flat in Athens and was used to the way they worked – or did not work, as the case may be. This involved them agreeing to do the job, turning up with all the tools and then disappearing for a few days. Never make the mistake of assuming that builders own only one set of tools. I think most of them must have at least five.

In fact, Daniel started out well when I hired him to do the work on the cottage, turning up almost every day and almost always on time. Admittedly he spent a lot of the day chatting to me while his helper did the work but he was clearly starved of English conversation and the job was getting done so I didn't mind too much. But slowly his appearances became less frequent. There was always an excuse. The usual one was about having to get another job finished, which again was understandable as all builders worked in this way. With so many builders around you couldn't say no to a new job for fear of it going to someone else. But by the end of the summer this was getting too much. Especially when he stopped answering his mobile phone. Whole days would go by when I couldn't get in touch with him.

This was a shame because I liked the guy. He was a fascinating character. His Greek was unbelievable. My wife was amazed by how well he spoke. He had somehow come to Methana and got involved with a local woman who already had children from a first husband. They then had their own and poor old Daniel had to support the whole lot.

Eventually Dad got to meet him. Deciding whether to give Daniel the job of building the big house was not a decision I was going to make on my own and it was important that Dad got on with him. It was a disaster from the start. Daniel was a very intelligent man. He knew an awful lot. About everything. And he liked to tell you so. This, of course, went down brilliantly with Dad, who clearly didn't know nearly enough about anything. When the subject stayed on building techniques things were fine. After all, Daniel really did seem to know his stuff. He was using laser levelling when the local builders were still using a plastic tube filled with water. His knowledge of building materials and methods was impressive. He used to work for the Ministry of Defence back in Britain but was made redundant, he said. It was when the conversation strayed off building that things started going horribly wrong. There was one memorable evening in late autumn when Daniel came for supper and I realised the relationship between him and Dad might not be completely trouble-free.

It was getting rather chilly by now and we had a fire going. Daniel knew the best way to lay a fire. He knew the best kindling to use. The best logs. And even, incredibly, the best way to scrunch up the newspaper that would light the kindling. I think he probably knew the best way to light a match but I had given up by then and had stopped listening.

Dad, as it happens, has managed to light one or two fires in his life reasonably successfully. In fact I remember one holiday he took us on when we were kids and in seven weeks we drove clear across the United States, down to Mexico and back to Washington the long way. For an eight-year-old boy it was the best holiday I could have had and I still remember it well. Most nights were spent in the big green canvas tent we had packed on top of our station wagon. Supper was always cooked on an open fire and Dad's *pièce de résistance* was managing to cook a turkey on a wood fire in the Sierra Nevada. Magical. But the turkey did not last long. The next night, when we were all in bed and Dad was sitting outside the tent reading in the light of a little gas lantern, a big black bear ambled up, looked at Dad, looked at our food store, ripped the lid off the freezer chest with one swipe of his paw, selected the turkey and walked off with it clamped between his jaws. God knows what would have happened to Dad if he had panicked or tried to do something heroic, but he sat there calmly throughout. 'I wasn't brave,' he said the following morning, 'just terrified.' But the point of the story is his fire-making ability. He does know how to do it.

Still, he let Daniel lecture him without registering too much disapproval. Things got a little more tense when Dad – who's a bit of a healthy food freak – got started on a pile of walnuts. Daniel, obviously, knew how to crack walnuts properly – which was, equally obviously, not the way Dad was doing it. Even then, he managed to restrain himself with no more than a barely audible 'One way of doing it might be to put them on your sodding head and hit them very hard with half a sodding house brick', but I don't think Daniel heard. He'd have been talking at the time. He never stopped talking. But Dad, as I say, more or less kept his cool. After all, Daniel was our guest and one shouldn't be rude to guests, should one? It was the question of how to fold plastic supermarket bags that pushed Dad over the edge.

When he'd finished the walnuts and emptied the bag, Dad rolled it up to get rid of it. I didn't take much notice of precisely how he rolled it up – well you don't, do you? – and neither did anyone else. Except Daniel.

'Ah, you don't know how to roll up plastic bags eh?' said Daniel, quite unaware of the risk he was running. I thought briefly about the bear and how one false move from Dad and it might have been him in the bear's mouth instead of the turkey. I wanted to warn Daniel, to tell him to stop, but I knew there'd be no point and anyway there is something about watching a disaster as it unfolds that causes you to freeze. Dad used a little irony at first.

'Really Daniel? You are, of course, absolutely right. I have led an utterly wasted – indeed entirely pointless – life until now. While I was struggling to become a reporter and foreign correspondent and news presenter and author and newspaper columnist and trying to earn enough money to bring up my family and educate my children and even build a sodding house in this sodding country employing ex-pat Englishmen who clearly couldn't manage to make a living in their own country I should, obviously, have been spending my time learning to scrunch up newspapers properly so that I could light a fire, practising a more effective way of cracking walnuts and learning to roll up plastic sodding bags. Thank God you came here this evening, Daniel, because had you chosen to stay at home rolling up your own bags to the delight and admiration of the entire population of Methana the rest of my life would have been as wasted and as pointless as the past forty-five years.'

By the end of this diatribe – which was delivered first very quietly and gradually increased to a volume that would have drowned out Tchaikovsky's cannons in the *1812 Overture* – I was hiding in the kitchen. Peppy had vanished entirely. And Daniel? Daniel nodded calmly, picked up the discarded plastic bag and showed Dad how to fold it.

That is the point about Daniel. He is utterly impervious to irony, sarcasm and even full-throated, maximum volume insults. And that, I promise you, is hard to deal with. Over the years I have seen some pretty tough characters collapse when Dad has wound himself up into one of his tirades. But not Daniel. He merely nods wisely and carries on saying whatever it was that sparked the tirade in the first place. It would be devastatingly effective as a tactic to disarm his critic, if that's what it was meant to be but I'm convinced it never was. Daniel is simply oblivious to insult and, therefore, utterly fireproof. It's infuriating.

Despite all this we gave him the job of building the big house. He convinced us that if he had a big enough job he wouldn't need to run around doing lots of little jobs for other people, which sounded reasonable. Yet again hope had triumphed over experience. As Dad is so fond of saying (with only a hint of sarcasm): it seemed a good idea at the time.

But before Daniel had been given a chance to show what he was capable of, we had another visitor and he proved to be not just a distraction from the business of building, but became the talk of the village – and still is.

# 8

*In which Henry the peacock is lured by sex and booze but stages a great escape*

It was June and I had gone down to the house, trying as usual to get things moving in time for one of Dad's dreaded visits: the ones where he arrives and wonders what I have been doing for the last few months. One of the locals had seen me arrive and greeted me from the beach in some excitement. He ran up to me and started to tell me something about our lemon trees. I wasn't sure exactly what he was saying because there were a few key words I couldn't quite make out. Something to do with the trees badly needing to be pruned maybe? I'm sure he was right, but I didn't want to get involved in a long conversation because when you do they tend to last for hours. In fact whole days can be lost having a little chat with the neighbours. Or at least, that's what I tell Dad.

I managed to keep the conversation quite short and when we parted I was still none the wiser. Sometimes it's just too difficult to work out the precise meaning of every obscure Greek word or phrase. I went to open the door of the cottage but realised that there was something different about the garden. My first thought was along the lines of: 'Oh, what a beautiful peacock!' My next, a split second later, was: 'Hang on a minute, what's a peacock doing under our lemon trees?'

On the manicured lawns of a stately pile a large male peacock looks completely at home, but we had no lawns – manicured or otherwise. All we had was a lemon grove that was badly in need of pruning and acres of garden and woodland that reflected the fact that they had not been touched by human hand for about forty years. Wilderness might have been a better word for it than gardens. Not that the peacock seemed to mind. He could scarcely have been more at home. Indeed, he looked as though he owned the place.

He was a big, healthy specimen, over two feet long with brilliant plumage. I finally realised what my neighbour had been trying to tell me and felt a bit stupid. If someone comes up to you when you are returning home and excitedly tells you that there is a bloody great peacock in your garden they probably expect a bit of a response. Mine had been a mumbled 'Yes, yes, I must see to that.' No wonder he had looked at me rather oddly when we parted. Then again knowing that I was British he may have assumed that we all had peacocks in our gardens. Half of them think we all live in castles as it is.

So here he was. I had a vague recollection of having seen one in a zoo before but that was about it for my peacock experiences. Having read this far, you will know that Dad regards me as more Greek than English, but my first reaction to the peacock gave the lie to that. Had I been Greek I would have nipped into the house, lifted the shotgun from its rack above the kitchen door, loaded it, nipped back out again and blasted the bird to kingdom come. It would have been roast peacock for dinner that night. Instead, I behaved the way the British do when they come across strange beasts. First I made a sort of clucking noise and then I tried to talk to him. He was not impressed. Neither was he scared of me. In fact, he raised his splendidly plumed head, gave me an imperious glare as if challenging my right to be on his territory, and carried on with whatever it was he'd been doing when I arrived.

Having spent a couple of hours admiring him (that's what I do with my time, Dad) I reluctantly got on with things. As I worked I tried to figure out where it had come from. I wasn't even sure if the things could fly. If it couldn't then how did it get to us? I couldn't see it strolling down the road for half a mile. Not when the locals would shoot it on sight. I had vaguely heard of peacocks on Poros but how would it have got all the way to us?

Peppy and Hector joined me the next day and the peacock became an instant hit. The kids loved him – especially my new baby daughter Amaryllis. They wanted to know what to call him, so we agreed on a fittingly regal name and the peacock became Henry. Henry was probably the first word that Amaryllis spoke. He was now officially part of the family.

But how do you look after peacocks? What do they eat? Where do they sleep? Henry certainly looked healthy enough but I was concerned about his food. I could see him grubbing about under the lemon trees but I wasn't sure if the odd insect would be enough for such a big bird. The next time I was in Athens I went to a large pet shop. There was a young guy behind the counter.

'Good morning, do you have any birdseed?' I asked.

'Of course, what kind of bird do you have?'

My Greek may not be perfect but I took a childish pleasure in being able to say peacock, a word I had learned the day before.

'You have a peacock?'

'Yes.'

'Are you sure?'

'Of course I'm sure,' I said. It's not like they can be mistaken for anything else, I thought.

'Please wait, I must phone someone,' he said.

I began to get worried. Perhaps, like swans in Britain, peacocks in Greece were somehow a protected bird. Unlikely, I know, given the Greek mania for shooting anything that can flap its wings but it would explain why Henry hadn't been bagged yet. By this time the guy was on the phone, and sure enough he was calling the bird society. He must have assumed that my Greek didn't stretch to much more than good morning and peacock. Not the most useful combination.

'Hello, I have a crazy foreigner here who has a peacock on his balcony!'

I tried to correct him but he wasn't listening to me.

'I know! These English really are crazy! He probably wants to fatten it up and eat it! No, he didn't say anything about having a swan yet but I wouldn't be surprised. I heard that they eat those in England as well. Or at least the Queen does. Yes, and the foxes! I saw it on the television! I know, it's disgusting. Po po.' I just couldn't be bothered explaining the whole story of Henry to this guy. I actually liked the idea that there were people in Athens who thought we were barbarians. He eventually decided on what sort of birdseed would be best for a peacock, and with much tutting he handed it over.

Henry made short work of it. Not that I needed to have bothered. Lest anyone else gets an unexpected visit from a peacock I can now tell you that they will eat just about anything. Grain, seed, flowers, grass, insects, bread, cat biscuits, even Weetabix left over from breakfast, they don't care. They are extremely hardy birds and they can live to forty years of age – not that that was very helpful given that I had not the faintest idea how old Henry was already. My only mild concern was how Dad would take to having his land invaded by an imperious peacock.

*J*: My first reaction when Christopher told me about Henry was to ask him: 'Is he any good at plumbing?' That's the trouble with building a house: you become a little obsessive with getting it finished. In fact, I rather liked the idea of having a peacock about the place. Might lend it a bit of class, I thought. That, of course, was before I realised quite how often peacocks vacate their bowels and how keen Henry would become on joining us for supper in the cottage. He was sociable to a fault. But all that was some little way into the future. What immediately endeared me to Henry was the way he dealt with Oscar, Christopher's psychotic cat, when he arrived at the cottage for his summer holiday.

You may recall that my first encounter with Oscar had been in Christopher's flat. He clearly regarded the flat as his territory and did his damnedest to drive me out. I wanted to see what he would make of a large male peacock invading his other home.

Henry was strutting his stuff in his favourite corner of the lemon grove nearest to the cottage when Christopher arrived from Athens with Oscar in his travelling box. The whole family gathered around – slightly apprehensively, it must be said – to witness what we were sure would be a classic encounter. Not that the outcome could be in much doubt, we thought. For all Henry's size, he was, after all, only a bird. He could scarcely compete with a scratching, biting, spitting bundle of fur, claws and very sharp teeth that had survived the mean streets of Athens and terrorised grown men and women. For all his failure to slaughter the rats, Oscar was a formidable fighter. He had even managed (admittedly with the loss of a large part of one ear) to challenge the feral cats that colonised our property. Henry stood no chance. One bite to that scrawny neck of his was all it would take and we'd all be dining like Henry VIII that night.

Not that we really wanted to eat Henry – as Christopher said, he had almost become part of the family – and we discussed at some length whether we shouldn't try to contain Oscar while Henry was about. Could we really forgive ourselves if we let Oscar slaughter him? But even if we tried, we realised it would never work. In the summer the doors and windows of the cottage were always wide open and if Oscar did not get out, Henry would surely get in. The other approach was to drive Henry away, but that wouldn't work either: he would simply come back again. So, given that a confrontation was inevitable sooner or later, it was probably best to get it over with. We removed the children from the scene lest they become traumatised by the carnage and offered a little prayer for Henry.

When Christopher released Oscar from his cage it took him a few minutes to realise that anything was amiss. He padded up the steps of the cottage to the veranda and then looked back at what had been his unchallenged domain. Then he froze. His back arched, his tail went stiff and his fur rose. He went into full stalking mode, moving silkily down the veranda steeps, onto the terrace, advancing low and slow like a hungry lioness with a young gazelle in her sights, into the lemon grove. Oh God, we thought, here we go, and somebody (it might have been me) shouted: 'Run, Henry!'

But Henry did not run. He glanced briefly at Oscar, glanced away again and calmly went back to what he'd been doing, pecking in the dirt at the base of the lemon trees in search of grubs. Oscar advanced a little further and froze again. He was now only a few feet away and in full crouch-before-pouncing mode. But he did not pounce. I have since formed a theory as to what was going through his vicious little mind at this point, probably something like: 'Cats kill birds. I have killed many. But this is a very big bird with a formidable beak and it appears to be not in the least afraid of me. This might be a fight best avoided. On the other hand, I have a reputation to live up to. My beloved owner Christopher is watching me and so are several other humans. Still, it might be wise to exercise a little discretion.'

At that point the decision was taken out of Oscar's claws. Henry advanced. He swished his tail fathers. He lowered his long neck and, beak thrust out, moved rapidly towards Oscar. Oscar moved back just as rapidly. Henry advanced again. Oscar moved back again. And so it went . . . a jerky, ungainly gavotte around the lemon grove, one large male peacock clearly toying with what had changed from killer cat to scaredy cat. Oscar had met his match. Then Henry got bored with the game – I swear that's all it was to him – turned his back on Oscar and went back to his grub-hunting.

If Oscar had wanted to retain a semblance of pride, this was his chance. He could have leaped onto Henry's back and finished him off with one quick bite to the throat. Instead he followed him around the orchard for the next half hour, approaching as close as he dared – which was not very close – and never taking his eyes off the bird. I wondered if he was sizing him up, planning an attack perhaps when Henry was least prepared, but it was exactly the opposite. Oscar, it seemed, was falling in love.

I know how foolish it is to anthropomorphise animals but I am tempted to say that, from then on, cat and bird became firm friends. Actually, that's not quite right. Oscar clearly wanted Henry's friendship but Henry simply wasn't interested. See one nasty little cat, he seemed to be saying, and you've seen 'em all. I'll tolerate your presence, but don't get any ideas, OK? But Oscar was oblivious to Henry's aloofness. He followed him around that August like a lovelorn little kitten, lying as close to him as he dared when he took a nap and even, when

Henry wasn't looking, drinking from his bowl. I almost felt sorry for Oscar. As for Henry, we were all becoming rather fond of him.

The only potential problem was the screeching. Peacocks, as I know from having once lived near a zoo, can make the most appalling racket and I prepared myself for the worst. The writer William Sitwell says a screeching peacock can 'chill the bones of the devil himself . . . and course through the veins like a vicious poison.' He likened it to 'a eunuch being strangled on the main stage at Glastonbury, accompanied by a choir of a thousand shrieking car alarms.'

Well, all I can say is that Henry did not screech. Maybe that's because he was himself a eunuch (how do you tell?) and had no need to screech to attract a mate – or maybe he was simply considerate. Instead, after a supper of bugs and corn, he would fly up to the top of his favourite tree as dusk descended and sleep the sleep of the just. He had chosen the tree and its location with some care. It was a good hundred feet high and although peacocks can fly perfectly well, getting airborne is not easy when they weigh as much as Henry. His approach was to plod patiently up the hill that stretches to our boundary fence and then race down it. As he gathered speed he would let out a triumphant 'Honk!' and, once he had reached maximum velocity, off he'd go – perhaps not quite with the grace or agility of a swallow, but perfectly capable of reaching his roosting place.

If Henry had a fault it was that he clearly regarded the veranda as part of his territory. In the early days it was slightly unnerving to be stretched out on a lounger, face buried in a book, and then to hear a little rustle and look up to see a peacock staring over your shoulder. He seemed particularly absorbed by the latest John le Carré, which I recall reading at the time.

Henry was, in short, good to have around: partly for the magnificent feathers which he donated generously to brighten up Peppy's floral displays in the cottage; partly because of his insatiable appetite for all manner of unpleasant bugs which meant there were fewer of them to bother us; partly because he brought such glorious flashes of colour when he suddenly appeared in view and mostly because he was obviously enjoying himself. He appeared to be, insofar as a human can tell, a very happy peacock. And then disaster struck. Henry's owner turned up and wanted him back.

I know we should have expected this to happen. It was pretty obvious by now that he had escaped from somewhere and, since there are no zoos nearby, it was likely to be a private owner. But it's not as though his arrival on our property was exactly unknown to the locals. On the contrary, it was all we could do to keep them away from him. Local men would appear, casually strolling around our boundaries from time to time. When Christopher struck up a conversation with them and wondered what they were doing in these parts they would look terribly innocent and mutter something about just happening to be passing by. The shotgun slung over the shoulder was a bit of a giveaway though.

But given that everyone in our area knew about him, it seemed odd that it had taken so long for Henry's owner to discover where he was. That, it turned out, was because of some local feud or other. Back in the mists of time there had been a dispute between our village and another one nearby where the owner lived. Everyone knew he kept peacocks and had done for years, but they did not like him. So why should they help him out by telling him where one of his prize birds had taken up residence – especially if there was the slightest chance that he (Henry, not the owner) might end up in their oven one fine day? It was a full three months from the day Henry first took possession of our lemon grove to the appearance of Dimitris, his owner. When Dimitris appeared at the cottage he made it very clear that he wanted Henry back – and the sooner the better.

Dimitris wasn't exactly threatening – he was an old man and those days were behind him – but he was certainly puzzled and a little suspicious. He appeared, at first, to think that we had kidnapped Henry (or 'that bird' as he disrespectfully called him) though quite how we could have done that without his being aware of it was never made clear. He also seemed surprised that Henry had decided to stay with us even though we hadn't locked him in a cage.

'Why hasn't he flown away?' he demanded.

'Because,' Christopher wanted to say, 'we did NOT try to lock him up and he obviously likes it here much more than he liked being penned up with you.'

But there wasn't much point. We shook our heads sadly and agreed that it was all very strange. The old man wanted Henry back and we knew that we would have to hand him over. After all, he was a valuable bird – apparently the best he had ever had – and peacocks were more than just a hobby for Dimitris: they were a good little retirement business too. The chicks sold for decent money and Henry's job was to make sure that the hens were serviced as and when required to ensure a regular supply of them – which put paid to my eunuch theory. Maybe, I thought, that's why Henry escaped; he'd had enough of being henpecked by three demanding females all at the same time.

So now we had to break the bad news to the children and arrange the handover. I imagined a Check Point Charlie scene resembling something from one of the le Carré novels that Henry and I had shared, where the prisoner is handed back to his own side. There were three big differences. The first was that we would be getting nothing in return. The second was that Henry is a peacock. The third was that he did not want to be handed back. What we did not know at the time was how determined he would be to stay.

It was agreed that Dimitris would return to the cottage later in the evening when Henry, if he followed his usual routine, would be feeding under the trees in the lemon grove. Not that Dimitris was anxious to leave us. By now he no longer suspected us of kidnap and he was more than happy to stay chatting. He was a small, wiry man, as sprightly and agile as a young goat. As Christopher pointed out later, he had other goat-like qualities too. Just as Oscar had fallen in love with Henry, so Henry's owner was instantly besotted with Peppy. He kissed her hand with slightly more enthusiasm than decorum strictly demanded, wondered why someone as beautiful as she was had not ended up in Hollywood, engaged her in as much intimate conversation as she would permit and would, we had no doubt, have followed her around the lemon grove given half the chance just as Oscar followed Henry.

But there was work to be done and Dimitris went off to fetch a big net and his young nephew, who would effect the capture. They never stood a chance.

They arrived at twilight when Henry was doing his final rounds before retiring for the evening, with the very large net on the end of a very long pole. At first Henry seemed a little surprised to see his old owner turn up at his new home. He was even more surprised when Dimitris and his nephew rushed at him with the net. As for us, the sad onlookers waiting to say farewell to our beloved Henry, we had no idea that peacocks could move so fast. In an instant he had transformed himself from a regal bird strutting in a stately manner round his kingdom to something more resembling the Roadrunner cartoon. Dimitris's nephew was a young, fit man with long legs who would probably have been able to outpace Henry on open, flat land but Henry had the advantage of being much lower to the ground, which meant that while he was running under the branches of the lemon trees, Dimitris and nephew were running into them. Constantly. Sometimes, for a bit of variation, they ran into each other. It was brilliant entertainment. The kids loved it. Christopher had to retire to the cottage at one stage because he was laughing so hard it was verging on the disrespectful. I suspect Henry was enjoying it too, but eventually he decided he'd had enough of the silly game, flapped his wings and disappeared into the surrounding woodland. End of chase.

We commiserated with Dimitris, agreed that it might prove to be a bit more difficult than we had thought to catch a peacock who does not want to be caught, and tried to look very sorry for him and his nephew. And then, once they had left, we raised a glass to Henry and waited for what the morning would bring. It brought Dimitris and nephew again with an even longer pole and a different plan of approach. Christopher thought he should show willing and join in.

The plan was altogether more subtle. There would be no rushing at Henry. Instead, they would creep up on him while he was taking his morning nap and catch him by surprise. Unfortunately it was at that point that Peppy appeared on the veranda and Dimitris, ever the gentleman, called out 'Good morning Madam.' Henry heard the voice of his legal owner and, this time, he was in no mood for chase-me-around-the-lemon-grove games. He took off – straight for the forest. Christopher, who was wearing shorts like everyone else, went no further. He knew what it was like in the undergrowth and did not particularly want his legs to be torn to ribbons by the brambles and thorn bushes. Neither did the nephew. But Dimitris did not hesitate. We lost sight of both him and Henry after a few minutes, but we could hear him well enough: cursing and swearing and crashing through the undergrowth like a rampaging rhino. Henry let out the occasional squawk but I suspect that was more to encourage Dimitris in his doomed pursuit than any fear on his part – probably to pay his master back for all those years of captivity. When Dimitris finally emerged he was in a bad way, blood flowing down his legs, his face an alarming shade of purple, and his torn hands clutching an empty net. Henry had triumphed again and Dimitris retired hurt.

For a while there was peace at Villa Artemis. Henry went back to his old routine. He would lie on the veranda with us in the late afternoon, come running if we rustled a bag of birdseed and always accompanied Christopher when he did the watering in the evening. But the moment the gate opened and Dimitris appeared Henry would be gone, leaving nothing more than a few feathers in his wake and a frustrated owner, who could be soothed only by another little heart-to-heart with Peppy. Clearly another plan was needed.

As it happened, it came straight out of the brilliant Roald Dahl book I had been reading to my small son only recently: *Danny the Champion of the World*. Danny's father was, of course, a devoted poacher and taught Danny everything he knew. One of his favourite techniques was to soak raisins in brandy, scatter them for the pheasants and collect them up when they had eaten enough to be incapable of flying or even running. In Henry's case, it was to be grain soaked in ouzo. This time, Dimitris assured us, there would be no mistake. He duly arrived the next day with a large tin can full of foul-smelling ouzo and corn, which he handed to me.

'You throw him a few grains, he gobbles them up and then . . . pouf! . . . he falls over. I rush out of the cottage, throw a net over him and it is done. Simple!'

'How much corn will it take?' I asked.

'Three . . . maybe four grains. Strong stuff, this ouzo.'

So, while Christopher stood by with the camera for the final shots of Henry, I rattled the tin and we waited for him to appear. It didn't take long. He looked at me expectantly and, feeling like a traitor, I threw him some corn – three or four grains. He gobbled them up. We waited. So did Henry. He wanted more. I threw him more. And more. Henry was clearly a peacock who could take his liquor. But after roughly a handful of corn the ouzo began to have an effect. Henry started swaying from side to side: a slow, rather graceful movement, but looking as though he would collapse at any moment. Dimitris, who had been watching the whole thing through the kitchen window, came rushing out yelling in triumph. Foolish man. Henry needed no runway to take off this time. He flapped his powerful wings and flew – in almost a straight line – to the top of his favourite fir tree. And there he stayed.

Dimitris left us – a broken man – or so we thought. Not even Peppy was able to soothe him this time. We, of course, were delighted. We had done our best to restore Henry to his rightful owner and it wasn't our fault that all our efforts had failed. There was just one little worry. How long could a drunken peacock stay in the top of a tree? Presumably, the alcohol would do what it does to humans and Henry would fall asleep and then . . . it did not bear thinking about. It was a very tall tree.

Christopher was nearby when the inevitable happened, watering the trees in the lemon grove and glancing up at the fir. He heard a honking and then a rustling sound which turned into a crashing sound – the sound of a large, drunken body falling through the branches. He rushed up the hill to the tree, fully expecting to see bits of Henry scattered around its base. Apart from a few feathers there was nothing. And then he heard the honking again. Henry had survived – no doubt with the mother and father of a hangover – but more or less in one piece.

Next day Christopher delivered the news to Dimitris, half expecting him to concede defeat. No such luck. A week or so later he appeared at the garden gate, once again with the big net and the nephew. Then he went back to the van and re-appeared – with another peacock. Or, to be more precise, a pea hen. Dimitris had tried the lure of hard liquor; this time it was to be the lure of sex. He calculated (though he would never have put it so crudely in the presence of Peppy) that Henry would, by now, be in need of a little sexual relief. So the plan was to tie the young lady to a tree and wait for nature to take its course. Henry would be so preoccupied performing his manly task that he would not even notice the net descending.

It might have worked, I suppose, but once again we had underestimated Henry's will to live in freedom. We had also underestimated Dimitris's determination. This was a high-risk gamble from his point of view: double or quits. Peahens may not be as beautiful as the males, but they are just as valuable as breeding stock and he must have been aware that it could go wrong. It did.

He tethered her to one of the lemon trees and everyone hid on the veranda, Dimitris with a new improved version of the net. But Henry did not appear. Maybe he wasn't so highly-sexed after all. Most of us got bored and went for a swim. Dimitris dozed off. And that's what Henry had been waiting for. He crept into the lemon grove, chewed through the tether holding his beloved and Dimitris woke up just in time to see the pair of them disappearing into the woods. The girlfriend was never seen again. Henry himself stayed away for several days – no doubt reacquainting himself with the joy of sex – and Dimitris grew despondent. As Lady Bracknell might have put it, to lose one peacock could be considered a misfortune but to lose two smacked of carelessness. At this rate by the time Christmas came around his entire flock would be living with us.

By the end of August Dimitris seemed to have given up. This was a bit of a relief to all of us. His daily visits were getting a bit tiring, not least because he always seemed to turn up just as we were about to eat. Christopher saw him one last time before he left for Athens at the end of the summer, assured him that he was welcome to come onto the property any time he felt like chasing Henry but assumed he wouldn't bother. He was wrong.

C: Two weeks later I went back for a long weekend and discovered that, far from giving up the battle, Dimitris had merely been re-arming. It had taken him a long time but he had built a giant peacock trap. This consisted of a five-foot diameter net with a metal hoop at the bottom. The whole thing was suspended from a tree. A pulley system was attached so that the net could be lowered via a fifty-foot rope from outside the front gate. This meant that the trap could be sprung even though Dimitris was out of sight. Beneath the huge net was Henry's food and water. Winter was approaching, it was getting colder and bugs were getting scarcer, so Henry would have to feed from under the net at some stage. At least, that's what Dimitris was banking on.

When we went to bed at night and when we awoke in the morning we could see him, resembling nothing so much as an outsized garden gnome, hunched outside the gate in thick coat and woolly hat, grimly hanging on to one end of the rope. We returned to Athens but our neighbour Nikos kept me posted on his vigil. He was enjoying the saga immensely. It went on for months. The temperatures were getting down towards freezing but Dimitris was still there every morning. As for Henry, he must have found another food source or he'd spotted his old enemy and it had become a test of wills. Dimitris, of course, cracked first. One morning he just stopped coming and the rope went with him. The trap was left where it was, gently mocking him as it swung in the breeze. I felt sure that this had to be the end of the story. If he couldn't catch his peacock in six months then what hope did he have of ever catching it?

I'm not sure if it was his own idea or whether someone in the village eventually took pity on Dimitris but somehow a new plan was hatched. I like to think that's because what was at stake here was the pride of the village. After all, these men are all great hunters. The idea that they were incapable of catching a single peacock made them look pretty foolish. To fail so abjectly in the presence of a couple of Englishmen added to their embarrassment. So this time serious reinforcements were brought in: four firemen and a very large fire engine. God knows how, but Dimitris had managed to persuade the local fire department that Henry had to be caught. This time there really was no escape. Henry had finally met his match. He stood no chance against the power of a high-pressure fire hose. His magnificent plumage soaked through, he had no chance of flying and escape was impossible. It was all over. The net was thrown, a sodden Henry bundled into it and his protesting, squawking form was unceremoniously carted out through the gate. Henry's reign over Villa Artemis had come to an end. I watched him being driven away, tried to conceal from the cheering fishermen who'd come up from the beach the slight pricking behind my eyes, and shouted to the disappearing truck: 'Farewell old friend! We'll come to see you on visiting days!'

I went to bed with a heavy heart and in the morning wandered, rather disconsolately, out to the lemon grove. And there was Henry.

'Hello,' I said. 'What are you doing here?'

He looked up at me with an expression that said: 'There ain't no prison in this town that can hold this old bird if he don't wanna be held!'

Dimitris arrived soon afterwards. The fight had gone out of him. He had met his match and he knew it. Would I like to buy Henry at a bargain price of 100 euros? I suppose I could have pointed out that Henry was, strictly speaking, no longer his to sell. He was a free bird, a liberated bird, the master of his own destiny and no man's property. But what the hell. Why kick a man when he's down? We shook hands on the deal and Henry is now, legally, our peacock. But only in a manner of speaking.

# 9

*In which we acquire several miles of fortifications and survive the terrible forest fires*

While Henry the peacock was strutting his stuff down in the lemon grove, Daniel the builder was doing much the same further up the hill on the building site. I suppose, with hindsight, that my first big mistake in dealing with him was my reaction when he told me he would need to build a retaining wall below the house. I said yes of course he would and left it at that. And why not? The hill is steep and the house pretty big and it seemed only sensible to build a wall to stop it sliding down the hill. In this part of Greece it's mostly dry but there is always the possibility of a big storm with a great torrent pouring down the mountain and causing a landslide. There is always the threat of an earthquake too. My mistake was in failing to ask Daniel to be a little more precise. I should have asked at least three questions. How many walls? How big? How much will they cost?

It began well enough. We were able to hack tons of stone out of the mountain directly behind the house, which gave us more space behind and also provided the material for the wall. Staring up at it from the cottage below it looked impressive – a beautifully built stone wall marching across the hillside. I went back to London, feeling pleased that we were actually making some real progress. When I returned to Greece months later there was another stone wall – even more impressive than the first – and another. And the bulldozers were well advanced clearing the base for a fourth. I advanced on Daniel.

'You know I agreed that we should have a retaining wall?'

'Yes of course . . .'

'I do not recall agreeing that we would build enough retaining walls to prevent the entire eastern half of the Peloponnesian mountain range collapsing into the sea. I did not expect a series of walls that will be a landmark for every navigator on every ship that passes within a hundred miles of our coastline, nor that our wall should be the only man-made object on earth visible from the moon with the single exception of the Great Wall of China. It's a bloody house that we're trying to retain, not a palace that would make Versailles look like a modest cottage in Dorset. We no longer have a house, we have a fortress that would withstand an earthquake, tsunami and combined nuclear attack from every B52 in the American air force all at the same time.'

I should have learned by now that my attempts at sarcasm with Daniel invariably fail. He looked pleased.

'Glad you think so,' he said. 'Better to be safe than sorry, eh?'

At that point I gave up and resigned myself to the fact that I'd have to add a couple of zeroes to the final bill for the house or alternatively scrap the plans for little luxuries such as bathrooms and a kitchen. I know when I'm beaten. In fairness to Daniel, the house has not slid down the hill into the sea – unlike the wall we built later which was supposed to keep the swimming pool where it was. But that was much later. First we had to get the house finished.

It was good to know that some of the most difficult work had already been done. The basic foundations had been laid and the pillars that would support the floors and the roof were in place – sunk deep into the rock according to the strict earthquake regulations. That's what we thought. When Thakis came to take a closer look at them he was not impressed. He sucked his teeth and frowned a lot. He dug a screwdriver into the concrete, chipped a bit away, examined the steel rods and then frowned a lot more. Finally he spoke. His English is pretty much on a level with my Greek and therefore I understood not a word of it. Christopher tried to translate but Thakis stopped him. He used one word that we both knew I would understand.

'Rubbish!' he said.

What he meant was that the pillars and foundations which, by law, must withstand the force of an earthquake that hits nine on the Richter Scale – in other words enough to flatten California – would barely withstand a modest tremor. And what that meant was that they would all have to be reinforced with an additional steel cage before we could do anything else. There was also the quality of the concrete to consider. Thakis said it might be good enough to build a single-storey kennel, but only for very small dogs.

This was serious. He took samples and we sent them off to the government laboratory to be analysed. Sure enough, they were sub-standard. I was beginning to yearn for a bit of old-fashioned building, the sort where you lay one brick on another and join them together with good old-fashioned mortar. I had assumed that building with concrete – although it might well be much tougher when the earthquakes came – was easy compared with the skills needed for 'proper' buildings. I was wrong – as I discovered when we finally started work on the top floors of the house, which needed yet more pillars.

Pouring concrete turns out to be an intricate, demanding job. You need experience and patience and even the weather matters. The concrete columns and beams are not just doing the obvious job of supporting the structure: they are the shock absorbers and safety cage of the house's defence against earthquakes. The process has as much to do with steel as it does concrete. Every column and beam has a precise number of steel rods of varying thickness running through them. How many and how thick is determined by the civil engineer who relies on a computer program to calculate the stress they will be under. Then they have to be connected to each other in fairly intricate patterns. Imagine using wicker to weave a box-like structure: fiddly but not too hard. Now try it with one inch thick steel – every twenty-foot length weighing a hundred pounds – and try doing that while you are perched on scaffolding sixty feet high. There is no room for error. Once all that is done and the wooden shuttering has been built the concrete can be poured – and again it's far from simple. While it's being poured the mix has to be pounded flat to make sure there are no air bubbles. They can be fatal. There's a lot at stake here – for the builders as well as the occupants. If a building does collapse during an earthquake the civil engineer and his team are held responsible and the man in charge can end up in jail.

So, once again, everything took far longer than we had expected, but at last we had a series of beautiful columns standing proudly to attention. That's when Christopher got roped in. He was told he had to water the columns. Naturally, he thought they were winding him up.

'What!' he said, 'Water concrete pillars as though I'm watering a tree or something?'

'Precisely,' they said.

That explains why, on one of my visits, I found him standing in his shorts and playing a hose-pipe on a concrete column. Silly it might have looked, but it was an important job. Thakis told him why. From the moment concrete is poured and starts to dry, it undergoes a chemical reaction that gives off a lot of heat and it takes about a week to cool off, which is why it's much easier to pour concrete somewhere cool and damp like Wales – not Greece in the middle of summer. So we had to waste yet more time waiting for the temperature to drop below a hundred and even then it was too hot – which was why, three times a day, morning, noon and night, Christopher could be seen standing on the top floor watering our new columns for all the world as though he was a gardener watering his new pepper plants. I suspect he rather enjoyed it: a stunning view; the occasional shower from the hose to cool him down and maybe even the sense that by watering well he was adding to the strength of our house.

He had been living in Greece long enough by then to know that earthquakes are not remote possibilities. They happen all the time – albeit with varying degrees of severity. I had my own experience of one shortly after buying the place. I was woken up in the cottage one night by my small son leaping onto my bed – something he often did when he woke up after a few hours' sleep and wanted company. I turned over to shove him out and tell him to go back to his own bed and let me sleep, but he wasn't there. Then I realised in my sleep-befuddled state that that was because he was in his own bed back in London and there was no one else in the cottage. It was an earthquake that had rocked my bed. And then it did it again. I was rather glad we had replaced the roof a few months earlier and buttressed the walls. Christopher's experience of earthquakes has been a little more dramatic.

C: My first experience of a proper Greek quake was scary as hell but also a bit comical. We were playing a lunchtime concert in a big hall as part of a conference for, fittingly, an insurance company. Without warning everything suddenly started shaking like mad. The whole stage was on hydraulics so that it could be raised and lowered, and this might have magnified the effect of the shaking, but it was strong enough to bring down some of the overhead lighting which showered us with glass. I have never seen an orchestra leave the stage so fast. Not even in Britain in the old days when the concert finished late and there were only five minutes left till last orders at the pub. Within probably a minute we were all standing outside in the sun, clutching our instruments and wondering what had happened.

The Greeks among us knew very well what was going on. Rather than being less scared on account of having seen it all before they were if anything more scared because they knew how bad it could be. Our new concert hall had the last word in earthquake design, the entire foundations sitting on giant rubber shock absorbers. There was no way it would collapse. But what about elsewhere?

Within only a few more minutes the concert hall was deserted and everyone had made for home. I did the same. If nothing else I wanted to be by the phone as mobiles had stopped working immediately. It was a surreal drive. This wasn't a devastating earthquake, but it had made its mark. I didn't see collapsed buildings and roads cracked in two but there was minor damage everywhere. A huge plate glass window from an office block had crashed to the ground. A few cars had been badly dented by falling masonry. Some of the lampposts were down. Racks of newspapers at newsstands had fallen over, spreading newspapers all over the pavement. It was as if the whole of Athens had suddenly suffered some pretty heavy vandalism.

Having made sure my friends were fine and reassured my family of the same, I sat in my garden. Being inside seemed like a bad idea and anyway it was still September, so nice and warm. My landlady spotted me and came to offer some advice. 'Don't worry about the house,' she said, 'it is very strong and has been through much worse than this. Just make sure you wear pyjamas when you go to bed tonight.'

This seemed rather odd advice. Surely if the house were to fall down a pair of pyjamas wouldn't save me? Or had she somehow noticed that due to the heat I slept without pyjamas? Not wanting to dwell on this for a second more I put it to the back of my mind. But for some reason I did wear pyjamas that night. Maybe it was superstition. I was still jittery. The aftershocks were nearly as strong as the initial quake and now that I was experiencing them outside it was the sound that got to me. An incredibly low-pitched roar would signal every aftershock. I've never heard a sound like it in my life. It was terrifying. So I and my pyjamas went to bed. In the middle of the night we had another big aftershock. I shot out of bed and out of the front door without really waking up. As I did I looked around at my landlady and all the other neighbours who had done the same. I then looked down at my nakedness to see the welcome sight of pyjamas and quietly thanked my landlady for her wise advice.

So far – since Dad bought Villa Artemis – we have been spared a serious earthquake in our area. With our luck it will probably arrive just as we have finally completed the whole project. I wish I could say the same for one of the other natural disasters that regularly threaten the Peloponnese: forest fires. This peninsula is blessed with millions of acres of magnificent forest. It is also blessed – or cursed, perhaps – with very long, hot, dry summers.

The children came running up from the beach one searingly hot afternoon, terribly excited because – as Hector put it in the colourful imagery of a four-year-old – the planes were dive-bombing our bay. In fact, they were fire-fighting planes especially adapted so that they can swoop down and scoop up great mouthfuls of sea water. That is what they were doing before flying off to dump it on the fires that, unbeknown to us, were beginning to break out all over the Peloponnese. The planes were to have tragically little effect.

In the weeks that followed whole areas of the peninsula were ravaged and more than sixty people lost their lives. They were the worst fires in Greece for many decades and even Athens, two hours' drive from us, was not spared. The fires devastated some of the last remaining forests on the hills surrounding the city – forests that act as the city's lungs and absorb much of the foul air pumped into the skies above. For days on end the people of Athens were unable to leave their homes because of the choking ash drifting down from the smoke-blackened skies. When I returned to my flat many weeks later everything in it was covered in a thick layer of dust and ash – even though we had closed it up while we were away.

The area worst hit was around the ancient site of Olympus in the western Peloponnese, the birthplace of the ancient Olympic Games almost three millennia ago. This glorious UNESCO world heritage site has been inhabited since prehistoric times. In the tenth century BC it became a centre for the worship of Zeus, the ancient Greeks' leading deity. Mercifully, the flames were diverted away only a few metres before they reached the buildings and ruins. But Mount Kronos (named after Zeus's father), which is next to the site and the museum, was burned to the ground.

The greatest tragedy was the human suffering – in lives lost and homes destroyed. As we watched those planes 'dive-bombing' our bay, we had no idea what lay in store over the coming days and weeks. We were among the lucky ones because of our position on the eastern side of the bay. The wind came to us across the water, rather than from the forest behind and did not carry the deadly sparks, so tiny and so potentially devastating. But even now, two years later, we see the scars left in the forests on the other side of our bay and offer up silent thanks.

Forest fires are usually acts of nature – the forest's way of regenerating itself. But many of these fires were linked to the very regulations that make it so difficult to build a house in Greece. It is particularly difficult if you want to build on what has been designated forestry land. It's meant to be impossible. The Greeks learned a bitter lesson from the way the city's population exploded after the Second World War. It was like the Wild West. Developers built wherever the fancy took them and a delightful small city became a hellish place to live in. In summer the air was unbreathable and in a few years the pollution began to destroy the ancient monuments. So the authorities imposed severe restrictions on motorists, built the Metro and prohibited all building on 'forestry' land. And what did some of the frustrated builders do? They set fire to the forests.

Everyone has always known about this and mostly they talk of it with a resigned shrug of the shoulders (these things happen eh?) or even a slight chuckle (such rascals, aren't they?). I have a friend who owes his charming home on the outskirts of Athens to one of the 'rascals'. But of course they are not rascals. They are murderers. They may not sneak out at night with a can of petrol and light the match themselves, but they pay others to do it for them. And there is not a soul in Greece who believes that it was merely the hot weather and powerful winds that caused those terrible fires. For the first time the other day I came into direct contact with the results of the tragedy.

I met someone who knows Naxos well and asked him if there had been any fires there that year. He said no, but with a look of great sadness. He then told me his own story. A good friend had been due to join him on Naxos for the summer but at the last minute had decided to go to a mountain village in the Peloponnese with his girlfriend.

'I was having lunch with some friends at the port and didn't hear my mobile. After a couple of hours I looked at it and saw that I had ten missed calls from my friend. I tried calling him back but his phone wasn't responding.'

By now my friend had tears in his eyes. 'He had been calling me just before the flames came. They found him in his car. They say he would have died from the smoke before the flames got him and that he didn't suffer too much. But who knows? He just changed his mind. He should have been in Naxos with me but just went to the mountains for three days. He was twenty-seven. Thank God his mother died six months before. Maybe she knew.'

If any good can come of this terrible tragedy, it must be the end of the arson. I cannot believe that the people of the Peloponnese or the Athenians themselves will ever again shrug it off as just one of those things that happens. The image of a mother and her children burned to a cinder in one devastated village will stay with them. But the Peloponnese will recover. The trees will grow again. Forest fires – however vicious – will not end three thousand years of proud history.

# 10

*In which John learns that sleeping on the job is the first lesson for successful olive farmers*

When I first told friends and colleagues that I was thinking of building a house in Greece the reaction varied from 'lucky you' to 'I suggest you lie down until the feeling goes away.' People who had already done something similar tended to purse their lips, look doubtful and wish me luck. One or two advised me strongly to abandon the idea and spend the money enjoying myself. The last time I had contemplated doing something vaguely similar I ignored all the advice and lived to regret it.

It was soon after I had returned to Britain following a decade as a foreign correspondent. I was thoroughly fed up with living out of suitcases and trying not to get killed by unpleasant people in nasty places and wanted a quiet, settled life running a dairy farm. I was too inexperienced in those days to spot the contradiction. I know now that you can have a quiet life OR you can have a dairy farm: you can't have both. The advice came from a dairy farmer and it was succinct: Don't do it. Do not, under any circumstances, buy a small farm. When I pressed him, he told me that running a farm – especially a dairy farm – will break your bank or break your heart or break your will. Probably all three. He was a wise man with a lifetime of farming behind him who knew what he was talking about, so obviously I ignored his advice and went ahead and did it anyway. There was never the slightest chance that I would heed his warning and behave sensibly.

That's because the two things I have wanted to do since I was a small child were become a reporter and own a farm. I achieved one of those ambitions when I was fifteen and got a job on my local weekly, the *Penarth Times*, though it's probably an offence under the Trade Description Act to describe what I did as 'reporting'. It was mostly asking people who had attended weddings and funerals for their names and writing them down – very, very carefully – in my notebook.

As for the farm, I had always wanted to grow things. The 'garden' of the house where I was born consisted of a small patch where we dumped the cinders from the coal fire and the vegetable peelings. Runner beans grew brilliantly in it and so did mint. I bundled up the mint and sold it door to door for tuppence a bunch (three pence for big bunches) but what I really hankered after was a proper garden with brown, not grey, earth. I rented an allotment when I was thirteen, which kept me happy for a while, but it wasn't enough: I wanted a farm.

It was not difficult to persuade my family. One mention of sweet little calves to be fed by hand and a frisky pony in the paddock was enough to convince my twelve-year-old daughter Catherine. Christopher rather liked the idea of learning to drive a tractor and my wife, Edna, would have liked anything that meant I was no longer leaping onto a plane with ten minutes' notice and disappearing to somewhere dangerous for a month or two.

I knew in my imagination exactly what the farm would look like: lush green fields in a sun-splashed valley; contented cows with big eyelashes and names like Daisy nibbling the grass until their rumbling bellies were full and their udders straining with rich milk. They would amble into the parlour at milking time, stand patiently while the milk spurted into big jars, smile at me in their bovine way and quietly amble out again.

That is not how it worked out. The place I ended up buying made Cold Comfort Farm seem a desirable property. The 134 acres were perfect for cows whose idea of a healthy diet was a combination of weeds, thistles and dock leaves. Normal cows, being notoriously picky eaters, like grass and clover, of which we had very little. The hedges enclosing the fields had more gaps in them than a prize-fighter's gums. The gates hung off their hinges and could not be closed. Mostly there were no gates at all so the cows ambled where they chose. Actually, marauded would be a more accurate description for what they did. Rather than a sun-dappled valley my farm was high up a Welsh hillside which probably had beautiful views. I say probably because it is hard to see far when the mist hangs low. Not that it was always misty. Sometimes the rain washed the mist away. Sometimes, I am told, the sun shone. But I was usually too knackered to notice.

The cows did not have names, just numbers, and they sneered rather than smiled at me. They hated me. Maybe they hated all humans because of the way they had been treated by their previous owner. Either way, the feeling was mutual. There were one or two that were not entirely psychotic and did not spend half their lives trying to kick me to death, but those were the very old ones who had scarcely enough energy to raise their tails when they needed to empty their bowels – the sort whose skinny bodies should have been supplying small children with tough old stewing steak for their school dinners rather than trying to squeeze a few drops of milk from their emaciated udders. On any self-respecting dairy farm they would have been culled years ago, but my farm had lost its self-respect long before I acquired it. I was just too much of a romantic to notice when I was negotiating the sale – or too much of an optimist, which amounts to the same thing.

I realised what a mistake I had made within about an hour of taking possession. Even with my pitifully small knowledge of farming (non-existent, if I'm to be honest) it should have occurred to me that if you suddenly find yourself the owner of sixty milking cows and forty of their offspring it is necessary to have something with which to feed them. We did not. It was March, so there was even less grass in the fields than usual. Not that they could have grazed it anyway: at that time of the year the fields resembled the battlefields of northern France in 1918. The cows would have sunk so deep into the mud we'd have never seen them again – which might, with hindsight, have been the perfect solution, if a little cruel.

In the winter cows are meant to eat silage or hay. The problem was that the previous owner, who'd clearly spotted me for the city-dwelling mug I was within about three seconds of my driving down his pot-holed track, had cleaned the place out. I swear I saw the rats leaving. When there's not even enough food for the rats, you know you have a problem. The silage clamp was empty and the hay barn contained not a single bale. He'd taken the lot with him – no doubt to sell to the next sucker with more hope in his heart than sense in his head.

Happily, the neighbours helped out. In fact, the neighbours were always helping out, which was one of the very few nice things about farming. I think they did it from a sense of pity combined with bafflement that anyone who did not know one end of a cow from another could have done something quite so barmy as to buy this godforsaken farm. The other good thing was Eddie, the manager whom I hired to run the place, and his wife Vicky but, hardworking though they were, even they needed to take holidays and then it was all down to me. And I was very, very bad at it.

In my own defence it must be said that dairy farming is difficult even for experienced farmers. You need to know an awful lot about cows, husbandry, grass, fertilisers, fields, machinery, dealing with the Department of Agriculture and the bank manager, filling in reams of forms and much, much more. I knew none of it. You also need to be prepared to work seven days a week and go without sleep when a cow is having a difficult birth. You need to be able to cope when things go wrong – which, in my case, was all the time. And you need to have a certain empathy with cows.

Don't believe all that soppy stuff about cows being gentle creatures whose only aim in life is to keep their owners happy by filling the milk tank twice a day, standing placidly in the milking parlour chewing the cud as they do so. It's not like that at all. They are big and strong and capable of kicking you to death if they decide you are incompetent – or at least if you are as incompetent as I was. I hated milking them and they knew it and they hated me back in return.

I stuck it out for nearly five years and then – with a broken marriage and kids who were by now teenagers more interested in London discos than west Wales milking parlours – decided to cut my losses. And I can still recall in sharp detail the glorious morning when I stood in the yard watching my neighbours bidding for the various lots in the final auction. When the hammer descended for the final time it brought to an end my short and unhappy life as a dairy farmer. It was all over. From now on the closest I would ever get to producing milk was pouring the stuff from the carton in the fridge. In the euphoria of the moment I gave no thought to the possibility that somewhere out there might be another kind of farming which offered a different kind of life.

It turned out that there was – and I discovered it nearly thirty years later and more than a thousand miles from west Wales.

They grow an awful lot of black olives in the Peloponnese – more than anywhere else in the world – and they have been doing it for thousands of years. I can't say I'm surprised. If there is an easier way for a farmer to make a living than producing olives I have yet to discover it. I learned just how easy from an old man I meet almost every day in the summer months when I take my early morning run. Actually, it's not quite true to say that I meet him; we have yet to exchange a single word. That's not because he is unsociable – though, as I said earlier, most very old Greeks tend to be a bit suspicious of foreigners like me – it's because he is always asleep when I come across him.

My run takes me through the olive groves that circle the bay, from the beach at the bottom of my land to the village above the top house and beyond. In the scorching summer the trees need water – ideally every day and preferably early in the morning before the sun has started to roast the land. Each tree is linked to the next by a length of narrow pipe running along the ground and there is one hole per tree. It is a simple and highly effective irrigation system, so long as someone is there to turn the water pump on and off. That is what the old man does. He drives to his olive grove from a nearby village as the sun is rising and switches on his pump. Then he lies down on his bench in the shade and dozes off. When he wakes up, he switches off the pump and drives back home for breakfast after which, I dare say, he takes another nap. That's it for the day. The next day he does the same all over again. Now *that* is my idea of farming. The greatest risk the old man faces is a slight crick in his neck from sleeping in an awkward position which, it seems to me, is marginally more acceptable than landing in a pile of pooh with three broken ribs while Number Nine cow plans her next attack.

I knew the first time I saw him that I wanted to be just like that man. I had discovered a new vocation: olive farming. And why not? I had plenty of olive trees on my land. Admittedly most of them were in pretty poor shape. They had been totally neglected over the years and the few olives they produced – scarcely, I thought, enough to bother harvesting – were shrivelled little specimens. But olive trees are incredibly hardy and I had no doubt that all they needed was a little care and attention, some judicious pruning and regular watering and before you could say 'extra virgin' I would be making my small contribution to the dinner tables of trendy families in Islington and growing richer by the day. Naturally I would have to learn to doze off on a bench in the shade but that, with a little practice, should not be too hard a skill to master.

At this point you might possibly be wondering whether this man ever learns, to which the obvious answer is no. Samuel Johnson is quoted as having said that a second marriage is the triumph of hope over experience. In my case it's farming rather than marrying, but the sentiment is the same. It took only a few months for me to realise that cracking the international olive oil market from my modest estate in the Peloponnese might present one or two problems I had not foreseen. Not that I'm bitter about it. My pathetic attempt at dairy farming had left me with some nasty bruises, a lifelong loathing for milking cows and a large hole in my bank account. Olive farming has had much the same effect on my bank account so far but that has been more than offset by a growing respect for olives and a sense of wonder that such an ugly little tree can have had such a profound influence over thousands of years of civilisation.

But of course, as with everything else in the intriguing, infuriating land of Greece, there were one or two problems to iron out before I could play my own small part in the great oil story. Such as, for instance, who actually owned MY trees.

It was one of those perfect summer mornings. I had been for my usual early morning jog, nodding politely at my sleeping friend as I passed him, and falling gratefully into the sea when I got back to the cottage. Battling waves can be fun for a few minutes but I prefer calm waters for serious swimming and on this particular morning the sea was perfect. When it's like this, the locals call it an olive oil sea: barely a ripple on its surface. The water was so clear I could watch tiny fish darting around beneath me and when I crossed the reef to swim in the deeper water it was like flying above a mountain range. In the skies above me I could hear the cry of a red kite and I turned to float on my back, watching her as she criss-crossed the bay, quartering her territory with that wonderful combination possessed by hunting birds: the power of a killer and the grace and ease of a dancer. Bliss. Wasn't this what I had dreamed of? Could there be a better place on earth at this exact time than this bay?

And then I heard my name being called – 'Meester John! Meester John!' – in a thick Albanian accent. I looked inland and there, charging down the hill from the building site, came the foreman, Apostolis. Even from this distance it was clear that he was worried. There was a crisis and I was the only man who could resolve it. But what the crisis was, I had not the vaguest idea, except that it was causing Apostolis great distress. The initial problem was that he spoke Albanian and Greek and no English – 'Meester John' was the extent of it – and I spoke only English. So we went through the timeless ritual of mutual incomprehension. He tried speaking ever more slowly in Greek and even more slowly in Albanian (I think), then more loudly in both. And I just kept shrugging my shoulders and looking wistfully at the sea. The magical hour was disappearing. Soon it would be too hot to swim. And anyway, there was a crisis to be resolved – if I could ever find out what it was.

I looked up at the building site. No obvious signs of any disaster. The massive retaining walls had not given way and the house was not in danger of sliding down the hill so far as I could tell. An accident maybe? One of the builders crushed by a falling boulder? No. Apostolis looked severely agitated rather than actually scared. Well maybe just a little bit scared. I needed an interpreter. I phoned Peppy. There then followed a bizarre three-way conversation with the phone being handed around like the parcel at a children's party – except that when the kiddies rip off each layer, the mystery of what has been wrapped begins to emerge. In this conversation the opposite was happening and by the end of it I was more puzzled than I had been at the beginning. Here, so far as I could tell, is what had happened.

An old man from a nearby village (probably in his nineties but no one knew for sure) had driven down the track leading to the big house on his ancient little motorbike, said nothing to anyone, and started wandering around the site, apparently making a pretty careful inspection. When he had finished he summoned Apostolis to his presence and demanded money. Lots of money.

When Apostolis asked him why the old man started getting angry.

'For my olive trees!' he shouted.

Apostolis, a mild-mannered man who generally takes life in his stride, inquired politely as to which trees he had in mind.

'These!' shouted the old man, gesticulating wildly around him. 'And these! These ones you have killed!'

He had a point there. It was indeed true that we had killed some trees, albeit unintentionally. They had been in the way of the heavy earth-moving equipment and we had been forced to remove them. We did so very carefully and wrapped their roots in sacks with the intention of keeping them damp and replanting them once the diggers had done their work. But of course they had been forgotten. The roots had not been watered and the olives had died. Another tree had been crushed under some falling boulders and another was run over by a bulldozer driver, anxious to get the job done and go home for his siesta.

But the other trees were very much alive. Indeed, we had gone out of our way to preserve and protect them – at considerable expense in one case. The biggest of the retaining walls should, by rights, have been built where the olive tree stood but it was such a splendid old tree we hadn't the heart to dig it out and there is now a great bulge in the wall. It looks odd, but the tree thrives to this day.

But what had any of this to do with this angry old man? They were my trees to do with as I wished. Or so I thought. Well, you would, wouldn't you? I doubt that you have ever bought a house with a nice garden and, a year after moving in, had a visit from a total stranger who tells you that the lovely old oak does not belong to you but to him and he wants you to pay him lots of money or else. But this is Greece and these are olives and Greek law is . . . well, it's Greek law. Need I say more? Sadly, yes. Lots more. But I'll let Christopher take up the story at this point.

C: I knew we had a problem when Peppy left a message on my mobile warning that I could expect a phone call from Dad at any minute. He was, she said, angry. Nothing new there then. But when she told me why, I was forced to admit that this time he had something to be angry about. I could also understand why he had told Peppy to deliver a simple message to the old man and his demand for compensation:

'Tell him to bugger off. I bought and paid for this land and the trees on it. They're mine.'

I don't think Peppy translated the nuances of bugger off precisely – I'm not sure there is an exact translation – but the old man was told that perhaps he should come back later when we were there. And then I got the call from Dad. It went something like this:

'You're telling me that I have spent a fortune on this blasted property and some old codger from the village decides that he owns my trees and wants me to pay another small fortune for them!'

'Well not exactly, Dad.'

'Well does he or doesn't he? You can't have it both ways!'

'I think he has the right to harvest the trees.'

'So now you're saying I don't even own my own olives!'

'You don't actually own the ones that come from those particular trees, no.'

'Ye gods! Perhaps you would like to tell me what I DO own. Are the lemon trees mine? Or maybe someone's about to present me with a bill for all the lemons we've picked and eaten in the past two years? And no doubt there's a hidden clause in the contract that says the entire village can drop in when they feel like it and help themselves to the contents of the fridge . . . or maybe my wardrobe? Or perhaps they'd like to nick the tiles off the roof? I'm sure someone must be able to find a use for them! But perhaps it would be easier just to sign the whole place over to the next passer-by and have done with the whole thing . . .'

I tried breaking it to him gently.

'I think it's just this one man and he just has the right to use the trees.'

'Oh great! So you're now telling me that after I have spent all this money someone can just walk onto my property whenever he feels like it and help himself to my olives.'

'Um, actually he wants you to pay him for the trees we killed off as well.'

'WHAT?'

'Well, legally he has a right to them and we destroyed them so he wants compensation.'

'So now you're telling me that not only do I not own my own trees but I have to pay somebody else for knocking them down ON MY OWN PROPERTY!'

'Yesss . . .'

'And what about the ones we did not actually kill off?'

'Those too.'

'And nobody warned me ahead of time?'

'Umm no, I'm afraid we didn't really know.'

Then Dad went quiet. When that happens you know he's REALLY angry. The next was said in almost a whisper: 'And how much does he want for these trees? Twenty euros apiece? Thirty? I'll bet the greedy old bugger wants a hundred apiece eh?'

'Umm, not exactly. Ten thousand . . .'

I tried to add: '. . . but that's for all twelve of them.' I didn't quite manage it. The volume had returned to normal by then and I'm afraid that's as much of the conversation as I can put on paper. The rest was pretty much unprintable. And I have to say he had a point. The truth of the matter is that we really did not own the trees. Yes, we owned the ground – but not those particular trees growing out of it.

How can it be possible to own your land but not the trees on it? As I explained earlier a comprehensive land registry is something that Greece still hasn't managed to finish. But to most people, especially a few generations back, it doesn't really matter. In a large country with a small population it was never so much the land that had value: it was the trees on it. Properties were mostly not even fenced because the land was worth so little. What mattered were the olive trees. It is common to see ancient olives with numbers carved or painted on them which mean that somewhere there will be a legal contract giving somebody rights or ownership to that tree. Those rights may have existed for centuries.

In fact, the history of olives in Greece is measured in millennia, not centuries. They have been prized and guarded by Greeks since long before the Roman occupation a couple of thousand years ago. Greek history, both ancient and modern, IS the olive tree. Lawrence Durrell put it like this in *Prospero's Cell*:

> Only the sea itself seems as ancient a part of the region as the olive and its oil that, like no other products of nature, have shaped civilizations from remotest antiquity to the present.

Most people know that Athens is named after the Goddess Athena, but it wouldn't have happened without the olive. The gods held a competition among themselves to decide who would have the honour of naming the city. The winner would be the god that offered the best gift. Poseidon came a close second. He offered the city a fresh spring for drinking water and promised a great navy to defend its seas. But Athena won. She gave the first olive tree. It was planted on the Acropolis. It was the olive that gave the Greeks an essential part of their diet as well as lighting, heating, medicine, perfume and ultimately wealth. Sophocles called it 'The tree that feeds the children.'

If the ancient Greeks wanted to placate the gods, they made offerings of olive oil. They still do – in a manner of speaking. Olive oil is used in Christian worship to this day as the sacred symbol of the cycle of life. In the Orthodox Church you can't be married, baptised or even die without the stuff. They even have a word for people who receive the christening oil from the same godmother or godfather – *ladadelfia* or oil-siblings – and the old tradition dictates that they should not marry each other – regardless of whether they share a blood relationship.

An ancient Cretan folk song says:

> O olive tree, blessed be the earth that nourishes you
> And blessed be the water you drink from the clouds
> And thrice blessed He who sent you
> For the poor man's lamp and the saints' candle.

It took a while, but we finally discovered what had happened with 'our' trees. Many years ago the person who then owned our land ran into debt. To raise money he sold a dozen of his trees to a man in the village, but the trees stayed where they were. There's no question as to the legality of it: the whole thing was recorded in a legal document and it's even mentioned in the contract of sale that took place forty years before we happened on it. It's just a pity that we didn't know when Dad bought the land. It wouldn't have made any difference – a deal is a deal – but it might have kept Dad's blood pressure to slightly below the danger level.

As Peppy discovered, none of this is unusual. People often own trees on someone else's property. You can even go to court to sue for your trees. You might think placing a value on an ancient olive could prove a bit tricky but it's not: there is an official table relating to the value of every tree according to its age, size and condition. It seems marginally less crazy when you think how much you pay for a litre of good olive oil. A good tree will yield a hundred euros a year or more. Multiply that by a hundred trees (the size of a decent olive grove) and it's a lot of money to people in rural Greece.

Good virgin oil may be considered a delicacy in northern Europe, but not in Greece – no more than a pint of milk or a loaf of bread would be. Life is simply unimaginable without it and they drink more of it than any other people in the world – roughly twenty-five litres per year for every man, woman and child. That's about a pint a week. Per person.

Given all this passion for olives and the legal reality, Dad recognised that he really didn't have any choice but to buy back his own trees. He's happy to go into battle on most things even if the odds are against him, but he knew he'd met his match when it came to three thousand years of history, a couple of Greek gods and one very angry old man. So he paid up with as good a grace as he could muster and then started thinking about how to get some of the cash back. The answer was obvious. We had to start making and selling our own oil. But first, of course, we had to harvest our olives.

Actually, that's not quite right. The very first thing we had to do was find all the trees. There were more of them than we had thought – and most were hidden among lots of other trees or covered in various climbers. As I've said, they were not exactly in prime condition. In fact, some of them were so old Dad suggested that maybe Athena herself had planted them and they probably hadn't been pruned since Aristotle started scribbling away. The other little problem was that we didn't have the first idea how to go about harvesting olives – I thought you probably just whacked the branches very hard with a stout stick – but we did have the wonderful Nikos, who offered to come and help. By 'help' I mean that he would provide all the tools, show us what to do and actually carry out most of the work himself – all of this at the crucial time when he should have been harvesting his own olives. This is what being a good neighbour really means.

It turned out that I was almost right. There was a time when they did beat the branches and the olives fell into a big sack, but that is no longer considered the right thing to do: it damages the trees. So now they have a slightly more sophisticated approach. It's still not exactly hi-tech, but it works. They rake them off – with a larger version of those bright plastic rakes children play with on sandy beaches – and the olives fall onto a big canvas sheet spread on the ground. You start at the top and work your way down, which means having to climb to the top of the tree first.

Ours, because they had not been pruned, were pretty tall and we worried about Nikos doing it. He's seventy years old with a bad leg, but he could have been a teenager the way he set about it. He put the rest of us to shame – bounding up a fifteen-foot ladder, balancing precariously on the top rung while holding on with one hand, stretching out as far as possible with the other arm and tugging the rake through the tough branches. I copied him – not entirely successfully. I ended up with bruises that matched the colour of the olives, but were considerably larger. Dad was his usual deeply sympathetic self, but he stopped laughing eventually.

Once all – or nearly all – the olives have been raked off, you have to sift the bits of twigs and leaves out – and that's it. Job done. We were at it for eight hours and managed five trees. I imagined doing a full olive grove and Dad began to see that olive farming did not consist entirely of sleeping on a bench. This was real work, but it beats milking. On that we agreed.

We learned a lot about olive oil over the next few days. As

someone who loves the stuff, I had always been puzzled by the various descriptions: cold-pressed; virgin; extra virgin; pure and so on. The extraction process is simple and very satisfying to watch – partly, I suppose, because it hasn't really changed for centuries.

The olives are ground fairly gently under a big millstone and the oil is left to settle and clarify. This is the quality stuff. This is what you want on your salad and once you've tasted it you will settle for nothing less. Real virgin oil: the first press with nothing added. If the olives are decent quality which, I'm proud to say, ours were, then it qualifies as extra virgin. That means its acidity level is no more than 0.8 per cent. Ours was around 0.5 per cent. Ordinary virgin oil can be up to 2 per cent. There's nothing wrong with that, but it's a bit like the wine grown on the wrong side of the vineyards – or so the experts told us. It was very hard not to feel smug about the quality of ours – not that we'd had anything whatsoever to do with it. Maybe that's the point. Our trees had not seen so much as an ounce of chemical fertiliser or herbicide in their long lives. This was exactly what the ancient Greeks were drinking thousands of years ago. Food, quite simply, does not get better than this.

Now a word of warning: do not be conned into buying 'pure' oil at fancy prices. Oil that is not virgin is fine for cooking, but that's it. And if the bottle does not say it's virgin, then it won't be. There may be some blended virgin oil in it, but the so-called 'pure' oil is vastly inferior to the real McCoy. Think of squeezing an orange. The juice will be wonderful and you will end up with skin, pulp and pips – which is more or less what remains when olives have been pressed for the first time. To get more out of the residue, chemicals and heat are used. Although these processes won't alter the chemical composition of the oil, it will most certainly affect the taste.

And don't be too impressed either by the term 'cold-pressed'. All genuine virgin oil is pressed at room temperature.

I learned something else about olives after I had loaded our sacks into the car to take them for pressing. In the short drive to the local co-operative, the scent hit me. It wasn't that the smell itself was so very different from sticking your noise into the top of a bottle of decent oil, but the intensity of it was almost overpowering – and quite wonderful. I was hooked on olive farming. But I wasn't so sure about Dad – especially after he had done the sums.

*J*: Well . . . the sums aren't exactly complicated and not exactly encouraging either. In that one day – one very long day – we managed to harvest about ninety kilos of olives. Admittedly, there were several small children helping, but even without them it was pretty hard work. Clearly, there's a bit more to this business of farming olives than switching on an irrigation pump and dozing off.

The co-operative press turned the olives into fifteen litres of oil, which was enough to fill one large tin. If we had sold every drop of our oil to a wholesaler it would have barely covered the cost of the labour involved in harvesting it. On top of that there's the cost of looking after the trees for the other 364 days of the year, cultivating and fertilising the ground around them, dealing with any pests (insects as well as children) and, of course, paying for the water during the dry summer months. There's also the small matter of buying the land in the first place and paying for the trees. Paying for them twice in my case. So, based on those sums it's fairly unlikely that my dream of retiring and living the good life on the income from my olive trees will ever be realised.

I suppose I knew that anyway. If I gained nothing else from

my previous farming experience I did at least learn that the only farmers who become rich are those who were rich to begin with. It helps quite a lot if your father is a duke and you inherit half of Leicestershire. If, on the other hand, you start out with a hundred acres of stony Welsh hillside and a small overdraft, the chances are you will end up with a hundred acres of stony Welsh hillside and a large overdraft. So perhaps I should have been disillusioned by the prospect of olive farming in the same way that I had been with dairy farming. Oddly enough, I wasn't. Quite the opposite.

Christopher wrote about the intense scent of the olives in a warm car. He's right about that. But equally wonderful is what the oil looks like when it has been pressed. Until I saw the real thing I had assumed that oil should be yellow. I was wrong. The best olive oil is a delicate, light green. If Athena existed and she had green eyes, they would surely be the colour of our oil.

Maybe that's too fanciful – my romantic side triumphing over the practical again. Well, quite possibly, but there is something mystical, even magical, about harvesting, pressing and then drinking the best oil in the world and knowing that what we did on that glorious autumn day in the heart of the Peloponnese was, in almost every detail, what men have been doing there for more than three thousand years. Some of the trees around us, themselves centuries old, can be traced back to root stock that would have existed when the Romans defeated the Greeks at Corinth only a few miles from us. The link between ancient history is here: in our land; in our trees; in the oil on our salad. They say that the nectar of the gods is wine. They're wrong. It's oil.

# 11

*In which Daniel disappears and Christopher has to get angry . . . in Greek*

Rewarding though it was, harvesting olives was a diversion from the main task: building a house. That was turning out to be altogether less rewarding. The wall-building had slowed down because of some sort of misunderstanding between Daniel and the stonemasons. On the one hand this did not seem too big a worry since by now there appeared to be only one very small patch of hillside that had not been walled in. Indeed, viewed from a distance, the site resembled nothing so much as a mediaeval fortress. On the other hand, the relatively small section of wall that remained to be built was crucial – for reasons I never properly understood – to the next stage. Without it we would not be able to make any real progress building the house itself which was, as I had to keep reminding myself and Daniel, the point of the walls in the first place.

But Daniel kept disappearing. He would do some splendid work for several days and then vanish. And by vanish, I really do mean vanish. It's not just that he would fail to turn up in the morning on time: he would not turn up at all. And then, when he did re-emerge, he would have absolutely no explanation for where he'd been. So I gave him an ultimatum. I told him I wanted to see him at nine the following morning because I was going back to London in a couple of days and we had lots to talk about. Or else. No problem, he said, he'd be there. But of course he wasn't. Nor was he there at ten . . . or eleven . . . or at any time at all. I tried his mobile on the hour every hour and got his voicemail. I left messages – lots of messages – but still no response. And then, halfway through the next day, he answered his phone.

'Where the hell have you been?' I enquired mildly.

'The dentist.'

'All day?'

'It was an emergency.'

'Why didn't you phone beforehand to tell me?'

No answer.

'Why didn't you phone after you'd left the dentist?'

No answer.

We gave him one more chance and told him he could put the roof on the house when we got to that stage. He gave us a rock solid guarantee that he'd have it finished by the end of the month. Once again, he did some sterling work – he really was a very good roofer – and then he vanished again. This time it wasn't a day or two . . . it was weeks, which stretched into months. We made enquiries at all his usual haunts but nobody had seen him. When he finally emerged yet again there was no explanation. Enough was enough. No more chances. We would have to go in search of someone else. I went back to London and it wasn't long before I got another one of those slightly excitable calls at my home in London from Christopher.

'I've found just the man.'

'Wonderful! And I bet he's yet another paragon of building virtue, patron saint of all the great builders there have ever been, a combination of Christopher Wren and Ramses III, who will complete the job by the weekend, leaving us only to decide the colour of the duvet covers and will pay us a vast sum of money for the privilege of being allowed to work for us.'

He ignored the sarcasm: he was learning.

'Look, I really do KNOW this man. He's been installing my new bathroom in Athens and doing the tiling and he's brilliant. He can do everything we need and he's utterly reliable. He says he'll stay in the cottage so that he's always on site and will supervise the entire project and charge us virtually nothing for the privilege. It's perfect.'

I agreed. Of course I did. By this stage I'd have agreed to the appointment of Beelzebub so long as he could recognise a washer. I really did want to get the house built while I was still physically capable of putting myself to bed in it. The name of the paragon was Vangelis and . . . well, you can guess what's coming.

I had to confess that I had serious misgivings from the start. If this man was everything Christopher said he was, how come he was able to leave Athens at the drop of a spanner and spend as long as it took to get our house built, living a hundred miles away in a little cottage on the beach? Why wasn't half the population of Athens beating his door down and imploring him to work for them? The answer to that, in a nutshell, was that he was not everything my son said he was. He was a lovely man but, like every other 'foreman' we employed, what he was best at was making promises that could not be kept.

I could handle his little eccentricities. I really didn't mind that before he went to bed at night he would go down to the beach, light flaming torches and plant them firmly in the shingle. We were never sure whether the purpose of this was to ward off any evil spirits that might be lurking in the sea, ready to crawl out at the dead of night, invade the cottage and suck the soul from his body, or whether it was a warning to the smugglers, who were known to use our coastline, to keep away. If that were the case I somehow doubt his cunning ruse would have worked. The smugglers are ruthless operators and their cargos are human beings – mostly from North Africa – who are so desperate to escape the grinding poverty at home that they hand over their entire savings and risk their lives in boats that are barely seaworthy. Some make it but, I suspect, most do not.

I could also handle (just about) his enormous enthusiasm for building things that I did not want to be built – such as a vast wood store in the corner of the lemon orchard nearest to the cottage. It was a construction of surpassing ugliness – one side nailed to a magnificent old cypress tree and the other propped up with spare bits of timber left lying around the place. He'd been busy up at the main house, too, building what appeared to be small shrines dotted all over what would one day be the garden. On closer inspection, they turned out to be part of an elaborate watering system. To this day I haven't figured out quite what the little shrines are meant to do that could not be done by taps hidden in the shrubbery . . . assuming we ever have any shrubbery, which seems unlikely.

Christopher's view, more or less, was that if doing slightly eccentric jobs like that kept Vangelis happy we should probably humour him because he was, after all, getting the real work done. Which would have been a convincing argument, except that he wasn't. What he was meant to be doing – with his own hands – was plumbing and tiling. What he preferred doing was supervising other people. So I set a deadline. I asked Christopher to tell him I was coming to Greece by a specific date with some very important guests and it was vital that the bathrooms were plumbed in and tiled and the house was liveable. I may have slightly exaggerated the importance of my guests (the Pope wasn't really one of them and Barack Obama had unaccountably failed to reply to the invitation) but it seemed to do the trick. No problem at all, said Vangelis, there was plenty of time and he'd make sure we had the finest bathrooms in Greece and living in the house would be a sheer joy.

I arrived on the date promised and the bathrooms were not, of course, finished – or even started. Nor were any of the other little things that make a house habitable. Just as well my important guests had been no more than a figment of my imagination. I doubt whether they would have been happy doing what Christopher and I were forced to do: cooking supper over a single-ring camping gas stove and trying to read by the light of a torch. But at least we had a floor. That may seem a modest enough achievement but it had caused Christopher a good deal of anguish.

C: A marble floor in Britain is considered pretty fancy. In Greece it is often the cheapest option. The 'mountain of the reclining lady', one of the ranges that forms our beautiful view, is full of the stuff. There's so much marble in Greece that you can even find kerbstones cut from it. What is really sought after here is wood. Dad decided that we would save the marble for the bathrooms and have wooden floors in the rest of the house. We also needed a wooden staircase. So off I went to find a carpenter.

My father-in-law suggested Giorgos, who lived in our neighbourhood in Athens and who seemed decent enough. I went round to his small workshop and we discussed what was needed. Giorgos was a big man with enormous hands that looked like they knew what they were doing. He was even missing the top of one finger as a kind of carpenter's guarantee of authenticity. I had forgotten that there is a certain band of gangsters in Japan who cut off the tip of a finger as a mark of membership and loyalty. He may have been a bit rough round the edges but I don't think he was a gangster. I liked the fact that he still worked with his father, who must have been well into his seventies by then.

They came down to the house to look at the job and knocked up a temporary staircase while they were there. This looked quite impressive to me. Within three hours we had a perfectly serviceable way of getting upstairs without having to use the very dodgy ladder that had been there before. I liked the way they had worked, was happy with their quote and found it convenient that the guy had his workshop just round the corner from me in Athens. So Giorgos became our floor man.

The problems didn't take long to start. Or rather they did because he didn't start. I had made the classic mistake of giving him a bit of money up front. This seemed reasonable at the time because Giorgos was providing and fitting all the doors as well. These he needed to buy and finish in his workshop before fitting on site. Nothing happened. Every time I called him his excuses became steadily more outrageous. They started out quite innocently. 'Mr Chrees (Greeks can't pronounce the 'i' sound), I'm very sorry but my wife is sick so I can't make it down for the next couple of days.'

I wished her a proper Greek get well soon and said not to worry.

'Mr Chrees, my father is sick now and I can't start the job on my own.'

Again, let's hope for a speedy recovery.

'Mr Chrees, I have to go to Kavala for a few days because my wife's brother is baptising his first son.'

Well, at least he isn't sick as well.

'Mr Chrees, on the way back from Kavala the car crashed into a cow and it's broken.'

I almost wished the cow a get well soon until I realised he meant the car was broken. Note that it was the car that crashed into the cow. It's very rare to find a Greek driver who will ever admit to an accident being his fault.

Eventually my father-in-law went round to Giorgos's cousin's shop and raised so much hell that the customers fled and the cousin promised to persuade Giorgos to get started. He had probably spent the deposit by now anyway and was keen to get his hands on some more cash.

Vangelis, as we said earlier, was living in the cottage at the time and was on site every day. Within a couple of days of Giorgos's arrival Vangelis was on the phone to me. He complained that they weren't working fast enough and the work was a bit shoddy. I didn't pay too much attention to this because Vangelis doesn't consider anyone capable of working as well he does himself. He doesn't just criticise work being done but will find fault in any previous work. He is a kind of archaeological building critic. No detail is too small for him. Vangelis likes nothing better than to find the corner of one tile hidden behind the loo that is slightly proud of the others. 'Po po! Look at that! I would never do such sloppy work. I can't believe someone has done a tiling job like this. Who was it? Did you do this yourself? You should let a real tiler do this work.' The truth is that Vangelis's tiling is no better than anyone else's. I have a fantasy of one day being able to take him to a house that he has forgotten he built and get him to criticise his own work.

So when Vangelis rang me to complain about Giorgos I wasn't too concerned. After all, I had watched him knock up a staircase in a few hours and he definitely knew his stuff. His tardiness in starting the job wasn't exactly unusual. And a lot of people, even a cow, had been sick. But Vangelis continued to express his concern to me.

'This Giorgos, he doesn't know anything about building floors. I looked at the floor this morning and do you know what he has done? He's made it crooked! I have the best eye in the business! I don't ever need a spirit level! Everybody tells me how good my eye is. And I told this to Giorgos! He didn't believe me and I told him, you go get your stupid spirit level now, you idiot, and see how good my eye is! Nobody has a better eye than me. I'm never wrong!'

Then Giorgos started calling me to complain about Vangelis. He threatened to walk off the job. This did get my attention so I had to go down and have a look for myself.

A very irate Vangelis was there to meet me. Giorgos, it seemed, had gone back to Athens the day before but had left two of his men on site to continue working. The problem was that he had left them with nothing. They had no transport and were staying in rooms in the small town of Galatas, a quarter of an hour's drive away. Vangelis had had to go and pick them up so that they could get to work. As Vangelis had to get back to Athens himself for the weekend I promised him I would sort it all out.

I rang Giorgos to find out what was going on. He claimed to have had an emergency in Athens and asked me to look after his workers. I was cross with him but at least work was continuing so I let it go and he promised that he would be back first thing on Monday. At five o'clock I went and told the two guys that I would run them back to their rooms in town. They were grateful to stop work but asked sheepishly if we could stop on the way at Tassos's shop. They hadn't eaten all day, they said.

They were the usual Albanian labourers who were no doubt illegal and could be picked up at any time by the police. When we got to the café I realised what their problem was. Giorgos had left them without a penny. I don't know how he thought they were going to survive. I stocked them up with food and a big bottle of wine, for which they were immensely grateful.

Giorgos didn't answer the phone all evening but I eventually tracked him down the following morning. He was completely unfazed by my shouting at him. 'Cool down,' he said, 'all you need to do is get them a couple of sandwiches. They can walk to town.' These guys were doing hard physical work for eight hours a day and Giorgos wanted to feed them with nothing but a sandwich and let them walk ten miles back to their cheap lodgings. He had effectively dumped them in the middle of nowhere, where they knew no one and had no money. And they were illegal. I had the feeling that Giorgos would not be winning the employer of the year award.

Giorgos naturally did not show on Monday morning and when I rang he told me something had 'come up'. I put his poor workers onto the bus back to Athens. Giorgos kept his head down for a few days but I eventually caught him. He treated me to the usual long story of family woes and the usual fervent promises that he would be straight back down next week and would work faster than ever.

What I really wanted to do was get rid of him there and then, but it's not easy to find a carpenter willing to take over after someone else has done half the job. Plus I would probably have to wait even longer for someone new to be able to start. We were running out of time as usual. The kitchen people were waiting, the plumber and the electrician were on standby and we couldn't even fit the doors until the floors were down. I argued with Giorgos until the point where he was walking out of the door, but finally he relented and eventually he laid the floor. That was when I sacked him. I told him I would find someone else to build the staircase and sand and polish the floors. He went berserk. *Malaka* roughly translates as tosser but its meaning depends on the tone in which it is used. As you can imagine, it wasn't being used in a very polite way in the following exchange.

'You can't sack me, *malaka*! Nobody does this to me! That Vangelis, what has he been saying? He's a *malaka*! He thinks he's the best builder in the world, the *malaka*. I'm not leaving until you pay me for all the wood I have bought for the *malakasmeni* staircase. I want four thousand, *malaka*, then we will see if I go.'

'Listen,' I said, 'I'm not paying you any more money. I don't like the way you treat your workers and I have no way of knowing whether you have paid for the wood for the staircase or not.'

'*Malaka*, I paid for it! If you don't give me the money then maybe you have to pay for something else. And maybe it's not so good for you . . .'

Now I had had enough. I am very patient (I've lived with Dad for many years) and it takes me a long time to lose my temper. But this guy really was a *malaka*. And Greek is a great language to shout in.

'Right! That is enough, *malaka*! If you bought all this wood then I want to see it. On my balcony. All of it! Tomorrow! Then you will get your money. Otherwise I don't want to hear another word from you. We are finished. If you want to sue me go ahead! I would love to spend four years fighting you in court.'

This was my trump card and he knew it. I was beginning to realise how useful it was to have a lawyer in the family, even if it had meant having to marry her. Giorgos capitulated. He knew he hadn't bought the wood and he knew that I knew too. But it was a Pyrrhic victory. I'd got rid of yet another builder, and that simply meant having to find someone else to replace him. And it was becoming increasingly difficult to explain to Dad why his house wasn't getting built.

# 12

*In which we learn the basics of Greek pronunciation and how to avoid insulting your Greek mother-in-law*

My problem – correction, ONE of my problems – was not being able to speak Greek or think like a Greek, which meant having to rely on Christopher at every stage rather than deal directly with the builders. He, by contrast, was more Greek than British by the time he had hit forty. Not that he was ever very British. He was three when I became a foreign correspondent for the BBC and for most of his childhood he and his younger sister Catherine were dragged around the world, living wherever I happened to be based. At the age of six – when we were living in Washington – he spoke fluent American, placed his right hand proudly on his heart when he sang the 'Star Spangled Banner' and thought football was played with an oval ball and enough body armour to withstand a Sherman tank at full throttle. By the time he was approaching his teens I decided I wanted my children to be British again and made my plans to return. But the BBC had other ideas.

The big story in the world had shifted from the United States, once President Nixon was forced to resign over the Watergate scandal, and had moved to southern Africa. The guerrilla war in Rhodesia was reaching its predictable climax and apartheid was in crisis in South Africa, so I was asked to move to Johannesburg and open a television news bureau there. I agreed – journalists always want to be where the big story is happening – and it was another four years before we finally made it back to Britain. I lost count of the number of different schools Christopher and Catherine attended during our years of foreign exile, but it didn't seem to matter to either of them. It took them roughly two days to adapt to their new comprehensive school in Oxfordshire. I remember waiting anxiously for them to come home from the first day, fully expecting them to be traumatised by their first experience of a British comprehensive.

'So how was it?' I asked Christopher.

'Great!' he said. And that was it. Not another word. Who says children aren't adaptable.

Once he had graduated from the Royal College of Music he started globetrotting again, this time under his own steam. There are precious few jobs for young musicians in Britain – which helps explain why so many end up busking on the underground – so he went to Spain to play for an orchestra there and then to Germany. Neither job lasted for long and when a friend told him a new orchestra in Athens was auditioning for string players he caught the next plane out. I assumed he would be back after a few months, if not days, but he has now been living in Greece longer than he has lived anywhere. One bizarre side effect is that when I hear him talking to a Greek male I assume they are about to kill each other. This is roughly how their conversation sounds – and looks – to me.

'You have the manners of a sewer rat and the appearance of a dog's rear end and if you care to step outside I will pound you into the dust.'

'And you have the manners of a dog and the face of a rat's rear end. Let's go!'

This, I learn later, is what they were actually saying:

'How lovely to see you again. We really must meet up for a nice cup of tea and perhaps a game of bridge.'

'What a jolly good idea. Your place or mine?'

That's the thing about the Greek language: when Greek men are talking together they almost always seem to be having a fierce argument. I wondered whether it stems from their desire to burnish the macho image they have of themselves – an image that is not borne out by the reality. Rather to my surprise I discovered fairly quickly that Greek men are actually pretty soppy and liable to burst into tears for no apparent reason. They are far more liable than northern Europeans (especially the British) to pour their hearts out to you even when they are entirely sober and sometimes weep on your shoulder over some sad episode in their lives. It can sometimes be endearing for a buttoned-up Brit to be exposed to this sort of behaviour, but mostly it is mildly embarrassing.

Christopher is not so sure that it's a macho thing because, as he points out, it's even worse when there are a group of Greeks together. It's a bit like listening to children in a school playground. What strikes you immediately is the incredible noise. When they are in a group, children naturally speak with the volume turned up all the way and the more of them there are, the louder it gets. That's because they have yet to learn the art of speaking one at a time. Greeks are the same – except, it seems, that they never learn it.

It's not just men either. Christopher complains that when his wife and friends are together, at least three will be speaking at the same time and all of them at full blast. Like me, he assumed when he first heard it that they were arguing. It helped when he had learned enough Greek to understand what they were saying, but even then he found Peppy's family meals a nightmare. What he learned is that you have to watch the person who is speaking as closely as you listen to them if you have any hope of catching what they are saying. He swears it's as important as learning vocabulary, grammar or accent, unless you want to spend your whole time avoiding groups.

I promise myself that when I have lots of spare time I shall knuckle down to learning Greek, but I know that's one of the many promises I won't be keeping. Watching Christopher struggling to learn over the years has persuaded me that I have simply left it too late. There has to be a very powerful motive to learn a language as difficult as this. Christopher denies it, but I noticed that he had been living in Athens for a very long time before he got really serious about it and, oddly enough, that coincided with him falling in love with a Greek girl. It concentrated his mind wonderfully.

C: There is an English newspaper in Athens which serves as a lifeline to foreigners living in the city. A weekly coverage of the Greek news, small ads and a guide to the more international cultural events mean that even newcomers to the city can get a feel for what is going on.

The back page used to be my favourite place. A British expat called Brian Church spent years writing a column with the revealing title: 'How To Speak Greek In Twenty Years.' When I was new to Athens I read it every week with some disdain. It does indeed talk about the Greek language, albeit the quirkier aspects. I blithely assumed that droll as the title was, it was surely not accurate. Fifteen years of struggling has taught me how ignorant I was and my respect for the man grows every year. Let me get my defence in first before you think of me as an abysmal linguist. Greek is a hard language. That is official. The foreign office league table of languages, used to reward diplomats according to their linguistic prowess, rates Greek as way harder than any average European language, and not far off the real monsters such as Mandarin and Finnish. Greek children spend many more years learning their own language than we do in Britain. Even then, less educated people are prone to making glaring grammatical mistakes. They must be glaring because even I am beginning to notice them.

In a way it does compare to learning something like Finnish because apart from a very demanding grammar that is on a par with Latin, it lacks any useful roots you can latch on to. Learn a bit of Spanish, Italian and French and you can soon be making educated guesses as to what a word may be. Try that in Greek and, unless the word is 'computer' you will always be wrong. In fact they even have a made up word for computer.

Here is the one notable exception: I got caught in a downpour downtown one day and ran into one of those shops that seem to sell everything. Being proud and stubborn about my hard-won Greek I started to explain that I wanted an umbrella. Easy enough if you know the word but I didn't.

A friend of mine here has solved her sad progress in the language by becoming a world-class mime artist. Need a 35 amp fuse for your garden shed? She can mime it intelligibly in five seconds flat. I am too stubborn for that and maybe a bit crap at miming so I laboriously started explaining that I had an urgent need for the thing you carry when the water is falling from the sky so that clothes they stay dry and you not get sick (you understand my level of Greek at this stage). After listening patiently and asking the obligatory 'Where you from?' the shop owner said 'Ah! Umbrella!' I was having none of it. My Greek was clearly superior to his pathetic attempt at English so I told him very sternly IN GREEK that yes I was after an umbrella, but more importantly I wanted to learn the GREEK for umbrella. 'Yes, yes, umbrella!' It had been a long day and it was raining so my temper was wearing thin. In my best Greek I started on a great tirade of how as I was bothering to learn his bloody language the least he could do was to respect my efforts and help me out by teaching me one bloody word. It probably didn't come off quite as fluently as I thought because he just looked at me like I was mad. I stormed out of the shop to ram my point home, of course forgetting the umbrella, and swore at the ingratitude of the Greeks.

In work the next day I asked a trusted Greek friend who was very supportive of my Greek efforts what the word for umbrella was.

'Umbrella?'

'Yes, what's the Greek for it?'

'Umbrella.'

'YES! How do you say it in Greek!'

'Umbrella!'

It dawned on me that I had stumbled on the one word in the Greek language that has come from us, rather than the other way around. With our climate I should have known.

We may not be able to make any guesses as to what a word might be but the great joy of learning Greek is that you simultaneously learn about English. Every other Greek word learned is an English root discovered. Half the time I find myself doing a Homer Simpson 'Doh!' afterwards because the root is so obvious. But only with hindsight.

As with any language, the more mistakes you make the faster you will learn. If you make the kind of mistakes described below only once, I guarantee you will never repeat them. Usually the mistakes can be laughed at, though you may require several years before you can laugh at them without cringing. Here is a selection of my favourites.

A sweetly-spoken English friend of mine walked into a bakery and tried to ask the baker for a small loaf. Unfortunately one letter can make a big difference. *Psomaki* would be a good way of asking for a small loaf. Substitute the *m* for an *l* as my friend did and you have just asked the baker if he has a small willy. She was lucky. The man was enormous. He went very quiet for a while and then said 'Eengleesh?' No physical harm was done although I still wonder how his pride coped.

The same friend spent some time as director of music at an international school where the most common language is 'Gringlish'. Getting a bit carried away in a demonstration to her class of twelve-year-olds, she tripped over her own shoes and decided to make light of it by telling them in Greek what she had done. 'Oops! I just tripped over my *Poutsa*!' she gaily told the class. Half of them stared in horror while the other half began giggling uncontrollably. None of the children would tell her what she had said but it definitely wasn't the word for shoes. In the staffroom after the class had finished she asked the first teacher she met what the word meant. The old Greek teacher she happened to ask went white and said: 'Where did you hear such a word?' Realising that perhaps it would be more than the old lady could take she fortunately said that she had heard it on the way to work. Just as well as she had just told her class in a very impolite way that she had tripped over her fanny.

I have my own bitter experiences to relate and while we are on the subject of rude body parts here is one of my own stories. It was the monthly visit to the Greek family whom I rented an apartment from. I paid the rent and had to endure several hours of ouzo, snacks and a tortured conversation that veered increasingly drunkenly from English to my abysmal Greek to French, which the mother spoke well. It was trying to think in three languages that was my undoing. I had been asked to bring a special cream back from my next visit to England for the mother. In trying to establish in Greek whether she needed a face cream or a hand cream I became a bit muddled (nothing to do with the ouzo) and managed to ask her if she was in need of a cream for her breasts. I now know that 'visage' is dangerously close to a quite different part of the body in Greek.

The hardest part of learning to speak Greek, especially for Brits, is that your accent must be pretty close to flawless. As English-speaking people we often fail to appreciate the wealth of accents, let alone dialects, with which our language is spoken. We are remarkably flexible when it comes to our mother tongue. Meet ten strangers on a train and there is a good chance you can place the origins of half of them to the nearest city, let alone county. Obviously we can also tell the Americans from the Australians from the Indians etc. We have a truly global language and can understand it no matter how wild the accent. Now think about Greek. Ten million people in Greece and a smattering in Chicago, New York and Australia. That is pretty much it. Of that total at least half live in Athens. There are no accents unless you count a slight difference in the way Cretans pronounce '*chi*' or Thessalonikians the double *l* which often crops up. This means that their ears are completely unused to hearing Greek spoken with an accent, let alone by a British foreigner with a fairly posh English accent. Ordering a beer can take a year to perfect. I am not joking. And I put in a lot of practice.

Here is a little test. Think of a Greek accent. Now say the name of the famous hotel chain Hilton in that accent. It's not that hard is it? My first very small victory in my Greek struggles came from that word. The Hilton in Athens is a landmark building and apart from its architectural merit it also serves as a great focal point for navigating your way round. Tell a taxi driver 'Hilton' and even he can't get lost. I was out with a Scottish friend of mine and we did just that. My friend had been in Greece a year longer than me and was fairly cocky about his Greek. We got in the cab and he told the driver 'Hilton'. There was no comprehension whatsoever. This went on for a while until I decided to have a go with the most absurd, over-the-top Greek accent I could muster. It worked first time. 'Why your friend no speak English?' demanded the taxi driver. It was tempting to explain about the whole Scottish angle but I could see he was pissed off as it was and we wouldn't be having much of a night out if I pushed it any further.

The point is that there is only one way to pronounce a word in Greek. Here is how you say Hilton:

- Forget H, it doesn't exist. The closest in the alphabet is *Xi*, sort of pronounced '*chi*'. I like to think of the noise a cat makes when it hisses.
- Forget I. Although there are three different I's in Greek none of them corresponds to the sound we make in Hilton. Think ee as in eel.
- The L has to go as well I'm afraid. Although it resembles our own letter the sound must be formed with the tongue further back in the mouth giving it a thicker

sound. A bit like slurring your words when you have had one too many.

- Yes the T is problematic too. I have spent hours with my wife trying to get this one right. I'm still not sure I get it. Something to do with the way the tongue meets the teeth as you make the hard sound, but I'm not convinced.
- By this stage you will be glad to hear that the last two letters are no problem at all. There are legions of Greek words ending in '*on*'. Oh, except that it must be pronounced as in to turn the light 'on' and not as in 'un', which is the way it sounds to Greek ears.

So there we have the quick and easy guide to pronouncing an ENGLISH word. What about the GREEK ones?

I must mention one example of the reverse, despite my arguing how flexible our English ears are. A colleague was teaching a young Greek girl cello. Now this was a little girl who clearly came from a rather well off background. She would arrive every week at my friend's house in a limo with two bodyguards. After a few months when my friend felt comfortable about it she finally asked the girl what her father did.

I met my colleague the next morning in work.

'You're not going to believe this,' she said.

'What?'

'You know my rich pupil? I asked her what her Dad does and she said he has lots of sheep!'

'No way. Nobody can have that many sheep. He must own half the sheep in Greece! It's impossible.'

The argument raged for some time until it finally dawned on me.

'Were you speaking in Greek or English?'

'We always speak English. She speaks it perfectly although she does have the Greek accent.'

I was fairly sure I could solve the mystery. 'How do the Greeks say sheep?' I asked.

'Sheep!' she replied.

'And how do they say ships?'

'Oh bugger,' my friend replied.

Luckily she hadn't told many people about the richest shepherd in the world and one little shipping magnate's daughter doesn't spend every summer helping Dad out with the flocks.

So we have grammar from hell and an accent that must be as perfect as the Queen's. Surely that is enough? Oh no. Next up is the important matter of stress. In musical notation the notes are arranged in bars so that the eye and the brain can make sense of them. Greek words have a similar arrangement and I like to think it is due to the ridiculous length of the words. We are not talking about German here where the odd technical word can stretch to a whole paragraph. I am talking about everyday words my young children use that can be six syllables long. Example: toy cars, *Aftokinitakia*. With words reaching five syllables in virtually every sentence it makes sense that you stress one of the five syllables. Otherwise they become almost nonsensical. The problem for someone learning the language is that this is a strict rule. Indeed in the old days the stress was marked when written. In the ancient days there were five different stress marks. What this boils down to is that if you stress the wrong syllable you will not be understood. You may as well not have bothered learning the word in the first place.

Having nearly completed Brian Church's advice to learn Greek in twenty years, I think I have earned the right to laugh at some of the Greek efforts with English. After all, I have provided my Greek friends and colleagues (not to mention my kids) with more than enough laughs over the years. This is the English website from a hotel I stayed in with Dad in the beautiful skiing village of Kalavrita. First let the website explain where the hotel is: 'We abstain 200kms from Athens, 28kms from Planitero where you can eat the alluring trout.' That's clear then. The hotel was very good, but not quite as the website described: 'The rooms are clean, the fireplace complements atmosphere, your bathroom is ready to enjoy it, autonomous heating and television. All rooms allocate nice furnishing, elevator, daily service and traditional morning.' I can vouch for the fact that the morning was indeed traditional. The sun rose just where it has been rising for a few billion years. No change there then. As for the staff, they were fine. Or as the website says, 'irreproachable, and always in your disposal'.

Although I've been to Kalavrita a few times it was nice to read a bit about the place. The website had an excellent guide. For train enthusiasts there is a famous narrow gauge line running up the mountain to Kalavrita. Or as the site says: 'Their connection becomes also with railway, the eminent and unique Cogged.' They put it much better than I could. The museum is worth a visit, or rather 'the monastery of Saint Layras with the most infrequent heirlooms and the historical Labarum'. OK, I have to admit to looking up the word labarum. And they are spot on. A famous banner or flag. The labarum is famous as it signalled the start of the revolution against the Turks here when Mr Germanos 'put under oath the lads'.

Of course there is the ski centre itself which the site explains perfectly: 'In order to enjoy the beauty of Helmos and the breeze of innumerable firs, that covers the slopes of legendary mountain. For SKI, if it is winter. Everyone can learn SKI, after functions faculty in SKI centre.'

If you were puzzled by the reference to 'alluring trout' earlier, all is made clear later: 'In foot of Helmos, front of rich sources of Aroaneioy river, under thousands leafy planes, it operates the trout factory, where the visitor can enjoy in the artificial lake the magnificence of swans, or the delicious fried trout.' I have to say, I find some of this quite poetic. How locals react to a reference to 'particularly dense – mainly Greek – tourists' is another matter.

# 13

*In which John is surprised by the man who cooked his dinner and Christopher learns how to ward off evil*

Here's one of the things I mugged up about Greece since I've started going there regularly: in the years between 800 BC and 300 BC the average size of the Greek household increased five times. That, when you come to think about it, is really quite remarkable and historians are not absolutely sure why it happened. Most make the assumption that it was because the region had became so much wealthier. The dark ages had come to an end and ancient Greece was entering its golden age, its classical period. I have now spent enough time in the country to have developed my own theory: it's because Greek boys simply didn't want to leave home. They still don't. Why should they? They're spoiled rotten by their indulgent parents. I started to get some inkling of precisely how spoiled once Christopher began going out with Peppy and making friends with young Greek men. Most of them were still living at home. Not only that but they were treated as if they were still toddlers – reliant on Mummy and Daddy for everything except getting dressed in the morning.

Christopher had called in at a friend's apartment one Saturday evening to collect him for a night out on the town. He made small talk with the parents and then, when Dimitris appeared, stood up to leave. On their way out his mother handed Dimitris some money.

'What was that for?' Christopher asked later.

'Oh, just a bit of spending money for the evening,' said Dimitris. 'They always do that . . . always have.'

Dimitris was in his late twenties, a qualified lawyer earning a fairly small but regular salary. He not only lived at home, paying no rent and making no contribution to the household expenses, but he actually got pocket money as though he were still a schoolboy in short trousers. And bear in mind that his parents were not exactly wealthy – just ordinary middle-class Greeks on modest incomes trying to keep body and soul together.

Dimitris is by no means the exception. When Christopher told me about him there was a hint of indignation in his voice but also, I detected, a certain amount of envy. Why didn't I still give *him* pocket money, I could imagine him thinking. But this parental largesse goes beyond a few euros on a Saturday night – way beyond. You might think it would end when the children get married. Quite the opposite. That's when it really begins.

The first time I stayed with Christopher and Peppy in their little apartment in Athens they treated me to a splendid dinner: several different Greek dishes, all beautifully cooked. This puzzled me. Christopher is capable of cooking an excellent meal, just so long as it consists of curry and rice. Since that's ALL he cooks, where did this excellent food come from? Certainly not from Peppy – who may possibly be capable of boiling an egg but that has yet to be established – for the very simple reason that she does not cook. She is a vegetarian who has absolutely no interest in food and will happily eat a plate of cold rice for breakfast, lunch and dinner – as long as it has some lemon juice squeezed on it. Greeks squeeze lemon juice onto everything. So I asked Christopher about the dinner.

'Oh that? That's from Thakis, Peppy's Dad.'

'Really?' I said. 'How very kind of him. Did he do it specially to welcome me to Athens or something?'

'Oh no,' said Christopher. 'He cooks most of our food and just drops by with it. That's pretty normal.'

Well it didn't sound very normal to me, but I ate it with some relish all the same. And then we got onto the subject of Christopher's apartment. I mentioned earlier that it was pretty small – very pleasant but not ideal for a young couple with a growing family – and I wondered whether they might be looking for something a bit larger to rent or even buy.

'Not really,' said Christopher. 'We'll probably move into Peppy's parents' apartment. It's much bigger than this.'

'What, big enough for ALL of you?' I asked. 'And surely you don't want to live with the in-laws?'

He smiled. A rather smug smile, I thought.

'Of course not,' he said. 'They'll move out.'

And that, a few years later, is precisely what happened. The dowry tradition has died out long since in most of Europe, but it's still going strong in Greece – along with God knows how many other traditions you might have expected to have vanished a century or two ago. Greece may appear to be a modern country, but you don't have to scratch far below the surface to see that the old traditions are still strong – and not just in the villages but in a big city like Athens too. Christopher is delighted and appalled in equal measure. Having married a Greek girl, he's especially delighted that the dowry remains.

C: When my new father-in-law first asked me whether I wanted to move into his home I declined. I explained that we wanted to build a new house outside Athens near the town of Megara where the family is from. We were promptly invited to choose from one of several plots of land that the family owned. When we had made our choice the land was signed over to my name. Fantastic. At least it appeared to be fantastic at the time. It turned out that we may not get the planning permission (what a surprise) and these days I don't think I care. The thought of having to build another house, even if it's for me rather than my father, makes me break out in a cold sweat. Even in the middle of a Greek summer. I think I've just about got the energy left to erect a small tent on the site, which will have the added benefit of not needing any kind of permit whatsoever.

A few years on, and with our second baby on the way, we were still living in Athens and realised it made sense to live near the in-laws, so I took my father-in-law up on his previous offer. As we moved in they moved out to a smaller flat across the road. This meant we had a three-bedroomed top floor apartment in the centre of Athens as well as a plot out of town for future development. I can just see my own father doing the same for my sister. Catherine would ring up Dad and say, 'By the way, we've decided to move to London. Can we have the house?'

I'm sure Dad wouldn't hesitate in saying 'Of course you can! Shall I move out next week? I won't have a problem finding a smaller place for myself. I never liked having such a big garden anyway. And while I'm at it, why don't I sign the land in Wales over to your name?'

My father-in-law wouldn't dream of doing otherwise. It is a matter of pride and honour. It also makes huge sense. They benefit from getting to see the grandchildren every day and we benefit from having a free apartment and having them on hand to help out. Or vice-versa as they get older. In fact if you have a young family in Greece and don't have at least one set of parents nearby to help out, people pity you. And so they should. I sometimes mention casually to friends living in London that we not only have a spacious apartment courtesy of the in-laws but permanent babysitting as well. Or at least I used to mention it. Now I find it's wiser not to. Jealousy is a terrible thing. But it's not as if the in-laws do it reluctantly. On the contrary, they love having the children so close and, of course, the children love it too. And so do Peppy and I. Mother-in-law jokes are just as normal in Greece as they are in Britain but I don't think many of them were made up by new parents with two kids under three and full-time jobs.

We also have Aunty Soula and cousin Katerina living round the corner. Katerina and Peppy are like sisters to each other and we see a lot of them. This means that my kids have grown up with a close family circle of about eight people who they see all the time. If this is what people mean in Britain when they talk sadly of the disappearance of the extended family, well, they have a point. It's a very good system.

Lest I start to sound a bit naive I should point out that there is a financial side to all of this. In many cases young Greeks can't afford to move out of the family home – certainly not before finishing their studies and getting a job, and often not even after. Since the majority study in the city where their family live there isn't much point in leaving the comforts of the family house, though moving out afterwards is not easy. The salaries are shocking. Peppy's starting salary as a trainee lawyer was 600 euros a month, for which she worked at least ten hours a day. A highly qualified secretary is lucky to make 800 a month even today. This is someone who probably speaks three languages and has a degree. How can employers get away with paying so little? Because most young people don't have to pay rent and for them their salary is effectively expenses. It's later on that things can get very tough indeed. Salaries don't shoot up after five years with a company. If you aren't lucky enough to have a family property then life is very hard. Yes, rents are low when compared to Britain but the cost of living is as expensive as anywhere else in Europe. This is one reason why Greeks have had a negative birth rate for so long. People can't afford large families.

Greek society is deceptive. On the surface it may look as if it's the man who is the boss and who heads the family. In reality the mother is all-important and ultimately holds the most power. The men are given long leads and allowed to think that they are in control. The length of the lead varies but it's fair to say that it stretches further than anything in politically correct Britain. Take the question of mistresses. Andreas Papandreou had been elected Prime Minister as an old man who had recently married his former mistress. Far from finding anything morally repugnant in the thirty-year age difference and the naked trade-off of sex for power, most Greeks just accepted it with a shrug. That's the way men behave, eh? In fact, many men applauded him. Mistresses are still reasonably acceptable. When we have a big gala concert, which tends to be more about the rich and powerful of Athens socialising rather than the music, it's always fun to look for the oldest man with the youngest partner. There's plenty of competition. The partner tends to be the mistress, not the wife. There's an old Greek joke that sums it up nicely:

Costas is out for an evening stroll with his wife when a pretty young girl runs up to him and greets him with a kiss. After she leaves the wife asks Costas, 'Who was that, darling?'

Costas replies, 'That was Dimitri's mistress.'

A little while later another pretty young thing runs up to kiss Costas.

'And who was that, darling?' asks the wife.

'That was my mistress,' says Costas.

They carry on walking for a while and the wife starts smiling.

'What are you smiling about?' asks Costas.

The wife replies, 'Our mistress is much prettier than Dimitri's mistress.'

That might make Greek mothers appear pretty pathetic. Any self-respecting woman – even if she had never burned a bra in her life – would surely regard with contempt one of the sisters who tolerated her husband's infidelity. Don't you believe it. I wouldn't dream (jokes apart) of suggesting that a typical Greek wife actually enjoys the idea of her husband having an affair with another, younger woman. Of course not. It's more a question of them accepting what they regard as the inevitable – and doing so from a position of strength rather than weakness. The reasoning seems to go something like this: I can't stop him taking a mistress but I can make damn sure that he will still value me – even if it's only because he knows I can make his life pretty hellish if I choose to do so. As often as not, the pressure is applied through the children. The children obey the mother, full stop. Even the most arrogant, obnoxious young Greek man becomes a little lamb when his mother snaps her fingers. The father knows that and will yield to her in much the same way if he wants to keep his family together – which he almost always does. Here's another Greek joke that illustrates the point:

Why was Jesus Greek?

1. He lived at home till he was thirty
2. He did the same job as his father
3. He thought his mother was a virgin
4. His mother thought he was God.

For the most part it is just a question of being old-fashioned and holding on to the traditions. In a society as homogenous as Greece the traditions seem to stay. I made a fairly big faux pas once when I met someone I hadn't seen for a long time. He was sporting a big bushy beard that I had never seen before. 'What's with the beard?' I asked lightly. 'Lost your razor have you?' I was politely ignored and a friend had to inform me that his father had recently died and he was in mourning.

The mourning process really can seem a bit too much for someone from our sanitised British society. Peppy's closest aunt lost her husband about ten years ago, around the same time that I lost my mother. They have two children who at the time were sixteen and fourteen. Coming from Megara, a town close to Athens, meant that tradition was followed even more closely even though these are modern, educated people. Giorgos, the son, is on his way to becoming a very successful architect and Katerina is a lawyer. They are wonderful people.

The day after her husband died, and before the funeral, Aunt Soula had to prepare her house to receive the mourners. This isn't a case of receiving your relatives and close friends. This means most of the town will pass by. Even people with only a passing acquaintance are entitled to drop in at any time. Chairs must be hired, special cakes baked or bought and brandy must be provided by the gallon. For several days the house will be full of people from morning to night. Maybe this is therapeutic for those most affected but I would have found it stifling. I didn't want to speak to anyone after my mother died, especially not crowds of people, some of whom I would barely know.

After the funeral you are in mourning, as are your children. Aunt Soula was an attractive, sociable woman of fifty-two when her husband died but her social life died with him. The black clothes were worn for five years. For the first few years any social outing was frowned upon. She couldn't even go to the hairdresser's in town because it would be seen as a sign that she wanted to make herself attractive, and the rules of mourning do not allow that. So she would drive half an hour away to Corinth just to get her hair done. Whereas, before her husband's death, she had been the life and soul of Megara and out all the time, now she had to stay at home. Only trips to close relatives were allowed. Even the children wore black for a while, although with Giorgos you wouldn't have known the difference. I remember going out with Peppy and Katerina maybe six months after her father's death and being puzzled as to why she didn't get up and dance when everyone else did. 'She's in mourning,' I was told.

I don't know whether this whole drawn-out process is healthier than our own way of dealing with death. Aunt Soula seemed to me to have been dealt a double blow. She lost her husband and was simultaneously ostracised from Megara society. But maybe being forced to acknowledge such heavy grief is ultimately better than the stiff upper lip approach of the Brits.

What I do know is that the relatively intact extended families with their respect for tradition make for a very pleasant society. Peppy and I live in a central area of Athens that has seen better days, as the strip club at the end of the road and the brothels hidden down a side street will attest, and yet I have never experienced the kind of unpleasant moment while walking down a street late at night that anybody living in a British city will be familiar with. More to the point, I know that Peppy doesn't feel threatened either. On her first trip to Britain we were walking back to Dad's house from a late show at the cinema when I saw three lads coming towards us. They looked a bit dodgy, not to mention drunk, and I thought it better to cross to the other side of the street.

'Why did we have to cross the street?' she asked me.

'I don't like the look of those three men over there,' I said.

'But why? What can they do?' she asked.

'It's not worth finding out,' I replied.

I felt cowardly and slightly foolish but the fact is that people who live in London, or any big city in Britain for that matter, have learned to develop a streetwise sixth sense that can help avoid you getting into trouble. Had I been walking on my own I might not have crossed the road but I had a pretty girl with me and there were three of them. It wouldn't have been the first time I had been hassled in this way. I took the easy option. Peppy didn't have the faintest idea what I was talking about and, given that she lives in Athens, there's no reason why she should have.

Greek traditions, on the whole, deal with the practical. They give a framework for daily life and all its complications. But surely a country that has given the world the wonders of Greek mythology has a more fantastical side to it? Don't worry, Greek superstition is alive and well.

Peppy came home from work one day looking rather peaky. She said she had a bad headache that had been with her most of the day. I suggested she take an aspirin but she said it would not help. I asked how she could be so sure.

'Because,' she said, 'someone has given me the Evil Eye. I'm sure it was when I was in court this morning.'

This can be very serious. The Evil Eye is a kind of telepathic curse. It is strongest when given by someone near you but it can also, apparently, be deployed at long range. Before you think I'm laughing at this quaint Greek superstition I should point out that the Evil Eye features as a belief in over a third of the world's cultures, from South America through the Med and as far as India. What I love about Greece is that it is still alive and well as a belief. It isn't just a 'village superstition', as one ignorant article I read suggests.

The Evil Eye gives a good insight into Greek society. First, it is as old as history. All the ancient Greek writers spoke of it. The blue eye that wards it off was painted on the sides of boats as old as the ancient triremes and can still be seen on the sides of fishing boats today. Many intelligent, educated, well-travelled Greeks have no problem with accommodating such an archaic belief in their modern lives.

When Peppy came home feeling 'eyed' she rang up a close friend and colleague of hers. Some people inherit the gift of 'de-eying' or removing the curse. This is normally passed down through the family from one sex to the other. Harris had been taught by his mother and will pass the knowledge on to his daughter, if he ever manages to settle down. The process involves the recital of some words, including prayers. Peppy began to yawn continuously, I heard some crying coming from the other end of the phone and that was that. Twenty minutes later Peppy was cured.

The Eye explains what seems to be a lot of curious behaviour in Greeks, particularly where children are concerned. Adults may say they suffer from headaches and nausea because of it but for young children it is believed to be much more serious, possibly even fatal. The curse is mainly believed to be a result of envy or jealousy, which is why newborn babies are the most susceptible. So the babies are given a blue protecting eye to be pinned on their clothes or their pram. When admirers – stranger or friend – stop to pay compliments to the mother on her beautiful child they must spit three times. In the past few years (maybe as a concession to modern hygiene) it is deemed sufficient just to make the spitting sound three times: 'ftou ftou ftou!' The first time I saw one of my Greek friends doing this I was amazed. I knew the practice existed but this was a woman with a degree in psychology who had spent ten years in Paris.

In some ancient cultures, such as those found in South

America, spitting wasn't enough to ensure that you dispelled any envy from your compliment and inadvertently 'eyed' the baby. It was important to touch the baby as well. Greeks are naturally more tactile than us stiff Northern Europeans but even so it would explain the almost obsessive stroking of poor Hector's hair whenever I took him out as a baby.

The Greek Orthodox Church is more than happy to accept this superstition. As a belief that has been around much longer than Christianity itself, one would think that the Church would want to have nothing to do with it. On the contrary, there are specific prayers for 'de-eying' and some priests go so far as to say that it is only they who should perform the ritual. As is often the case the Church chose to embrace an older tradition and use it to its own advantage rather than try to eradicate it. A wise move, I think, as the Eye is one of the ancient traditions that to this day helps to bind the family, and thus the society, together in Greece. Inheritance in Greece means much more than just passing on money or land. It is about passing on knowledge and tradition. It matters.

# 14

*In which we are treated to a display of the finest swearing known to man and finally achieve a functioning kitchen*

There were times, given the slow progress we were making, when I wondered whether our old enemy Douskos – the original engineer on our building site – had 'eyed' us. Maybe we should paint the magic eye on the side of the house . . . but given our luck the painter would probably fall off his ladder. Still, it's not as if we weren't making some progress. In fact we were now at the stage, after two years of building, where we had to get a proper electricity supply to the site. We had managed so far by running a very long lead from the cottage all the way up the hill, which would have given any British health and safety inspector a heart attack. It was fine so long as all we needed to do was charge an electric toothbrush, but anything that needed more juice caused serious problems for our neighbours who were in the next bay and next in line on the grid. They were delightful people but strangely unenthusiastic about having to sit in the dark during the long winter nights and manage without a fridge during the searing summer heat because we had overloaded the circuit. Sometimes it worked the other way. Sitting in the cottage, we could always tell when our neighbour's fridge kicked in or one of them took a shower because our lights would dim so low it was impossible to read. The supply was, to say the least, both erratic and inadequate. The supply to the new house was also illegal. So we had to apply to the electricity company to be connected properly.

Yet again I am tempted to blame Christopher and his Pollyanna approach for what happened next. He believed what he had been told by the electricity company. Privatisation has yet to reach the power supply industry and so, because they are a part of the all-encompassing State and therefore civil servants, they operate by different rules. It's not so much that they set out to lie to their 'customers' – more that they cannot be bothered to tell the truth if the truth is likely to be unwelcome. There are a clear set of rules which go more or less as follows:

Rule 1: It's Not My Fault. Someone else is to blame because you do not have an electricity supply.
Rule 2: There's Nothing I Can Do.
Any further (pointless) question is answered with . . .
Rule 3: I Don't Know.

And that is pretty well that. They don't need to say anything else. It is simple and effective. Anybody silly enough to try to take things further will simply be given The Condescending Smile. At that stage acceptance of defeat is the only option.

Once we had built our pylon and Christos, our excellent electrician, had installed all the necessary wiring and junction boxes, we made the formal application to be connected to the mains. At this stage, incidentally, we were applying for only a temporary connection. The real McCoy would not be granted until every last detail of the house had been completed and we could prove that we had paid the state insurance for every worker who had ever set foot on the site. Such are the ways of the bureaucrats. We were told that our 'temporary' supply would be connected within ten days, so Christopher figured it was reasonable to assume that we would have it within a month or so. Nothing happened. Not after ten days and not after two months. Then they went on strike, which lasted ten days. That, we were to learn, did not mean it would add ten days to our waiting time. What it actually meant was that all promises previously made no longer applied. Whenever Christopher tried chasing them up and pointing out that it was now six months since the application had been made and we had been promised we would have our supply within ten days, the conversation would go something like this:

'Why have you not connected me up yet?'

'Because there has been a strike.'

'But it is now six months since I made the application and the strike lasted for ten days.'

'Yes, but there is a backlog of work as a result of the strike.'

'But a strike of ten days means a backlog of only ten days' work and I have been waiting for six months.'

'That is not the point.'

And, of course, they were right. It was not the point. The point was that there had never been the slightest intention to honour the original promise and provide a supply within ten days. They might as easily have said ten minutes or ten years: it was simply a notional figure sucked out of the air so that Christopher would get off the phone and leave them to do whatever it is that bored bureaucrats do who have never felt the hot breath of competition on their necks. As always, Christopher told me relatively little about the problems – I think he feared for my blood pressure – but I could sense that he was getting a bit panicky.

C: There was a reason for that. Dad was due to arrive in only a few weeks for another of his visits – welcome but scary in just about equal measure. I had rashly assured him that we had finally started making real progress and by the time he arrived there would finally be something to show for all the money he had been spending. Not only did we have walls, a roof and floors by now, but a kitchen and bathrooms as well, fully equipped with the finest fittings Dad's money could buy. What we did not have was electricity and there is limited value in big fridges, swanky cookers and dishwashing machines if they cannot be switched on.

Dad arrived just when he said he would. The electricity supply did not. Which was why he spent the first evening trying to read by candlelight while I tried to cook on a tiny single-ring camping stove powered by a half-empty can of camping gas. In the end he gave up trying to read and instead produced a small calculator so that he could while away the hours happily working out roughly how much it had cost him to live pretty much the way he had lived when he was a penniless seventeen-year-old reporter in his first bedsit. As for me, I gave up cooking when the gas ran out – which it did when the rice was still as hard as a bureaucrat's heart. I lay in bed the following morning waiting for the sun to come up (there was no point in switching on the lights) and trying to work out how best to persuade Dad that cooking over an open fire in the middle of winter was the very latest thing in international cuisine. I needn't have bothered. Over a dish of cold porridge he ordered me to ring the electricity board again and warn them that if they gave me the usual run-around he would personally drive to their headquarters in Athens and . . . but he never finished that ominous sentence because something quite remarkable happened. The electricity men arrived.

We heard their van coming down the dirt road above the house and saw it stop at the pylon at the top of our drive. One man got out, glanced at the junction box and, with the van's engine still running, started to get back in again. Before he could slam the door and drive off again Vangelis appeared, making a passable imitation of an Olympic sprinter as he hared up the drive towards them. Dad was all for joining him but I advised him that his version of tactful diplomacy and persuasion might be counterproductive, so we both watched through the kitchen window. It didn't take long. A few minutes later the van door slammed very firmly shut, the van took off and Vangelis retreated down the drive, clearly a broken man. We could hear him muttering to himself: 'The bastards! The bastards!'

What had happened was that in his ten-second inspection of the junction box the electricity man had spotted that the last wire had not been connected; the final connection had not been made. There was a very good reason for that. Christos had said it would take only a few seconds to do it and it was best to leave it until we knew we had a secure supply lest anything go wrong. But the man wanted it connected. Vangelis had his screwdriver with him.

'Look!' he had said. 'I am doing it now. There! It is done!'

But the electricity man would not have it.

'It is a job for the original installer, not for you,' he snapped.

Vangelis produced what is normally a trump card in these circumstances: a fifty-euro note, which he tried to thrust into the man's hand. Maybe the man was incorruptible as well as officious. Maybe fifty euros wasn't enough. More probably, they had never seriously had any intention of connecting us up to the main supply: they'd paid us a visit so that it could be entered into the records and now we could be forgotten about for another six months. Whatever the reasoning, they drove off and I swear that their tail lights, as they receded into the distance, gave us a small, knowing wink.

I tried to look on the bright side. Yes, it had taken six months to get them out to the house and they had driven off without doing what was needed and it would probably take another six months to get them back again – but at least Dad had seen for himself how the system worked. Surely from now on he would be more sympathetic when I moaned about the problems of dealing with the bureaucrats. In the meantime, I knew what had to be done if we were to stand any chance of ever living in the house. We had to get Christos to come and make the connection and sign a bit of paper to say that he had done so.

As the noise of the van died away I phoned him and begged him to do the following: drive to Piraeus from his home in Athens tomorrow morning; catch the early boat to Poros; get a taxi to the house ten miles away; disconnect the wire that Vangelis had already connected; join it back up again; stamp a piece of paper that said he had made the connection and get a boat back home again. In other words, I was asking a skilled electrician to put in a very long day in order to do a thirty-second job that had, in fact, already been done. But that is what The State, in the person of two taciturn officials, decreed had to be done and there is no arguing with The State.

Christos was not, it's fair to say, a happy man. He was swearing when he arrived and he did not stop swearing until he left. To give him his due, he swears with great fluency and colour. He is almost as good at swearing as he is at wiring up a house. After greeting Dad he started asking Vangelis what had happened. The entire conversation was conducted in swear words so loud that Dad thought the situation was going to get violent. Christos then swore non-stop for the next hour while fixing the fuse box, stamping the paper and having a coffee. Some of his invective was so imaginative I felt I had to translate it for Dad. The general theme was the nature of the mothers of the people who worked for the electricity company. Sometimes this tirade was directed at the public sector more generally, occasionally against the type of people living in an area such as ours. I only understood half of what was said but it was the most impressive scatological display I have ever witnessed in my life.

But at least we were now in with a fighting chance of getting a proper electricity supply which meant that we could cook decent meals. If there's one thing on which Dad and I (and just about every Greek I have ever met) are in total agreement, it is the importance of good food. The British make small talk about the weather; the Greeks make small talk about food. And big talk too. When you live in Greece you quickly realise that food is the default conversation in almost any situation. I have sat through many a meal with Greek family and friends where food took up the majority of the conversation. After asking after my health and that of my children, the most common question from the in-laws is about food. Have I had lunch? What did I have? What am I planning on eating for supper? What about the kids? How about some roast lamb at the weekend?

Hours can be spent discussing where to find the best ingredients. This is a vast topic because it can range from local shops to the big supermarkets and on to the weekly farmer's markets. Then you can argue the merits of various products from different regions of Greece. Are the mountain greens better in Megara or Methana? Which part of Greece has the best feta? When the conversation switches to recipes – which it usually does – things can turn quite nasty. I have heard plenty of innocent discussions about the best way to make a cheese pie end in shouting matches. Every family has its own recipes and they guard them with all the ferocity that would normally be reserved for defending the honour of your wife or daughter.

It is, in short, a great mistake to take Greek food lightly. I have learned to my cost how foolish it is to go to a friend's parents for dinner and even hint that actually you're not terribly hungry. Worse still to suggest that goat, for instance, is not really your favourite dish. It has probably taken them two days to prepare the goat dish from a recipe handed down by a revered great grandmother. I once failed to wipe my plate clean of a particularly pungent goat dish and managed to insult four generations of Papadopouloses.

*J*: When Christopher waxes lyrical about Greek food, I tend to be a bit sceptical. It's certainly true that older people like Thakis produce some wonderful dishes and if you're lucky enough to eat in a Greek home you will almost certainly eat very well indeed. As he says, they take it seriously. But what most of us know about Greek food comes from eating in tavernas and anyone who has spent a week on a certain kind of Greek holiday island will know what to expect: taramasalata that owes its shocking pink colour more to the contents of a test tube than the natural world; thin chips with everything; all the dishes arriving at the same time and almost everything tasting a bit like everything else. The first meal might be okay, but by the end of the week you'd happily slaughter the taverna owner's cat if you thought you could get it cooked in a red wine sauce.

Christopher gets cross when I complain about eating out in Greece. For one thing, he says, it's daft to talk about restaurants and tavernas in the same breath. A restaurant might have Greek food but it might equally have French,

Italian, German or Chinese food as well and it will have table cloths on the tables and cost twice as much. A taverna will have only Greek food and no tablecloths and will be cheap – unless it's some sort of tourist clip joint. He says it's my own fault for not finding the right ones and points out that every country has rotten restaurants as well as good ones. Of course that's true, but ask him how you identify the good tavernas and he is less than helpful. He has only two rules and the first one is common sense: avoid the ones that are obviously aimed at tourists; they will have little flags of half the world's nations displayed outside and the only people inside will be foreigners. If there are three tavernas on the same street – as there often are – and all the locals are in the same one, then that's your choice. That really is all the help he can offer.

What about asking around? The problem with that is who to ask. The manager of your hotel will probably think that you are after chicken 'Gordon Blue', as it is so often described, and will direct you to the horrible 'international cuisine' restaurant where he will receive a commission. If you stray further than the hotel and perhaps ask someone in a shop or café then your answer will depend on the shopkeeper's relatives. The odds are that at least one of them will work in, or own, a taverna, so that's the one you'll be sent to. There is another tactic that Christopher says sometimes works: find the local priest. If you spot him sitting in a taverna, then it is a fairly safe bet that you have found the best taverna in town. Unless of course, it is the worst but happens to be owned by the priest's brother, nephew or uncle.

In my own, rather more limited, experience it is wise to avoid tavernas with menus – especially if they have pictures on them and offer set meals. Any decent, traditional taverna will offer you food that is in season and fresh, which means they'd have to print new menus every other day. It becomes a little more difficult to order if your Greek is less than fluent, but not entirely impossible. Christopher and I had some slightly surreal encounters in the days before he was able to order food with the confidence of a native. The most important thing to remember is that it is unwise to expect a waiter to approach and ask whether sir or madam is ready to order. They won't do that, so you will have to try to catch the waiter's eye – which is not always easy given that it is not entirely obvious who the waiter is. Timid hand gestures are fairly pointless, too, and so is the classically British, apologetic 'Sorry . . . excuse me . . .' The waiter will be puzzled by this, given that he can see no obvious reason why you should be apologising, assuming he can understand you in the first place.

# 15

*In which John marvels at an ancient theatre and Christopher confronts the neighbour who tried to cut us off from the outside world*

It was now almost three years since I first stood on the foundations of the building site and looked out across the Argo Saronic Gulf. What was then not much more than a few pillars and slabs of concrete was now well on the way to becoming the house I dreamed of – not so much because of *what* it is but *where* it is. I have seen many beautiful bays, many beautiful islands and many beautiful mountains. What makes the Peloponnese unique is the combination of all that and its ancient history too. This was the beating heart of classical Greece. I can stand on a balcony and look out across the bay and, on a clear day, see the finest amphitheatre of the classical world. It sits on the top of a hill above Epidavros: a breathtaking semi-circle of benches carved from limestone, worn smooth over the ages by countless bottoms that might once have been covered in robes and are now more likely to be covered in denim jeans. There is seating for 15,000 people and the acoustics are good enough to make a modern sound engineer, with all his fancy equipment, wonder how they did it more than two millennia ago. It is possible to sit in the back row, from where you can barely see the actor on the stage far below, and hear the click of his fingers. The scale of the achievement defies the imagination, and so does the scale of the ambition.

Might those craftsmen have imagined, as they laboured at their stupendous task four centuries before the birth of Christ, that their theatre would still be used regularly for live performances long after the end of their own civilisation and even the collapse of the mighty Roman empire? Perhaps they knew that they were building something that might very well outlive the last human beings on earth. Or perhaps they were simply doing what they were told, grumbling as they carved out yet another row of seats about how little they were paid and why they had to work such long hours to earn a living wage and why was so much money being spent on something to entertain the middle classes when it was cheap housing and hospitals and decent schools that were really needed?

I like to think they took the view of an old stonemason I interviewed when I was a television reporter for the BBC in Liverpool. He had spent his entire life since completing his apprenticeship working on the building of the new Anglican cathedral. I was a youngster at the time, bored with local news and desperate to make my mark as a foreign correspondent. How could he do the same job for so long, I asked him? Surely he found it boring, cutting and placing one stone after another, day in day out for years on end? He looked at me with a degree of incomprehension.

'But that's not what I'm doing,' he said. 'I am building a great cathedral.'

Of course he was right and I, in my youthful ignorance and arrogance, was embarrassed by the naivety of my question. No doubt he has been dead these many years but I imagine how he must have felt in his retirement with his task complete and the cathedral consecrated, its great spire reaching into the sky above the city where he was born and lived all his life. I like to think of him gazing up at it, his grandson by his side, and murmuring proudly: 'That's what I did with my life, son, I built a cathedral.'

Naturally, one of the first things I wanted to do as soon as we had settled into the cottage at Metamorfosi was to go to see the ancient theatre. It would, I thought, take no more than twenty minutes to drive there. I had not allowed for the fact that Greeks do not approve of maps – or at least, not the sort of maps that enable an averagely intelligent human being to get from point A to point B without beginning to lose the will to live. I remembered my first trip to the Peloponnese and the amused reaction at the tourist office in Athens when Christopher asked for a map to help us find the Lousios Gorge. But surely it would be different with Epidavros, a unique attraction that must be worth a fortune to the vitally important Greek tourist industry? It is, after all, a UNESCO world heritage site visited by millions of people every year from countries far and wide. All I can say to that is: heaven knows how they manage to find it without a guide. I was lucky enough to have two people to guide me – Christopher and Peppy – who know the area well. They suggested that they should come with me. Quite unnecessary, I said, I shall have no trouble finding it by myself if you tell me how to get there. They looked a little uneasy but set about giving me detailed instructions.

I had assumed – not unreasonably, you might think – that it would be sensible to follow the signs to Epidavros. That was my first mistake. Epidavros does not exist. There is NEW Epidavros. I have seen a signpost to it and it is marked on some maps. There is also OLD Epidavros and I know THAT exists because Christopher has stayed there many times. Indeed, it was where he first met Peppy. I was also vaguely aware that there was a place called ANCIENT Epidavros, but that, it turns out, is just their little joke. Christopher, I know, has played many times in the ancient theatre of Epidavros. But which ancient theatre? There are two. If you follow the signs to the ancient theatre when you are in Old Epidavros (assuming you can find the signs) you will find yourself in a charming but modest little ancient theatre on the sea. It is only recently that it has been excavated. This is obviously not the one that sits so proudly on the hilltop across my bay. That is the one I wanted to find and that, it turns out, is not in Epidavros at all – Old or New – but somewhere else entirely. It is close to the town of Asklipiion, which is what Christopher had told me. All I needed to do was head for Asklipiion and follow the signposts from there. That is pretty much what Christopher had said. He had even found a map of sorts (though it looked more like something little Hector had scribbled with his crayons) and circled Asklipiion on it. Then he sent me off, obviously confident that the combination of my infallible sense of direction and his local knowledge meant there was no way I could go wrong. I phoned him about an hour later.

'Right, I've done everything you said and I know I turned left at Old Epidavros or whatever it's called but I'm damned if I can see a sign to Asklipiion, let alone the theatre!'

'But that's not possible. I know there's a town by the theatre because I've stayed there and I know it's called Asklipiion. It's on the map, dammit!'

'I don't care where you've stayed or what the map says, I'm telling you there is no such place!'

We were saved by Peppy who, slowly and calmly, pointed out that I was right – in a manner of speaking. There is no such place as Asklipiion. Or, to be a little more precise, there is such a place but it is not really called Asklipiion. It is called Ligourio. Why? Who knows. Certainly none of the local people asked by Christopher and Peppy knew. When they enquire about it the locals just look at them as if to say: 'Why does it matter? We know how to find our way around. Can't we just leave it at that?'

I found the ancient theatre in the end, of course, and if it had taken me ten times as long it would have been worth it. There are few places that make you catch your breath when you first see them, but this is one. If you remove the cars and the car park, it must look just as it had when the first theatre-goers sat on these seats millennia ago. Not that there were many cars. Most people, it seems, arrive by coach. How wise.

It is not entirely true to say that there are no maps of Greece. You will be handed one when you hire a car and it's fine if you never leave the main road, but it took Christopher years to find something that vaguely resembles an ordinance survey map. Detailed maps of Greece simply do not exist. The army have them (or so they say) but it seems it just wouldn't do to let them fall into the hands of civilians. What if a stray map of the Peloponnese were to be found by a Turk! The people of Greece would probably wake up the next morning to find Turkish soldiers on every street corner and the entire Greek government hanging from the lamp posts.

Most archaeological sites in Greece get scarcely any visitors at all, which is unsurprising given how many of them there are and given that you probably won't even know they exist until you stumble on them. I remember going for a stroll a few miles from the house one fine winter's day. We saw a rough old piece of wood nailed to a tree with the words 'Temple of Hippolytus' scrawled on it and a sign pointing up a dirt road. We followed the arrow and at the end of the road came to a rusty old gate. On the other side of the gate were ancient ruins which, in any other country in Europe, would be regarded as a national treasure. This, of course, was no Epidavros – nothing else is – but just as remarkable in its own way.

These were the substantial remains of an early Byzantine church and the partly excavated ruins of the temple, which had been used as a place of healing at roughly the same time the first theatre-goers were taking their seats in Epidavros. You might have expected the site to be patrolled by men in peaked caps; ticket booths with queues of people waiting to pay their fiver for entry and signs everywhere warning you not to step over the ropes surrounding the ruins and ON NO ACCOUNT remove anything from the site. Here there were no fences, no guards, no warning notices and no people. We had this glorious piece of ancient history to ourselves. It really is a rare privilege to stand in the centre of ruins as ancient as these and allow your imagination to take you back thousands of years, unhindered by hordes of other visitors, the only sound the breeze rustling the leaves in the surrounding lemon groves and the hint of a murmur from the mountain stream that was once fed into the channels marking the limits of the temple.

Even Christopher, with his local knowledge, had no idea the site existed and when he finally went there he was as impressed as I had been. He took Spiros and Freya, his archaeologist friends with him and Spiros agreed that, yes, it was indeed a marvellous site but, no, he wasn't surprised that nobody bothered to guard its treasures. Christopher picked up a few pieces of tile and shards of pottery and pointed to a stone with an inscription carved on it.

'Ah yes,' said Spiros, 'this is almost certainly a stone from the original temple that was plundered to build the Byzantine church. The inscription on it was probably made several centuries before Christ.'

'But this is crazy,' said Christopher. 'Anyone can come here and take away as much of this stuff as they want and there's no one here to stop them.'

'So what?' said Spiros. 'Even if we wanted to protect every

piece of ancient pottery or tile we couldn't possibly do it. There are maybe a thousand sites scattered over the country and only a tiny fraction are being excavated. If we guarded every last archaeological treasure we'd never be able to look after them all.'

I got some idea of what he meant on my first visit to Naxos and my first encounter with a Kouros statue. He was a pretty hefty chap who would have stood as tall as a giant had he been standing, but he wasn't. He was lying in the corner of an overgrown field, totally neglected and unprotected apart from a bit of rope which was originally meant to cordon him off but had long since rotted away. He was magnificent.

The people of Naxos have been sculpting marble for five thousand years. Their earliest work would not have looked out of place in a modern art gallery: abstract forms, simple and serene, that might have inspired Henry Moore or Modigliani. Then they moved on to producing the sort of statues that lay in this field. The Kouroi were found all over ancient and classical Greece – usually depicting the god Apollo and carved from one solid block of marble – and nowadays all over the world. No major international museum would be seen dead without their own Kouros.

And here this one lies – at least three times as tall as a man – in a scarcely visited corner of the island near the village of Melanes, where anyone out for an afternoon's walk might stumble upon it. He almost merged into the dry stone wall behind, wild flowers and herbs growing around and beneath him, as though he were sleeping on a soft green bed. One of his legs was broken at the knee and the other was missing a foot, but otherwise the Kouros was intact. All his graceful contours were clear, no more than slightly softened by millennia of rain and wind. In some ways he seemed to have grown out of the ground beneath him and looked surprisingly lifelike. Christopher and I might not have been too surprised if he had raised his massive head and fixed his unseeing eyes on us.

The local people seemed to have no idea as to how or why he came to be lying here, why he had not been carted away, installed on a plinth to be admired by a stream of visitors. Indeed, they seemed scarcely aware of his presence. Perhaps he was carved where he lies from marble hewn from a nearby ancient quarry. Perhaps he had never been completed to the satisfaction of the sculptor because he discovered flaws in the marble. Perhaps the sculptor had died as he worked to complete him, chisel and mallet in hand, or perhaps there had been a row among the locals over the best place to put him. Maybe the sculptor had not been paid for his work and refused to hand it over. Whatever the reason, here he lies and will continue to lie for centuries to come, a magnificent sight and an endless source of wonder to everyone who happens across it.

Scholars who know about the Melanes Kouros speculate that his intended destination might well have been Delos, the sacred island of the Cycladics that has been a centre of worship of the gods for three thousand years. Many of the giant marble statues there have come from Naxos, including the massive lions guarding the Sacred Way, an avenue a bit like the avenue of sphinxes in Egypt. Delos is a World Heritage site, a protected island, where tourists are allowed to visit for the day but are forbidden from staying overnight. Perhaps that would have been a more fitting home for this giant than the corner of a field – but perhaps not.

I suppose you could argue that it is simply wrong for a great piece of art to be abandoned like this. Surely ancient art should be protected, kept out of harm's way, admired from a respectable distance beneath signs that warn 'Do not touch!' I'm not so sure. As I looked down at this handsome giant and ran my hand over the weathered head, I thought about works of art locked away in private collections, admired by their wealthy owners and select groups of friends, or bought as investments in the same way as one might buy shares in a pork pie company.

Before we get too sniffy about the way the Greeks deal with their unique archaeological heritage it's worth remembering what they did nearly two centuries ago when the Acropolis came under threat. The Ottoman Empire was still a mighty force across the Middle East and parts of Europe, but in Greece, which the Turks had occupied for four centuries, they were finally beginning to meet some pretty stiff resistance. In 1822 they were holed up on the Acropolis – by any standards one of the greatest glories of Classical Greece. The ancient Greeks started building the Parthenon on top of the hill in 447 BC: a temple to the Greek goddess Athena, whose great pillars stand to this day. The Greeks see it as the ultimate symbol of ancient Greece and Athenian democracy and are immensely proud of it. But the Turkish soldiers getting fired at by rebellious Greeks saw it as something else: shelter from the Greek guns and a useful source of ammunition.

When the Turks ran out of anything to fire back at the Greeks they started tearing down the columns and gouging out the lead, which was wrapped around the iron rods inside them, melting it down and turning it into musket balls. The Greeks saw what was happening and said, in effect: If you stop destroying our temple we will give you what you need to defend yourselves against us. The Turks gratefully accepted. A shipment of lead was handed over by the Greeks and promptly returned in smaller, more lethal, form. History does not record whether this is the only example of one side in a war supplying the other side with ammunition to fire at them, but the gods rewarded the Greeks and a few years later – with a lot of help from other countries as well as the gods – the

Turks were driven out. Greece was finally recognised as an independent nation in 1832.

By the closing years of the next century it wasn't the Turks who were threatening the Parthenon; it was the motor car. There were so many of them clogging the streets of Athens that within a couple of decades the pollution from their exhausts had done more damage to the ancient temple than the entire Turkish army and two millennia of wear and tear. As I mentioned earlier, this was *nefos* – an acid, acrid smog that burned your eyes, choked your lungs and rotted the ancient stonework of the Parthenon and every other monument. Something had to be done. Before they built the Metro, they tried various schemes to keep cars out of the city centre – including the ingenious one of banning every other car on alternate days. If you had an even number plate you could enter only on, say, Monday, Wednesday and Friday; if you had an odd number you'd be restricted to Tuesday, Thursday and Saturday. It didn't work. People either had two cars with different plates or they simply cheated.

If the Parthenon was a triumph of ancient Greece, the Metro (admittedly for rather different reasons) is a triumph of modern Greece. The first time I used it was to get out to the airport from the city centre for an early morning flight to London. I was worried that I wouldn't be able to read the signs and might get on the wrong train. Christopher assured me there was no danger of that.

'Your train will arrive at 6.34 a.m. and that's the one you get on.'

'But what if it comes at 6.32?'

'Then it will be the wrong one. Yours will come at 6.34.'

He was right. I got to the station much too early and sat nervously on the spotlessly clean platform, soothed somewhat by the classical music relayed over a magnificent speaker system. I wondered how everything could be quite so clean, given the huge numbers of people who use the Metro. I understood when I saw a young man come onto the platform with an open drinks can in his hand. Another passenger pointed to it and said something fairly sharply. The young man looked embarrassed and promptly dumped the can in a bin. Christopher told me that was typical: it is illegal to eat or drink on the Metro and the rule is enforced by other passengers as well as officials. Athenians take great pride in their Metro and it shows. He was right about the punctuality too. I watched a few trains come and go, was tempted by the 6.31 but held my nerve and then, as the station clock changed to 6.34, my train arrived. I was at the airport forty minutes later.

It has taken an awfully long time to build the Metro. The law says that if builders come across ancient ruins, they must stop until archaeologists have been called in and given their permission for the work to be carried out. The thing about Athens, of course, is that you need only dig a spade in the ground to find something or other that dates back a couple of thousand years or more. Imagine trying to build a station near the Acropolis. They got around the problem wonderfully by lining the excavation with thick sheets of Perspex rather than coating it in a foot of concrete. So it is now possible, while you're waiting for a train, to inspect various levels of archaeological excavation dating back five thousand years. This is not just a Metro: it's a history lesson with a unique perspective. Quite wonderful. And the trains run on time too.

It is tempting to wonder what future generations will make of modern buildings, assuming they survive for long enough to achieve any sort of archaeological significance. No doubt my own house will have slid down the hill and vanished into the ocean long before some 29th-century archaeologist decides to make a study of our area, but there is one small structure that I hope will survive. It bears a striking resemblance to a pile of old breeze blocks – unsurprisingly really because that's precisely what it is. It sits proudly near the entrance to our drive: a symbol of a rare victory in our endless battle with the forces of darkness ranged against our modest building project.

When I saw the van stop at the top of our drive – actually not a drive at all, more a dirt track, but still the only way to get to the house – I assumed it was making a delivery. But it seemed a bit odd that the driver started unloading the concrete blocks there, rather than delivering them to the building site. Odder still was the sense of urgency. It is fair to say that at the height of a hot summer, builders and delivery men tend to take things pretty easy. You can't blame them really in that heat. But this man – not exactly in the first flush of youth – seemed very anxious to offload the blocks as swiftly as possible and then, odder still, begin to pile them up rather than just leave them in the usual heap.

Vangelis, who was still our foreman at the time, was not expecting a delivery, so he wandered up to find out what was going on. Christopher and I watched them chatting, then arguing, then appearing to become very heated indeed. By the time we got there they were going at it hammer and tongs – voices at full volume, veins throbbing in foreheads, fists clenched. Even Christopher, with his fluent Greek, was puzzled by what the row was about. Eventually he managed to discern that the man intended to build a wall – which might have been fine given how much building we needed doing one way and another. What we did not need was a wall clear across our drive so that we could not get out of our property and nobody else could get in. Yet that was precisely what the angry man was planning to do. The question was why.

Christopher sent Vangelis away before the argument came to blows and tried to get some explanation. It seems we were the (almost) accidental victims of an ancient feud between neighbours. The would-be wall builder turned out to be the owner of a plot of land that bordered a few hundred feet of our boundary from where our drive started. We had seen him only once, when he'd come to harvest his olives, but we had heard about him from our friend Nikos. His name was Panos and he had grown up in the village and had been at school with Nikos. For many years they had been good friends and neighbours: Panos's land bordered Nikos's property.

The problem started when Panos announced that he wanted to build a house on his land that he could use as a dowry for his daughter. In order to get planning permission he needed access down to the beach road and that would mean driving a road smack through Nikos's land, which anyone could use. Nikos was not madly keen on losing his privacy and having a road running through his delightful garden, so he said no. Panos never got his planning permission and never spoke to Nikos again. But he did not give up. His daughter might have been married long since without her dowry, but he still wanted to build the house. All that happened many years before we ever set foot in the Peloponnese so you might think it had nothing to do with us. You would be wrong.

Christopher and I were chatting one day about how best to build a footpath from the house down to the beach and he idly mentioned that one of the neighbours had told him that what he really needed was a road. Think how much easier it would be, he said. Rather than the arduous five-minute walk through the trees down to the beach and then all the way back up again, we could simply get in a car and drive down there. Christopher thought he was joking.

'A brilliant idea!' he said. 'In fact, let's make it a two-lane highway and then we can turn it into a toll road and charge everyone who wants to drive from the main road down to the beach to use it. True, we'll have to destroy the woodland and the entire character of the bay, but what do a few old trees matter and anyway the sound of cars revving up the hill are far more pleasant than all those irritating birds. Let's do it – I'll get the bulldozers in before the week's out!'

The irony was wasted on the neighbour because he was, of course, Panos and, as we were to discover, he had never given up on his dream of building a house. He had calculated that if Nikos would not agree to an access road on his property, then we might. In his eyes it seemed to help that we were foreigners and therefore, presumably, more inclined to take the advice of a local – especially since we had no notion at the time of his ulterior motive. When he realised that Christopher thought he was joking and it was more likely that all thirty-two of Methana's volcanoes would erupt simultaneously than his father would agree to construct a road and destroy the tranquillity that had attracted him here in the first place, a new feud was initiated. The business with the concrete blocks was the opening salvo and suddenly made sense. If he could block our access from the road running down from the village, we might have to consider a new access down to the beach road. The problem was that he had a slight – a very slight – hold over us. He claimed that he was building the wall across our drive because we had stolen part of his land.

What we had actually done was use a tiny corner of his property – no bigger than a dining table – to open out the curve where our drive meets the farm road. It meant we could get vehicles larger than a child's tricycle to the house without having to execute a six-point turn. It had absolutely no effect at all on Panos. There was nothing he could do with the tiny square of stony land except admire the few weeds that grew there, though I doubt he'd even set foot on it before this assault. But that was not the point. It was his land and we greedy foreigners had violated his rights and we would be punished. Natural justice demanded no less.

Christopher, I have to say, was remarkably calm. He adopted what he told me later was his Greek Respectful Voice, the one he normally reserves for difficult bureaucrats and unreasonable fathers, and Panos began to calm down. What we need, said Christopher, is some sort of compromise. After all, we were neighbours and it would be very sad if we became enemies. Perhaps some sort of compensation might be the answer? It was like throwing a light switch. Panos changed from aggression to charm in an instant. You could see the calculator whirring behind his eyes. How much could he cream off these naive foreigners for a couple of metres of waste ground? It would certainly be enough to enable him to spend happy hours in the local café boasting of how he had fleeced the stupid British and how they had caved in at the first hint of aggression. Before he could come up with a figure, Christopher offered a suggestion, still in his most respectful tone.

'Naturally, we want to compensate you fully for the loss of this land,' he said.

'Of course, of course,' said Panos.

'Since there are no olives or any other trees of any kind on it, perhaps you would agree that it is the land itself that is important and not the fact of what is on it and where it happens to be?'

'Yes, that is precisely my point.'

'Then we should reimburse you fully for that land.'

'Indeed.'

'So,' said Christopher, who had now switched from respectful supplicant to a pose not unlike that of Portia facing Shylock in Shakespeare's Venetian courtroom: 'You must choose a piece of our land on our boundary that is exactly the same size as this piece here and regard it as your own. I am sure my wife, the lawyer, will be able to draw up the appropriate deed.'

And as he said it, he smiled. What could possibly be more reasonable than that . . . an eye for an eye? Panos did not smile back. Instead, he got in his pick-up truck, slammed the door, revved the engine, made a tight turn using his own two metres of land and avoiding his concrete blocks, and shot off in a cloud of dust. We have never heard from him since and the concrete blocks sit there to this day.

# 16

*In which John despairs of the Athens traffic and Christopher spends the night in jail*

I mentioned at the start of this book that the drive from Athens to our village of Metamorfosi could be both hellish and stunning. Stunning on clear days because of the magnificent views, but hellish on dark, wet winter nights because of the two mountains that had to be negotiated. And then the gods smiled on us: a new stretch of road was opened on the coast which cut out the mountains altogether and shaved an hour off the journey from Athens airport. There is, though, still one potential hazard to be negotiated: the city of Athens itself. In theory there is no reason to drive through it because of the motorway that bypasses the city. The problem for the unwary is failing to follow the right signs and ending up in the centre of Athens. If that happens there are only two possible strategies. One is to abandon the car and, if necessary, any luggage and children, and hail a taxi: the police will eventually tow away the car and the hire company will collect it from them and the Greeks really do like children so they'll be fine. The other is simply to pray. The one thing to be avoided at all costs is any attempt to negotiate your way through the streets of Athens. It cannot be done. I know. I have tried and I have the bills from the doctor who treated my nervous breakdown to prove it.

It's not that I am intimidated at the thought of driving in strange cities: I've done it all over the world from Calcutta to Mexico City and even Birmingham. But I am scared in Athens.

That's not for the reasons people are usually nervous in big, strange cities – getting mugged or duffed up by drunken yobs on a Saturday night. There's remarkably little of that here. No, it's driving. And, yes, I know every big city claims to have the worst drivers in the world – Rome, Paris, Istanbul, they take a perverse pride in it – but Athens really is nightmarish if you haven't spent half your life getting used to Greek drivers. The accident figures are bad enough – three times as many deaths proportionately as there are in Britain, for instance – but it's not just that. It is, for instance, literally impossible to follow the road signs. In my experience they are designed to get you lost so that you will be deterred from ever trying again. And the reason for that is the traffic jams.

It's true that there are worse jams in other cities – Lagos, for instance – but in most European cities, traffic jams are tolerated even as they are cursed. You know that you have no alternative but to sit and wait and perhaps swear from time to time. In Athens they are not so much a nuisance as a challenge and anyone who meekly accepts them is a sissy. As with double lines down the centre of the road, such things as traffic lights and No Entry signs are scarcely more than advisory. If an Athenian motorist spots someone escaping from a snarl-up by nipping the wrong way down a one-way street he will follow. And so will everyone else. The result? Well, you can guess.

One answer for residents – assuming you have no fear of death or permanent disability – is to use a motorbike. I expressly forbade Christopher from buying one but he said he could not afford a car and had no choice. So, when he returned to London for a few days, I told him he could take my car back with him. He accepted graciously as though it was him doing me a favour and then, when he got back to Athens, he bought a motorbike anyway – though naturally he kept the car too. I mention this only to give you some idea of the respect I command in our relationship.

But at least he wore a helmet when he was driving on his bike, which is hardly surprising given that when Greece joined the European Union the law said everyone on a motorbike had to wear one. The problem was that it did not say where. So, for years, young men would roar around the lethal streets of Athens with their helmets strapped neatly to their elbows. Then the law was amended to stipulate that the helmet had to be worn on the head. For a long time the young men just ignored it on the basis, presumably, that it was more important to be seen to be cool than to be alive. Then the police decided they would really crack down and now, as Christopher says, things have changed. A little.

C: You know you have lived somewhere a long time when you catch yourself saying, 'It's not like the old days.' I've been doing this in Athens for years. The old days of driving in Athens resembled the Wild West – only with cars rather than horses. There was complete lawlessness. Drive as fast as you like. Park anywhere. Use your horn constantly. All traffic lights are turned off at 2 a.m. just as most people are leaving the bars. Don't worry about driving home drunk because everybody else is doing the same thing and it makes the evening more fun. It's probably why the traffic lights are turned off. It was complete madness.

I never used my motorbike at night. That really would have

been crazy. Night-time was like the dodgems ring at a fairground. I have seen someone so drunk he could neither stop nor steer in a straight line and used a whole street of parked cars as a sort of crash barrier along which to scrape. A friend of mine had a famous accident in his old Range Rover – famous by Athens nightlife standards at least. He had parked his car up against the wall of a bar where he spent the evening and when he left he was not what you might call sober. Sadly he had left the car in gear and when he started it up with a great rev of the huge engine it smashed clean through the wall of the bar he had just left. Whether the bar owner gave him one more for the road or a punch on the nose I cannot recall. I once did something similar, though I was entirely sober and it was by way of accepting a dare. I parked, late at night, in a souvlaki shop. Literally in the shop. Admittedly, it had a very wide entrance. The owner looked at me deadpan, and said, 'On a stick or with pitta?'

Fifteen years later I am appalled at my behaviour. I blame it on getting married and having babies. What seems like an amusing escapade when you are a single young man out on the town becomes boorish and inconsiderate when you are pushing a pram around the place. The one thing that hasn't changed is that Athenians still park in the most inconsiderate manner. We once had an elderly English conductor whose accent came straight out of a 1950s BBC broadcast and who would take no nonsense from anyone – which may be why he was such a good conductor. He came into work one morning in a state of high dudgeon.

'I say, old boy,' he said when he saw me, 'these bloody Greeks and their parking are a bit much aren't they?'

I asked him what had happened.

'There I was, walking along the pavement minding my own business, when this young fool decides to mount the bloody pavement right in front of me and park his car there!'

I asked if he had been hurt.

'Of course not! The point is I was buggered if I was going to stop walking just because of some silly Greek driver. So I climbed up on his bonnet, walked over the roof and carried on in a damn straight line. That should show him, doncha think?'

Inevitably, I have had my share of crashes in Athens – usually not my fault. I once tried to turn left at a busy junction after my light had turned green but the Jeep coming from the opposite direction did not stop at his red light and smashed into me. Thank God I was driving the big old Rover that Dad had given me. Peppy and I had nothing but a few bruises to show for it. So far, so reasonably good. But one of the young women in the Jeep had a broken nose so the police were obliged to ask her if she wanted to prosecute someone for her injury. They had observed that her boyfriend had been smoking something rather stronger than tobacco so were a bit surprised when she said 'Yes!' and pointed at me.

'Him!' she snapped – or, rather, snuffled.

The policeman had no choice but to arrest me and a few hours later, having been fingerprinted and checked out with Interpol, I found myself locked up, which seemed a bit unfair, given that I was the innocent party. The policeman in charge of me was friendly enough when he learned that the other driver had quite a criminal record and had done time in prison. He even let me send out for coffee and sandwiches. I was treated rather less well when they took me to court the following morning.

Peppy, when they finally allowed her to see me, was more worried than me – maybe because she is a lawyer and knows the system. After hours of waiting we were finally ushered into the presence of the judge. It all felt vaguely unreal. There I was, entirely innocent of the slightest offence, having been driving home, carefully and entirely sober when I had my car wrecked by a stoned ex-convict, spent a night in the cells and now, for all I knew, was facing the chance of spending the rest of my life behind bars. A shade melodramatic, maybe, but you have to understand that I was very tired and genuinely a bit scared. I felt as though I were a character in a bad television police drama.

Still, I thought, once I'd got a chance to speak to the judge, played on my vulnerability as a foreigner and deployed a bit of British charm, everything would be sorted and they'd send me home with an apology and prosecute the real villain. But the judge did not like me. She was a middle-aged woman with a tired, unhappy look about her and she clearly did not enjoy her work. Or her life. I was asked where I was from and then I was asked if I spoke Greek. I said that I was learning the language but still had a long way to go. This clearly wasn't good enough.

'Do you speak Greek or not?' she demanded.

What could I say? By then I had completed the intermediate class at a good Greek language school but had spent rather too much time competing for the attention of the very attractive young teacher with another one of the students. Peppy had not properly taken me in hand and turned me into the fluent Greek speaker I am now. But she was very much in command in that court room, bless her. She whispered to me to say yes, because otherwise the hearing would have been postponed until an official interpreter was found and I would remain in jail. By now, given the hostility of the judge, I was even more apprehensive. After all, it was my word against the word of the other driver and I was the foreigner. That small fact had not escaped the attention of the judge. After hearing a brief account of what happened she pronounced: 'The case will be heard in three days' time. The foreigner will stay in custody until the trial.'

Peppy was on her feet immediately and started shouting at the judge. She pointed out that, unlike the other driver, I had no criminal record and a respectable job, had lived in Greece for many years and would most certainly not be fleeing the country before the trial. The judge grudgingly relented and said that 'the foreigner' could go if Peppy vouched for me. We hadn't been married for long at that stage so Peppy agreed.

Having resisted the temptation to flee to South America and spend the rest of my life on a cattle ranch I duly turned up for the trial three days later. If the previous hearing felt like television drama, this felt like a Hollywood film. Peppy had pulled out all the stops and I now had a legal team that consisted of herself as chief witness, my manager as a character witness and a hotshot young lawyer from her office who looked a lot like Tom Cruise. We had spent hours discussing what would be said, I had an official interpreter should I need one and nothing had been left to chance. Mercifully, there was a different judge, but I nearly blew it with my answer to his first question: 'Mr Humphrys, had you been drinking at the time of the accident?'

Safe in the knowledge that the breathalyser had shown I was under the legal limit I breezily answered: 'Only a few beers'. It turns out my Greek word for a 'few' might easily have meant 'many' and Greeks aren't big beer drinkers anyway. I wondered why the judge's eyebrows went up as the heads of my legal team went down but knew I had not got off to the best possible start. Things began to pick up when we realised how stupid the opposing lawyer was. She insisted that it must have been my fault because I was foreign. Not that foreigners can't drive, she charitably explained, but because I was driving a foreign car. Wasn't it true that my car had the steering wheel on the right side? I happily admitted that this was indeed true, not having a clue where she was going with this. And wasn't it true that I was turning left at the time of the accident? I could hardly deny this either. 'Well there you are!' she said triumphantly. 'He obviously couldn't see properly because his steering wheel was on the wrong side!'

The new judge – a fairly jovial chap – would not allow Peppy to reply, presumably because he could see there was some fun to be had from this. 'Please explain to the court Madam Lawyer how, if this is so, Greeks miraculously manage to turn to the right without crashing regularly even though their steering wheel is on the left?'

This was a judge who clearly enjoyed his work and apparently had a bit of a reputation in the public gallery for providing some entertainment. They showed their appreciation, laughing and clapping until the court officer shut them up. From then on things went our way and it was clear I was not going to die in jail. Even better than that, I was to get my revenge on the other driver who had so nearly consigned Peppy and me to oblivion. The charges, remember, had been brought by the injured girlfriend who was of course present, with a suitably big bandage on the end of what was already a suitably big Greek nose. As it became completely clear who was to blame for the accident the judge turned to the girl with the nose and asked her, 'Are you absolutely sure you want to prosecute the person responsible for this?'

'Yes, I want to prosecute the English one!' she said.

'That's not what I asked. Do you want to prosecute the person responsible?'

Even her lawyer could see where this was heading and was frantically shaking her head at her client. But the girl was looking at the judge and did not notice.

'Yes, I want to prosecute the one responsible!'

So her boyfriend and I swapped places in the dock and he ended up being sent to jail for a year. I came out of the courthouse punching the air in victory and hearing in my head a big, uplifting movie soundtrack as the final credits rolled. It was a fantastic feeling. Justice had been served. Tom Cruise and me . . . we'd shown 'em! Well, okay . . . maybe with a little help from my lovely wife too.

# 17

*In which we distract ourselves from housebuilding with the help of bream and bouzouki*

Christopher suggested once that perhaps I have a claim to sainthood. That came as a bit of a surprise given that we have a fairly typical father/son relationship in which reverence has never been exactly the dominant feature, but it seems it has something to do with the precedent set by Saint Neot. St Francis, as everyone knows, is the patron saint of animals but Saint Neot is the patron saint of fish. It is, apparently, because of my own relationship with fish that I may qualify for canonisation even though I am neither devout nor a Roman Catholic. Nor, for that matter, am I only fifteen inches tall, as Neot was said to be. But there is one area in which, Christopher points out, I can claim to have out-performed him: my relationship with fish.

It seems that Neot spent a large part of every day standing in a well (a very shallow well, obviously) praying and reciting from his prayer book. One day he was visited by an angel who told him there were fish in the well and he could help himself to them so long as he never took more than one at a time. Soon after that Neot fell ill and had to abandon his visits to the well, with the consequence that he could no longer feast on his daily fish. But unbeknown to him his servant nipped down to the well and, thinking he was doing the right thing for his master, brought back not one but two fish. Neot, naturally enough, was deeply dismayed. The consequences of disobeying an angel could, one imagines, be pretty severe. So he returned the fish to the well and miraculously they came back to life. And that, it seems, is the miracle that helped him qualify for his sainthood.

Now I'm not going to suggest for a moment that saving a couple of dead fish isn't a worthy achievement, though whether it should qualify a chap for sainthood is for others more theologically inclined to judge. Christopher's point is that I, his revered father, have saved many, many more fish from certain death than Neot – and I have done it without the help of an angel. My power is such that all I have to do is stand on the bank of a river, a lake or a seashore where anglers are reeling in countless fish and bashing them on the head before taking them home for tea and the fish are saved. It's not that I restore them to life – rather that I save them from a ghastly death in the first place. It is quite uncanny. All I need is a fishing rod. One cast from me and the hungry fish, who had been deluded into snatching at wicked hooks disguised as food, simply vanish.

I am aware that for miracles to be accepted by the Vatican there must be witnesses. Well, I have plenty. All my children, at some time or another, have witnessed my uncanny powers. I hire a boat and tackle and spend a few minutes on a well-stocked lake guaranteed to provide enough fresh fish for every angler for a week and they all disappear.

Owen, my youngest son, has been a keen fisherman ever since he caught a small mackerel from the end of a pier on the Isle of Wight. Obviously I was not there at the time. I have had to develop various strategies since then to persuade him that he should find company other than mine for subsequent fishing trips, but it is not easy when it's just the two of us together in Greece. I am torn between the pleasure of standing with him at the shoreline casting into the sea and the disappointment he finds so hard to conceal when we both come away with our buckets empty. Which is why what happened one lovely summer's morning seemed an opportunity sent by the equivalent of Neot's angel.

We were driving back from an ice cream expedition in Methana and as we rounded the bend onto our beach road, we saw two men fishing. Nothing remarkable in that: there are usually people fishing from our beach and sometimes they catch fish and sometimes they don't. These two were catching fish in a way I have never seen before. Their buckets were so full the fish had spilled out onto the shingle and formed a scaly carpet around their feet. The beach looked like a stall in a busy market just after the trawlers had returned from a week at sea.

Owen and I recalled a wonderful David Attenborough programme we had watched about the great sardine run, when countless millions of the little fish migrate from the cool waters south of the African continent and form into vast, swirling shoals as they swim up the Wild Coast. Often they are driven too close to shore by thousands of predators such as dolphins and sharks that come to feast on them and all the local people have to do is cast their nets into the sea at the right time and haul them in. The two men Owen and I watched had no nets but they did have rods and every time they cast their lines into the water they caught a fish. Every time. It was hypnotically repetitive. Bait the hook. Cast. Reel in. Unhook a fish. Bait the hook again. Cast. Reel in. Unhook a fish. And they were beautiful fish: plump, delicious, every single one of them the perfect size for a fish dinner for two.

They were, I learned, *Tsipoura* – better known to us as gilt-head bream. A kilo of *Tsipoura* in a fish taverna can cost forty euros. This was seriously good fish. Naturally enough, I assumed that we were witnessing the Aegean Sea equivalent of the great sardine run – only with bream instead of sardine – and as we stood and watched, the beach began filling up with more and more fishermen. Clearly word of the Great Bream Run was spreading. Owen and I looked at each other, thought the same thing, got back in the car and drove swiftly to the cottage. This was it! This was the moment when I would be able to prove to the world – more importantly, to my small son – that I'd had enough of being the patron saint of fish and was just as capable of catching them as the next man. What's more, we had a clear advantage over the other fishermen, who by now were jostling for space on the beach. We had a raft – built from scrap timber and chunks of polystyrene – that was perfect for the job at hand.

We hauled it down the beach and into the surf, paddled out to the reef that crosses the bay, in which the biggest shoal of sea bream known to man had been trapped, cast our lines and reeled them in.

Nothing.

We tried again. Nothing. We paddled to another spot and tried again. Nothing. We watched the men, women and children on the shore doing exactly the same as we were doing only with different results – by which I mean they were catching fish and we were not. Owen looked at me with an expression that said something like: 'You're not *really* a bad father but . . .', and I nodded. There was nothing I could say. We paddled back to the beach, hauled the raft back onto the shingle and I went into the cottage to find some money – enough to buy a kilo or two of plump sea bream from any one of a hundred fishermen.

When Christopher arrived later that evening I toyed with the idea of pretending that I had caught them, but I knew there was no point. Yet more humiliation was to come.

Christopher had brought with him a friend, Spiros, who had a copy of the local evening newspaper with him. On its front page was a photograph of a fish farm a few miles further down the coast and the headline 'The Great Escape!' What we had seen was not, it turned out, one of nature's natural phenomena – the equivalent of the great sardine run – and the fish were not wild creatures migrating in search of warmer waters. They had been born, bred and raised in captivity only a few miles away and, until the walls of their aquatic prison were breached, had spent their whole lives being fattened up for a hungry market.

No wonder they were so anxious to grab at every baited hook they saw: they'd grown accustomed throughout their short lives to being fed regularly and well. What they had not learned to do was fend for themselves, nor to develop that sixth sense that wily old fish seem to have when they spot a bit of shrimp dangling on a hook. There was not one gilthead bream among the ten thousand escapees with the wit to warn its friends: 'Hang on! How come every time one of our mates takes a nibble at all these bits of shrimp he gets hauled out of the water and we never see him again?' No wonder they all looked the same size and weight. And no wonder that every amateur fisherman within a fifty-mile radius of our little bay was tonight sitting down to a magnificent dinner of sea bream and blessing his luck. Better make that every fishermen save two: Owen and me.

C: It was hard not to feel a twinge of sympathy for Dad, but by this stage in the building project I was beginning to feel a little sorry for myself too. I hadn't come to Greece all those years ago to wage war against a colony of rats and be given the run-around by half-drunken peacocks and half-crazed plumbers on a building site. I'd come to play music. It was music that earned me my living and music that gave me my enjoyment – at least, some of the time. Admittedly, it varied. Perhaps that was part of the joy of working for an orchestra like the Camerata.

One evening we would be playing Mozart to an elegant audience in the best concert hall in one of the world's great cities, receiving a standing ovation for an electrifying performance of a Haydn symphony conducted by the great Christopher Warren Green. The next we might be on a remote island playing to an audience of two children, a handsome white horse and grumpy donkey in the only public space, the local taverna. The animals were not actually in the taverna, but listening through the open windows; I think the donkey was the more appreciative. Actually, we do a lot of that sort of thing: touring Greece giving educational concerts to people, many of whom may never have ventured beyond their villages and never set eyes on an orchestra.

As it happened, the entire island of Kimolos was good enough to turn out for our next performance, and horses were banned. At a guess I'd say a third of the audience loved it, a third were bored stiff and a third obviously didn't know (or care) where they were. This would include the elderly gent whose mobile phone rang halfway through. I knew he didn't have a clue what was going on because he kept telling the person on the other end of the phone exactly that. Very loudly. He then started to ask after the health of the caller's family and what they were having for supper, until one of the more appreciative islanders managed to shut him up. Still, it made our one hundredth performance of a dreaded Vivaldi guitar concerto a little bit more interesting.

After the concert we were introduced to a bit of the local culture. A couple of my younger male colleagues got talking to some of the younger female audience members and it was decided that we should all go out for drinks. We would join them after we had eaten something. Knowing where to go wasn't difficult because the town had only two places open and they were next door to each other: one a bar and the other a bouzouki club. After a couple of drinks at the bar it was time for some dancing, we were told. So we poked our heads round the door of the bouzouki club and were blasted by the noise. Half the population of this little, sedate island seemed to be dancing like crazy to the loudest Greek music I have ever heard.

Bouzouki music has now come to mean pop music but its roots are much older and the more traditional singers will be performing songs written decades ago, which guarantees an audience ranging from teenagers to grannies. The easiest way to describe the experience is to think of a very noisy cabaret: live music with a starring singer and possibly a support act. Most importantly, this is where Greeks do their serious drinking.

Foreigners often get the wrong impression of Greeks and their alcohol. If all you do is stick to bars or even western style clubs then you won't see much drunkenness. Go to the bouzoukia and it's a very different story. 'Bouzouki' is the name of the instrument: a three-string member of the lute family. It was brought over from Turkey with the hordes of Greek refugees in the 1920s. By the end of the Second World war bouzouki clubs had become the places where Greeks could display the full range of their emotions through music, drink and camaraderie. Office outings are common.

Rather against my better instincts, I was dragged along to one with Peppy and it turned out to be an instructive – I almost wrote 'sobering' – experience. They were mostly lawyers, lots of them, packed into a fairly small club in Piraeus the size of a large restaurant with basic tables and chairs set up, whisky bottles on the tables and a few plates of snacks. The food was incidental. People had come here to drink in vast quantities – apart from Peppy and me, that is. She seldom drinks and I had insisted on driving so I would have an excuse to leave early and sober. That was wise.

Since it was one of the more traditional 'clubs', the music started off quite well: old *rembetika* songs from the 1930s and 1940s that have a real charm. But the later the evening got, the worse the music became and the more people joined in. The evening followed a pattern typical of these clubs wherever they are in Greece.

After an hour or so of steady drinking many people are joining in with the songs, most of which have been around since their grandparents' time. Not just singing the odd chorus, though: they know every word. After several hours every single person is singing to every single song and many are dancing. The songs are traditional and so is the dancing. The themes are familiar ones of love and loss, infused with a melancholy that only a Greek can understand. They talk of the considerable suffering of the people from the horror of Smyrna in the 1920s when the town was destroyed and 400,000 Greeks left homeless, the World War that followed, the civil war that followed that and the horrors of the military junta which rounded it all off. People are laughing one minute and crying the next as a song about Turkish oppression is followed by one about a jilted lover and another about the loss of a child.

Towards the end of the night the scene is one of almost religious hysteria. People who can hardly stand are performing great swooping dances while their friends cheer them on, punctuating their encouragement by smashing their glasses on the floor. But that is as violent as it gets. Even at the end of the night when everything on the table has been smashed on the floor it doesn't seem aggressive. It is just an outpouring of emotion aided by alcohol but mostly helped by the power the music has over the people. If you haven't been brought up with this history, with the music in your blood, with the essence of it all then it is impossible to understand. The bill for such a night of mayhem may be high but the cathartic effect of the evening on a group of lawyers working sixteen hours a day probably saves a fortune in psychiatrist's bills.

The clubs started out modestly enough but are now big business. The top performers, a mix of Elvis, Tom Jones, Johnny Cash and Sinatra, can make 20,000 euros a night. Think Las Vegas meets Istanbul. The venues are equally surreal. Old factories have been converted into giant clubs that can hold thousands of people. Huge effort is spent on creating a theme that can be Arabian Nights or modern industrial with lots of lights and lasers. But however large the venue, the tables are packed together. You are squashed onto a narrow taverna chair and crammed around a too-small table. Then you order the drinks. This means bottles of spirits. The minimum cover charge is one bottle of whisky for four people. Or vodka if you prefer. This will come with plenty of mixers and an ice bucket. It will cost anything from a hundred euros to three times as much, depending on the club. Nobody has just one bottle on the table. Drinking half a bottle each is average. A bottle each is not uncommon.

So far the night has been fairly expensive but not – depending on how many bottles you drink – ruinously so. But now there are flowers to be added to the night's bill and this is not really optional. The flowers are bought to throw at the singers in appreciation of their act and then, after the show has ended, at their friends, who provide the second stage of the entertainment. They are almost all girls and almost all dressed to kill in high heels and low-cut dresses with very short skirts. They are dancing on the tables – partly because the place is so packed there's nowhere else to dance and partly because they obviously enjoy the attention they get. At this stage in the evening it is fair to say that modesty is not at a premium and, to show their approval, the young men throw flowers. Hundreds of them. Thousands of them. These are real flowers, not paper or plastic which could easily be swept up and re-used (not to mention re-sold). They are carnation heads and are sold by the tray for between thirty and fifty euros. It's perfectly normal to see a table spend a thousand euros on flowers. Somebody, somewhere, is making a great deal of money from the Greek passion for bouzouki.

# 18

*In which our guests get a shock in the showers . . . and other potentially dangerous scenarios*

By the summer of 2008 the house was well on the way to being finished. It was not, of course, the house I had envisaged three years earlier. When Christopher and I first looked at the plans that had come with the property I had some pretty fancy ideas as to how to improve on them. For a start, there would be one magnificent bedroom spanning the width of the house at the front with a balcony overlooking the bay and a ceiling of wooden beams soaring into the sky, reminiscent of a great cathedral. When I went to see how it was getting on what I found was a rabbit hutch. It seemed there had been some mistake, some minor misunderstanding over the plans. Instead of checking with us, the bricklayers had simply gone ahead and done what they guessed was right. It wasn't. So . . . back to the drawing board.

In the end, we compromised: still no cathedral roof soaring skywards, but something slightly more inspiring than a rabbit hutch. Think dog kennel with a pointy roof. The one thing you learn about building a house from scratch – especially if you are trying to do it at a distance of a thousand miles – is that everything is a compromise. I did not, however, expect to have to compromise on safety. I most certainly did not expect to electrocute any of my visitors. Maybe there's something to be said for a system of getting rid of visitors who outstay their welcome, but in this case they happened to be very welcome and anyway it wasn't only them who were electrocuted.

The first I knew of it was when Rebecca came downstairs in the morning looking shaken. But she's not the sort of woman to make a fuss – unlike her husband, Matthew, who is one of Britain's sharpest and funniest newspaper columnists and makes a fuss for a living. It wasn't until Matthew said he'd be late for breakfast because he had to call his lawyer and begin compensation proceedings that I started feeling a little nervous. It turned out that Rebecca had been shocked in the shower. She'd lifted the shower head off the hook to wash her hair and a great bolt of electricity had arced across to her head, knocking her flat, stopping her heart, causing her eyebrows to vanish into the back of her sockets and her tongue to protrude, so when Matthew rushed into the bathroom he thought she was dead and managed to bring her back to life only after intensive mouth-to-mouth resuscitation and chest massage.

That's a slight exaggeration, but she really did get an electric shock and it was a bit worrying. We checked the other bathrooms and discovered there was a definite tingly feeling in the water in another one of them. So, yet again, we had to make an emergency phone call to Christos, the profane but brilliant electrician who'd done all the wiring, and he caught the next boat from Athens. He was obviously a bit worried too, checked out every tap in the house with a special little meter and found . . . nothing. Not so much as one little errant amp of electricity. So he caught the next boat back again, clearly wishing that he'd never had anything to do with these strange British people and their house in the Peloponnese. And obviously, the moment he left the tingly stuff started again. Then, after a couple of days, it vanished and never came back and to this day no one has the faintest idea what might have caused it. My own theory is that it was an attempt at sabotage by one of the many builders we had sacked over the years: he had sneaked into the house one dark night and wired the immersion heater up to the taps or something. As it happens I was mildly disappointed – I rather enjoyed the tingly sensation – but on balance I suppose it's better not to electrocute your guests. The whole thing did make me think about what we'd do if we really did have a medical emergency. I found out soon afterwards.

Some illnesses and injuries command more respect than others. Tell someone you broke your leg skiing down a black run in the Alps and you will get precious little sympathy but a fair amount of respect, if not envy. But tell someone that you're as deaf as a post because you have a build-up of wax in your ears and you get neither respect nor sympathy. Trust me, I know. There's just no dignity in it and anyway it's easily dealt with. It takes a few minutes for the wax to be removed in an almost painless procedure (you probably don't want to know the details) behind closed doors in the privacy of your doctor's surgery – which is as it should be. That is not, to judge by my own bizarre experience, the way it happens in Greece.

I had lost my hearing, probably because of spending too much time under water, so I went to Galatas in search of treatment. I tried the ironmonger first, which is not quite as reckless as it seems. The woman who runs the shop speaks good English and I had heard her brother was a doctor but, sadly, he was not the sort of doctor who could deal with my little problem. So she sent me off to the health centre. I would recognise it, she said, by the Red Cross symbol outside. It was surprisingly luxurious, I thought, for a public health centre. The doctor who eventually appeared was attractive and elegant in her white coat and she too spoke decent English. I told her what my problem was and she seemed surprised.

'Are you sure you want me to deal with it?' she asked, with the hint of what struck me as a slightly superior smile.

'Why not?' I asked her. 'It's a very common complaint, isn't it?'

'Indeed it is,' she said, 'and I dare say I could drill through it for you if I really tried but I'm not sure I would recommend it. Dentists usually drill teeth.'

I made my apologies for my mistake and left, thinking that on balance even the ironmonger might have been a better option, and eventually found the health centre. The doctor who saw me was extremely small and extremely fierce. She was not remotely interested in my complaint but wanted to know how I came to be in Galatas and why I had built a house in Greece without even bothering to learn her language. Then she produced a vast form with so many pages it could have been a British MP's expenses claim in the bad old days and, with two young trainee doctors looking on and many little sideways sallies, the four of us spent the next half hour filling it in.

I made several half-hearted attempts to explain that all I wanted was to have my ears syringed and was it really necessary to know the state of my father's health and whether any member of my family had ever had a communicable disease, but I am, at heart, a coward. If this fierce little woman was going to be poking things into my delicate ears any minute now it might be wise not to upset her any more than my simple physical presence appeared to have done already. I needn't have worried. She had not the remotest intention of doing anything to my ears. It was far too late to embark on any treatment now, she said, and anyway this was not the correct day for treating outpatients, so I would have to come back the next day to see a doctor who might actually do the necessary. Which I did.

Everything seemed to go smoothly at first. I was given one

of those little tickets with a number to make sure nobody jumps the queue and took a seat in the waiting room. It was rather enjoyable for the first hour. This was clearly more than somewhere to come to see the doctor: it was a chance to catch up with old friends, swap stories about various ailments and generally enjoy a sociable hour or two. Some of the old women had brought vacuum flasks with them and light refreshments to while away the waiting hours. The problem was that no one seemed actually to be seeing the doctor. Every so often the door of the surgery would open for someone to come out or go in, but it appeared never to be a patient: various doctors and nurses and men with bits of equipment, but no numbers were called. So the waiting room became more and more crowded and more and more hot until, eventually, signs of a mutiny began to develop.

The first to break ranks was a fat old lady sitting opposite me. She shouted something at her rather timid husband, marched across the room, pulled open the door of the surgery and marched in. I waited for the hospital security to be called, or at least for somebody to show a little concern. You can't have people barging into a doctor's surgery when he may be in the middle of treating someone who is seriously ill, can you? Apparently you can. No one took the slightest bit of notice. Eventually she came marching out and then marched straight back in again, this time dragging her husband with her by his arm. That seemed to be the sign that everyone else was waiting for. For the next hour or so it was anarchy. No one bothered to look at their little numbers any longer. When they got tired of waiting and, presumably, reckoned that the doctor had had quite long enough to deal with his last patient, they opened the door and in they went. Everyone, it seemed, was going to be treated – except me.

And then the fierce little doctor appeared on the scene, having apparently undergone a personality transplant overnight. She gave me a warm smile and greeted me as though I were an old friend. When I told her what was going on and wondered whether I would ever be seen by the doctor, she nodded sympathetically, took my arm, opened the surgery door and pushed me through. I was in! And then I saw why there had been such chaos. There really had been a patient in the surgery all this time and he was still there, lying on a trolley in full view of anyone who happened to wander in, with various tubes attached to him and looking extremely unwell. The two young trainee doctors were there as well, who also treated me like an old friend, and another doctor – presumably the man qualified to perform my modest little operation. Naturally, there were many more questions to be asked before we could proceed. I think it was at that point I realised what they were actually doing was using me to practise their English – which would have been fine except that I really did want to have my ears syringed.

By the time the doctor finally got around to it the little surgery was even more crowded. A mechanic had wandered in to fix the light and someone else had arrived with the syringing equipment. It turned out to be a pretty sociable event one way and another, though on balance I think I prefer to engage in light chat when someone is not trying to force a gallon or two of warm water into my ear. Still, it worked in the end. What happened to the poor chap lying on the trolley I never did find out.

C: The big problem with the Greek health service – in many respects far better than the NHS – is when it comes up against the inevitable bureaucracy. Emergency care is great, hospitals work well and even the pharmacies put Britain's chemists to shame, but what happens if you need a non-urgent appointment with a consultant and a doctor's note for work? This is when it gets tricky.

When I crashed my motorbike into the side of a taxi that came out of nowhere and broke my collarbone the emergency care was quick, thorough and effective as usual. But it meant that I would be off work for ten weeks and would need the paperwork necessary to ensure I received my sick pay. After all, I could hardly be expected to spend two months recuperating on Naxos without enough money for essentials like beer. The first week of a broken collarbone is painful and you pretty much have to stay in bed. Because it can't be set in plaster any sudden movement grinds the ends of the broken bone against each other and makes you go 'Ow' a lot. The worst part is turning over in your sleep, having forgotten about the injury, and being woken by excruciating pain. After a week your body seems to learn what not to move, which was just as well because in order to get the necessary paperwork to claim my sick pay I had to appear before a committee. You must appear in person before the committee. How somebody who has just had a leg amputated is supposed to manage I'm not quite sure. As the incurable optimist that Dad always accuses me of being, I assumed this would be straightforward: a telephone call to arrange an appointment with the committee and perhaps half an hour chatting with the doctors. Not quite.

It is not possible to make an appointment by phone and nor is it possible to see the doctor who might arrange the appointment for you. You must go to the local healthcare office, which opens at eight in the morning. I went at nine, which turned out to be a big mistake. The place was heaving with old people who knew how the system worked.

'I was here ten minutes before the doors opened at seven,' I heard one old lady boasting.

'Po po! That's nothing! I arrived before the sun rose and spent an hour and a half sitting on the door step!' said her neighbour.

After three hours my optimism was beginning to drain away. I knew the place would close at two but figured that they would at least see the people who had been waiting patiently all morning. Not a chance. I watched the doctor leave his room at two o'clock sharp. A frail old lady pleaded with him to be seen but was rudely brushed aside. I went home and contemplated getting a folding bed and sleeping bag to spend the night camping outside. We'd see who had the boasting rights around this place, I thought. But I didn't and instead went the following morning at eight sharp. Another mistake. I stood no chance against the professional waiters.

The goal was to be the first one through the door when it opened, thereby winning the prize of an instant meeting with the doctor. I had the advantage of age but it turned out to be useless. These old people had the advantage of experience and, I quickly came to realise, utter ruthlessness. They knew where I was vulnerable because I was wearing a bright blue sling. Whenever I tried to get near the door an old lady would jab her bony elbow into my bad arm, causing me to wince.

'Sorry, dear,' she would mutter, but her look said: 'Don't even think about trying to get in front of me.' I didn't. The only people I beat through the door were on crutches or in wheelchairs and even then it was a close thing. But at least it meant that I had an outside chance of being seen by a doctor some time that day. Incredibly, I had to wait for a mere four hours. I gave the surly doctor my most polite, respectful greeting. He did not respond. 'What's wrong with you?' he asked bluntly.

'This,' I said, gesturing to my arm.

'And?'

'I play the cello.'

'So?'

I had to take a very deep breath. Getting annoyed would be suicidal. He would throw me back to the old people with absolutely no mercy.

'I need to take time off from my job with an orchestra because I can't play the cello with a broken collarbone,' I explained very carefully.

'Why didn't you just say that? Take this paper and go and get it stamped. Then see the office to arrange your appointment with the committee.'

That was it. He sat down and ignored me.

It took me a couple of false starts before I worked out where to get my stamp. There is nothing worse than spending half an hour in the wrong line. It means that when you get to the front and ask for what you want you have given the person behind the desk or counter the ultimate pleasure of being able to say to you: 'This is the wrong desk, I can't help you.' People whose job it is to sit behind a desk and stamp pieces of paper live for these moments. It gives their meaningless job a little bit of malicious purpose. Don't even think about checking if you are in the right queue before you join it. That would mean approaching the desk and looking like you were trying to jump the queue. Five or six old people would instantly turn on you. You'd stand no chance and they'd get away with it in court. No jury would convict.

By the time I had my stamp it was two o'clock again so I had no chance of going to the office where I could eventually arrange my appointment with the committee. The only bright side, if it could be called that, was that I couldn't see all these old people needing to see the committee as they were clearly too old to be working. So the next morning I finally got my appointment.

I was a little nervous about this committee, judging by the way the previous doctor had treated me. And when I arrived it did indeed look a bit imposing. Four men were seated on one side of a table with an empty chair facing them. It reminded me of an audition, which is the worst possible experience any musician can go through. Playing in front of just the same sort of table, you are given five or possibly ten minutes to show what you can do after twenty years of practice. So I was quite nervous when I sat down. I had to remind myself that I didn't have a cello and that I wasn't being interrogated. Then again maybe I was.

It didn't start well.

'Name?' asked one of them without even looking up from the paper he was holding.

'Christopher Humphrys,' I said, in the poshest English accent I could manage. My surname is so unpronounceable in Greek that I don't even bother trying. This made the man who had asked me my name look up in surprise.

'You are English?' he asked me in English.

'Yes. Well, Welsh actually.'

'Ah, a Welshman! How wonderful! I spent three years in Cardiff studying, it was a very good time. How did you come to be in Greece?'

This was very good news indeed. If you can make personal contact with even one person working in the bureaucratic system your life becomes much, much easier. I had hit the jackpot.

I quickly explained about the cello, the orchestra and my slight difficulty in playing the cello with a broken collarbone.

'Of course, of course! You must take off as much time as you need. Would three months be enough or would you like six? Normally we are only allowed to approve six weeks and then you must see the committee again but I can easily fix that for you. A Welshman playing the cello in Athens, this really is wonderful!'

I couldn't get away. He wanted to know all about me, the orchestra and what I thought about Greece. It was only when his colleagues pointed out that there were other people waiting that he reluctantly let me leave, and only after assuring me that if I needed anything else he would be only too happy to help. Sometimes my optimism is justified.

# 19

*In which we brace ourselves for defeat at the hands of the bureaucrats and Thakis throws a wobbly to save the day*

The engine of the crane came to life with a great roar, black diesel smoke pouring from its exhaust, and the driver hauled on a lever. At the end of a chain hanging from the crane's arm a great wrecking ball swung slowly from side to side. The driver revved the engine and the ball picked up speed. Faster and faster it swung as the grinning driver approached the cottage, the powerful crane crushing everything in its path. And then, with the ball arcing upwards, he swung the arm of the crane so that it towered just above our little cottage and threw the lever again. The massive ball could travel in only one direction as it arced downwards. With a mighty thump it smashed into the end wall of the cottage, bringing the wall crashing down and most of the roof with it. For the next hour the driver worked methodically: a rev of the engine, the thump of the wrecking ball, the crashing of concrete, wood and glass until everything that had made this such a delightful little home lay smashed and flattened. Villa Artemis, on whose balcony my family and I had so often sat watching the sun set, was just a pile of rubble. As I gazed at the wrecking ball, now at rest, its job done, I realised that it bore an image of a face: the triumphant face of Douskos, the engineer. And then I woke up.

As nightmares go, I accept it's not the worst. It is, when all's said and done, only a little cottage. But the thought of having to knock it down was horrible and everything depended on the co-operation of Douskos, the original engineer and our old enemy. What we had come to realise was that if he did not formally 'sign off' the project even the big house, which we had now finished, would never be legal. We would not be able to obtain a permanent water and electricity supply and a bureaucrat with a clipboard could come knocking at any time and order us out. We would also have to go ahead with demolishing the cottage.

This was not quite how I had imagined things turning out in those innocent days when I had stood on the foundations gazing across the bay. True, there would always be some sense of achievement in having finally defeated the rats, turned the cottage into a delightful little home again and built the house on the hill in spite of everything. But only up to a point. While it was very nice owning a home in such a beautiful part of the world, it really would be even nicer actually to be able to live in it. And to do that, we had to have the right pieces of paper signed by Douskos. Without them, we would for ever be waiting for the knock on the door.

In short, we needed Douskos and we needed him badly, and Douskos was not a friend. It was he, remember, whom I'd fired from the project right at the beginning and it was he whom I'd told to get stuffed when he made his outrageous demands for payment for work that he had done for the previous owner. This was not an encouraging scenario. So I did what I've always done in Greece when things have looked particularly tricky: I handed the problem over to Christopher.

C: When my father-in-law Thakis, who had ousted Douskos as the site engineer, had explained the final process to me it sounded like a formality. That was until he mentioned Douskos. It was like mentioning Dracula. We thought we'd dealt with him – buried him at the crossroads at midnight – but we must have forgotten to hammer the stake through his heart and now he was rising from his coffin. When a house is finished in Greece there is a sting in the tail. The civil engineer has to give his final consent. Having spent years getting Douskos off our backs we were once more beholden to him. I realised – too late – that he must have been aware of this procedure right from the start. He had probably been biding his time, secure in the knowledge that revenge is a dish best eaten cold.

It took me a few days to prepare myself for calling him – I confess I was a bit scared – and when I summoned up the courage and dialled his mobile there was no answer. I tried again later with the same result and again and again until it was clear that he was not going to answer. We tracked down an office number for him in Poros and I tried that. Eventually someone answered but it wasn't Douskos. It was one of his minions who assured me, in a somewhat supercilious manner, that Mr Douskos would get back to me. He did not. After a week of phoning I realised I had no choice but to track him down in person. I thought that if I could catch him unawares, with the papers ready to sign, then he just might forget our previous battles and play along, especially as he would receive a small fee for his signature. While I knew Dad would rather cut off his own arm with a blunt penknife than give him another penny, we had no choice.

I remembered where his office was from my earlier visits: a large old house a little way out of the town on the top of a hill – not unlike Dracula's castle in my fevered imagination.

It was April and the weather was suitably gloomy as I climbed the hill. Rather than march up to the front door and ring the bell, I wanted to make sure he was there first so that I would be prepared for our meeting. I crept round the side of the house, keeping low, and peered through the window of what I thought was his office. Nothing. No coffin. No chairs. No desks and definitely no Douskos. He must have moved his lair. Perhaps the villagers were on to him.

So he would not answer his phones and appeared no longer to have an office. I spent hours the next day wandering the narrow streets of Poros hoping to stumble across a new office with the name of Douskos on the door. I found lawyers, solicitors, accountants and even an acupuncturist but no Douskos. So I tried to tune in to the village gossip on the basis that the smaller the community, the more people like to bitch about each other. Plus, I had friends from Athens with connections on Poros. One was the sister of someone I knew who ran a bar in Poros harbour. She promised to spread the message that if Douskos would not meet us we would do whatever it took to make his life a misery. It worked. Within a week he answered my call and – yes, you've guessed – could not have been more helpful. In fact, it was a bit of an anti-climax.

'But of course I'll sign the documents,' he assured me, as though we were old friends kept apart for too long through circumstances beyond our control. Naturally there would be a fee involved – a fairly substantial one at that. I knew it would infuriate Dad – he'd written an oath in blood swearing that he'd never pay him a penny – but I reckoned that what he didn't know couldn't hurt him, and I assured Douskos the fee was no problem. I told Dad eventually. At the risk of sounding smug, I timed it perfectly – a jubilant telephone call, telling him we'd finally got the documents we needed and then a casual mention that it might mean a modest fee for Douskos. And so I paid up and Douskos signed on the dotted line. And that was it. We were home and dry. More to the point, we'd be able to live in the home . . . but not just yet.

There was one final hurdle to overcome and this time we had to rely on Thakis. It was he who would have to deal with the dreaded planning office. It was he, as our civil engineer, who would have to produce all the paperwork, satisfy all the bureaucrats that we had jumped through every hoop, bowed before every official, collected every stamp from every department and he who would walk away with the final document that would make the house legal and the cottage safe. Given our experiences of the past three years, I should have viewed this final encounter with trepidation if not fear. The planning officers had not exactly made our lives easy in the past and I'd heard many cases of people who had reached this final stage in the process, galloped right up to the last fence, only to find the three-bar wooden fence replaced by an insurmountable brick wall with rolls of barbed wire on the top. What was particularly scary in our case was that we knew the man who ran the planning office in Poros did not approve of us (swayed a little by Douskos perhaps?). He'd already made that very clear. But before I could get down to some serious worrying, Thakis arrived with news of a miracle. He summed it up in seven words: 'The planning office has moved to Piraeus.' He was ecstatic.

'Don't you see?' he told me. 'It means we don't have to deal with that idiot from Poros any longer! The Piraeus office is huge! Who knows how many *meson* we will find there!'

*Meson* is yet another one of those essential concepts that you can't live without in Greece. It means 'insider' or 'contact'. Somebody you know, or your aunt knows, or one of your mates from the local café is married to. It means, in short, someone who will do you a favour. We had to find a *meson* – and we did. He turned out to be the mother of all *mesons* . . . an old friend of Thakis's from his childhood in Megara who was now a Director of the Piraeus planning office. We had struck gold. A meeting was arranged and, after the obligatory reminiscences about the old days, Thakis laid it on the line:

'Listen old friend, I have a bit of a problem,' he explained. 'My one and only daughter is married to a foreigner. An English. Don't worry, he's a good boy and he comes from a very good family. Po po, his father is a very famous journalist, a very big man in England! Now he has built this house near Poros. A beautiful house and there are no problems. We have all the papers ready, it's all legal. We just have a tiny problem with the old cottage that was already there. This is where my daughter will stay. It is a real doll of a cottage, right by the sea and with some excellent fish. Next time I come I will bring you some. Because of the idiot in the Poros office we have had some silly little problems with the cottage. Nothing serious for sure, but maybe you could just keep an eye on it for us?'

The old friend promised he would do just that and Thakis left, a happy man. It was in the bag. Now all that remained was for the final papers to be processed and one more meeting to be arranged at which everything would be signed in the presence of the Director and Thakis would walk away with the document that said, in effect: 'This house and this cottage are legal. Nightmare over. Dream realised.' The meeting was set for a Monday morning. I told Dad I would phone him that night.

*J*: Normally I turn my phones off fairly early in the evening. If you get up, as I do, long before the sun has even started thinking about rising, it is necessary to go to bed very early: that's the only way to survive on the *Today* programme. But not this time. Christopher had prepared me for the best – or the worst – and I was ready when the call came. Christopher's opening words were: 'You won't believe what happened . . .'

I knew it! How many times in the past three years had my son started a conversation with those words. Yes OF COURSE I would believe what had happened. Yes OF COURSE I would believe that the Director had turned out not to be a friend at all, but the Devil incarnate, Satan in a suit and sober tie who had not only failed to approve our final application but had ordered us to demolish the cottage and the house and the walls block by block, remove every last piece of building debris and restore the hillside to the state it was in before Socrates had gone on trial for treason. Why shouldn't I believe it?

Christopher calmed me down, or tried to, and told me what had happened.

Thakis had gone to the meeting as arranged and arrived at Christopher's flat several hours later, looking rather shaken, demanding a large whisky and repeating over and over again that he had had the worst day of his life.

'I was there at nine o'clock,' he said. 'I went straight to see the Director and I gave him a pot of that special honey I get from Megara. It's the best honey in the world. He thanked me but he looked a little strange.

'"Ach, Thakis," he said to me, "why did you leave it so late? I'm afraid I can't help you any more."

'What do you mean?' I asked him.

'"Your file has gone! Didn't you see the trucks? They are

moving the planning office back to Poros! Your file is already on the truck and it's about to board the boat to Poros!"

'Po po, at that moment I thought we were finished. It was over. I lost my composure in that office, I can tell you. I became very, very emotional: I was shouting, I was crying, all the office was looking at me. I said that this was my daughter's house and that if it was destroyed I would die from the shame. I said I might just die right there and then. I said that only three times in my life had I been so upset. Once when the German soldiers hit me when I was a small boy, once when I was put in prison during my military service and once when Olympiakos lost the final to Panathinaikos. But then I was young and now I am an old man. I really thought I might die. I told him that I would leave that office in only two ways. Either with the paper in my hand or in a coffin. And it would be his choice. He must decide whether I would live or die of shame.'

Thakis, you will have gathered, is not a man given to understatement or to restraining his emotions. He paused while Christopher refreshed his glass and brought him some tissues to wipe his eyes.

'He knew that I meant it. He could see the look in my eyes. So you know what he did? He called the driver of the truck and told him to come back. The driver said they had already punched the ticket for the boat and he was on the boarding ramp! But the Director insisted. He made him back off the ramp and return to the offices. And then we unloaded every box from the van and went through the files one by one.'

Thakis was beginning to smile now . . . a big smile that spread all over his face.

'And then we found it! Our file! Our papers! I made the director sign them in front of me. People came and congratulated me. One person told me he had never seen such a great performance in all his life. But it wasn't a performance. I meant it! Four hours it took me! In those four hours I saved your house! If our file had gone back to that idiot in Poros it would have all been over. I knew it.'

And with that he thrust the papers into Christopher's hand and took another very large swig of whisky. He'd earned it.

# 20

*In which Christopher experiences the horror of Ikea . . . and we all learn a lesson from our house martins*

If it's true that the optimist sees the glass as half full and the pessimist sees it as half empty there needs to be a separate category for Welsh pessimists. We not only see it as half empty, but with a jagged crack down its side and the contents seeping through. Except when it comes to building houses in Greece. For reasons I still find hard to fathom, I never really had any doubt that everything would work out in the end, in spite of all the evidence to the contrary. I knew exactly how it would be: my closest friends and family enjoying a magnificent dinner around a huge dining table on the balcony as the sun set behind the purple mountains; a gentle breeze blowing off the sea carrying the scent of the forested hillside to us; the glorious sound of Christopher's string quartet playing in the background; a witty toast from one of my guests congratulating me on what I had created in this idyllic corner of Greece. It may not surprise you at this stage in the narrative to learn that things did not turn out quite like that. As various friends will attest, my irrational optimism led to them having to change their holiday plans more than once.

'Keep a space in your diary for next summer,' I would tell

them. 'I'm going to have a big house party at my place in Greece and you must come and stay.'

'Wonderful!' they would say. 'But are you sure it'll be finished in time?'

'Good heavens, yes,' I would say. 'It's just a matter of getting the roof on . . . fitting the bathrooms and kitchen . . . plastering the walls . . . laying the floors . . . painting everything . . . installing the pool . . . we're almost there and there are *months* to get it done. No problem!'

They would look a little dubious and make vague noises about booking flights and then wait for me to tell them that I'd been a little too optimistic and actually the house wouldn't be ready this year. But maybe next year . . .?

After two years I was beginning to run out of friends – gullible friends anyway. And then, by the summer of 2008, it really was finished. This time the invitations could be sent out with utter confidence. They would not only have a roof over their heads, but windows and doors and bedrooms. The house really was habitable. Actually I suppose I should be a little more specific. The top half of the house had bedrooms, bathrooms and a kitchen. The bottom half, where the friends would stay if the top half was filled with family, did not. But that wasn't a problem – just a matter of painting walls, finishing off the bathrooms and kitchen and cleaning up the mess accumulated during three years of building work. No problem . . . plenty of time to get it done. I might have omitted to mention this to my friends.

Actually, there was another little problem too. Furniture. Christopher pointed out to me that, since I had invited a total of fourteen people to stay, most of whom were fully grown adults, it was fairly likely that they would expect beds to sleep in and chairs to sit on and all the other little luxuries that western softies like us have become accustomed to. I had to concede he had a point.

C: Imagine winning a competition and being given an open cheque to spend on furniture. Pretty cool, huh? Now imagine it has to be spent in Ikea. Still not bad, is it? Now imagine that it's not only furniture – chairs and beds and stuff – but everything you need to make an empty house liveable. Everything. And finally imagine that all that stuff has to be bought and loaded onto a huge truck that you have rented at vast expense which is waiting outside Ikea while you shop. And you have only three hours to do it all in. Not so cool now, huh?

As an Athenian of long standing there was a time when I rather enjoyed going to Ikea. It's cheap, has great design and sells all sorts of useful stuff that you just can't find anywhere else in Greece. The snag is that unless you are insane or Greek (or both) you go there only on weekday mornings. You do not even think about trying to go on a Thursday afternoon or, God forbid, a Saturday. These times have been unofficially designated 'family times'. People come from miles away, not because they need a new wardrobe, but because they want to see Ikea. Greece had never had a shop this big before. It was fortuitous that they built it next to the airport: when the enormous Ikea car park overflowed, they were able to use a disused runway for extra parking. Entire extended families happily spend six hours getting lost there. They could probably have charged admission.

If you've ever tried furnishing a large house in three hours at Ikea, you will appreciate why the prices are so reasonable. You're on your own. Don't even think about getting help. I knew they didn't deliver, which is why I had the truck meeting me, but I had vaguely assumed that if you were spending a great deal of money they might make a bit of an effort. Not a chance. I made sure I was the first person on the shop floor when they opened – not just to get off to a quick start, but to make sure that I claimed everything I needed before anyone else did. That's another Ikea secret – not holding too much stock. The day before the big shop I had planned my strategy carefully and calculated that it was quicker to ignore all the helpful arrows and go the wrong way round.

Having bagged everything on my list it was time to go downstairs to what they mockingly call 'self-service'. Self-hell would be more appropriate. How many flat-packed double beds can you get on one trolley? Two. So that was my first six trolleys. Plus another two trolleys for the mattresses. By the time I had filled ten trolleys I started looking for help but to no avail. It's not policy. Eventually I managed to get twenty trolleys to the check out. The woman behind the till asked me if I was opening a hotel and I asked her if anyone could help me. She must have spotted the desperation in my eyes – or maybe it was the way I allowed my legs to fold beneath me as I slid slowly to the floor – and realised that if I died on the spot all that stuff I'd bought would have to be returned from whence it came. Either way, she took pity on me and beckoned to a couple of colleagues and together we created a trolley train that could have handled the month's output of a sizeable factory.

Several hours later all those flat-packs had been unloaded into their new home. That was the easy bit. You will know what I mean if you have ever tried turning an Ikea flat-pack into a recognisable piece of furniture, wasting a whole afternoon when you discover that they've left out the vital screws and then wasting several more hours when you discover that they haven't and it's your mistake and now you're going to have to start all over again. If you have, you must now imagine going through that exercise not once, but over and over and over again. If you think Sisyphus you will have a fairly accurate picture.

He, you will recall, was the mythical king of Corinth, just up the road from our house, who was punished by the gods by being forced to roll a huge rock up a hill, only to watch it roll back down, and to repeat this throughout eternity. My punishment was to assemble a flat-pack chest and when it was finished, start all over again assembling another. And when the chests were done, I'd have to start on the beds (ten beds) and then the chairs (thirty chairs) and then the tables and the book cases and the wardrobes and everything else. The difference between Sisyphus and me was that his rock did not come out of a flat-pack and he had eternity in which to complete his task. I did not.

I became an Ikea expert. Double bed? Twenty-five minutes. Double wardrobe? My record, after five of them, was twenty minutes but that doesn't count the shelves. I became obsessed with Ikea. I went to bed at night dreaming of the stuff. The names don't help. Half of them sound so strange they take on a life of their own in dreams. The Poangs and the Ektorps would join forces with the Heffalumps from *Winnie the Pooh* – that my kids watched – and chase me round the house. And every morning I would wake up and have another bedside table to assemble. I had to pace myself with these because although they were small they took forever. And I had ten of them to do.

Still, I was getting through it all and felt fairly confident that I was on track for the arrival of Dad and his friends. Then, halfway through assembling a Bjursta, he rang.

'How's it going?'

'Could be worse. At least I'll be able to get a job as a flat-pack assembler if the orchestra ever folds.'

'Right,' he said, 'I'll see you next week.'

'You mean in two weeks,' I said.

'No, next week.'

'No, two weeks!'

'Look, I may be getting on a bit but I think I can remember when I booked my flight.'

I couldn't believe what I was hearing. I had timed everything down to the day of his arrival and now he was telling me that day was a week earlier. Apart from the Ikea furniture, there were still a couple of windows to be fitted in the basement, all of which needed painting and the carpenter still had to fit the banisters on the landing and there was a massive clean-up job. I had written the date down months ago. It was clearly printed in the place where I record my entire life.

'But Dad, I've written it down. It's on the fridge!'

This, admittedly, was a mistake. Had I told Dad that I had entered the date in my leather-bound desk diary (which I do not possess) and backed it up on my computer (which I use for different purposes) he might have been a tiny bit more understanding.

'Oh, I see! Well, if it's on the fridge then obviously you are absolutely right and I must have it wrong. That must explain why I keep confusing my *Mastermind* recordings with the *Today* programme and end up asking Cabinet ministers the date of the Battle of Hastings and *Mastermind* contestants why they haven't sorted out the economy yet and why I'm happily dozing in bed when I should be interviewing Gordon Brown at ten past eight. I'm going to start using a fridge door and carry it around with me. SO much more reliable than a boring old diary!'

As I may have already mentioned, Dad does go over the top with his sarcasm from time to time. Still, I had to concede he had a point. I had clearly got the date wrong and I realised something had to be done about it. Maybe I needed to buy a new fridge.

*J*: So I arrived on the appointed day and, a couple of days later, the first of my guests started arriving too. Our inaugural evening was not quite the idyllic occasion I had imagined. There was no string quartet for a start, which was probably just as well. If they HAD been there, I'd have set them to work on the many remaining flat-packs. Oddly enough, no one seemed to notice that their home for the next week or two looked very much like a furniture assembly plant and that where there was paint it was still wet and the path down to the sea was still in a state that would have been child's play for a young mountain goat and the bottom half of the house was a perfect setting for a post-Armageddon movie.

What they did notice was the single thing that had melted the hearts of Christopher and me when we had first seen it all those years ago. The view. Friends who had been baffled that I had spent a big chunk of my life and an even bigger chunk of my savings building a house in a fairly remote corner of Europe that most of them had never even heard of were baffled no longer.

I don't suppose the house will ever be just as Christopher and I had planned it. That's the thing about houses – old and new. There's usually something you wish you'd done differently and always something to go wrong. I could have done without the massive rain storms that swept torrents of water down our mountain that winter, undermined the foundations of the swimming pool and threatened to send it crashing down the hill into the sea. I could have done without the wooden floors in the bedrooms deciding to buckle up like a discarded sweet wrapper. I did not particularly enjoy having to get out of bed one very dark and stormy night and balance on a narrow ledge in a force ten gale trying (unsuccessfully) to stop the canopy over the balcony being ripped out of its moorings. It was just like being a lone yachtsman but without everyone telling you how brave you were. I had to boast about it the following morning, but I don't think anyone was impressed.

So plenty has gone wrong with the house and every time Christopher and I go there we find something to do when we should be lounging around enjoying ourselves. But, as someone famous once said, it's location that matters and, however many times I do it, I never tire of standing on the balcony and looking across the bay at the setting sun and counting myself massively blessed. The beauty of the view never fails to work its magic, never fails to lift my spirits.

As for Christopher and our relationship, well that's another reason to count my blessings. I had every reason to throttle him at least half a dozen times during the past few years and he had even more reasons to throttle me. But, remarkably, we seem to have come through it. He's put an enormous amount of time and energy into getting it done and it wouldn't have happened without him. I've also got to know him better and that's nice. I worry about only one thing and it has to do with house martins.

When we first saw the building site I had noticed a house martins' nest built in what would become the basement living room. It was a beautiful little thing: a half-shell with an entrance tunnel fixed with great care to the underside of a concrete beam: not unlike a tiny upside-down igloo made from pellets of mud. When I next went back, its builders had returned from their winter break in southern Africa and taken up residence again. We spent hours watching the parents darting to and fro, swooping and gliding through the sky and returning with beaks full of insects for their squawking brood.

I knew that when the building started, the nest would have to go and I worried about it. For two years we managed to leave it untouched and kept a gap in the wall so that the birds could keep coming and going – which they did, seemingly oblivious to the racket of cement mixers and shouting builders. But eventually, with heavy heart, Christopher told me the builders had been forced to fill in the gap. We couldn't really go without a floor for the sake of a pair of house martins, could we? I supposed we couldn't. The nest was destroyed and I wondered how the birds would cope when they next returned from their long journey. I imagined their despair when they saw that their home of – how many years? – had disappeared. I need not have worried.

The following spring the house martins returned and promptly set about building a new nest in the covered porch to the basement. They are there to this day and every morning in the spring and early summer we watch them performing their breathtaking aerial acrobatics, often swooping down at extraordinary speed to take a sip from the swimming pool, sometimes missing the swimmers by inches.

So why do I worry about them? It was something Christopher said when we saw the nest had been built again.

'How long d'you think it took them to build their new home? A few days at most. Amazing, eh? You know, I reckon you'd really love a nice little house somewhere near the Acropolis in Athens and given how much we've learned here . . .'

I did not let him finish.